Classical Sociological Theory

Classical Sociological Theory

IRVING M. ZEITLIN

Ⓢ CANADIAN
SCHOLARS

Toronto | Vancouver

Classical Sociological Theory
Irving M. Zeitlin

First published in 2019 by
Canadian Scholars, an imprint of CSP Books Inc.
425 Adelaide Street West, Suite 200
Toronto, Ontario
M5V 3C1

www.canadianscholars.ca

Library and Archives Canada Cataloguing in Publication

Zeitlin, Irving M., author
      Classical sociological theory / Irving M. Zeitlin.

Abridgment of: Zeitlin, Irving M. Ideology and the development of sociological theory.
Includes bibliographical references and index.
Issued also in print and electronic formats.
ISBN 978-1-77338-100-8 (softcover).--ISBN 978-1-77338-101-5 (PDF).
--ISBN 978-1-77338-102-2 (EPUB)

      1. Sociology--History. I. Title. II. Zeitlin, Irving M. Ideology and the development of sociological theory

HM435.Z452 2019   301   C2018-906053-0
                                       C2018-906054-9

Text design by Elisabeth Springate
Cover design by Em Dash

Printed and bound in Ontario, Canada

Canada

For my wife, Esther;
for my wonderful children,
Ruth, Michael, Beth, and Jeremy;
and for my beloved grandchildren,
Rebekka, Jacob, Kayla, Isaiah, Albert, Caleb, Ethan, Daniel,
Jonathan, Leo, and Finlay

Contents

Preface   xi

Chapter 1   The Enlightenment: Philosophical Foundations   1

Chapter 2   Mary Wollstonecraft (1759–1797)   8
Vindication of the Rights of Woman   10

Chapter 3   The Romantic-Conservative Reaction   16
Hegel's Historical Synthesis   22
Conservative Philosophy and Sociology: A Summary   25

Chapter 4   Auguste Comte (1798–1857)   29
The Advent of Positive Philosophy   33
The Positive Method in Its Application to Social Phenomena   36

Chapter 5   The Philosophical Orientations of Karl Marx
(1818–1883)   41

Chapter 6   Marx's Relation to Hegel and Feuerbach   50

Chapter 7   Marx's Historical Sociology   57
Marx's Famous "Preface"   58
Tribal Ownership   61
Productive Forces: Did Marx in Fact Assign Them Causal
    Priority?   67
The Feudal Mode of Production   71
The Asiatic Mode of Production: Its Significance for Marx's
    Theory   74
Theoretical Implications   78
The Capitalist Mode of Production   79
Was Marx a Social Evolutionist?   83

Chapter 8   Max Weber (1864–1920)   93

Weber's Dialogue with Marxism   96

Feudalism: Weber's View and Its Affinities with That of Marx   105

The Asiatic Mode of Production: Weber's Fruitful Elaboration of
    Marx's Concept   110

Asian Religions   114

Western Capitalism: Weber's Complementary Analysis   134

Social Class and Other Aspects of Social Organization: Weber's
    Revision of Marx's Class Theory   137

Bureaucracy   142

The Charismatic Political Leader: Weber's Error   146

The Historical-Sociological Method   149

Chapter 9   Vilfredo Pareto (1848–1923)   154

Pareto's Repudiation of The Enlightenment's Legacy   156

Pareto and Science   156

Les Systèmes Socialistes   158

Pareto's Sociology   162

Society, Elites, and Force   166

Pareto and Fascism   173

Chapter 10   Gaetano Mosca (1858–1941)   176

The Ruling Class   178

Aristotle and Montesquieu   184

Juridical Defence   190

Universal Suffrage   194

Parliamentarism   196

Standing Armies   198

Chapter 11   Robert Michels (1876–1936)   202

Chapter 12 Émile Durkheim (1858–1917)   222

Durkheim and Saint-Simon   223

The Problem of Order   229

Order and Justice   236

Durkheim's Sociology of Deviant Behaviour   239

Crime and Punishment   241

Durkheim's Sociology of Religion   245

Methodological Rules and Values   254

The Study of Suicide   257

Chapter 13 Karl Mannheim (1893–1947)   264

Ideology and Utopia   265

The Intelligentsia   270

Chapter 14 George Herbert Mead (1863–1931)   274

Mind, Self, and Society   275

Meaning   278

The Self   281

The "I" and the "Me"   282

The "Biologic I"   283

The Philosophy of the Act   285

More on Mead's Pragmatic Epistemology   286

Epilogue   *292*

Index   *293*

Preface

More than fifty years ago, I was inspired to write *Ideology and the Development of Sociological Theory*, now in its 7th edition. In this abridged version, I have retained only those who are officially considered to be classical sociological theorists. If, however, teachers wish to enrich this version with great non-sociological thinkers, they should feel free to consult the 7th edition of *Ideology and the Development of Sociological Theory*.

I demonstrate in this and in all editions of my original book that the classic tradition of sociological thinking had developed in the course of a long and intense debate—first with the eighteenth-century Enlightenment, and later with its true heir in the nineteenth century, Karl Marx. It is not far from the historical truth to propose that the classical tradition began with the Enlightenment thinkers. For it was they who pioneered in studying the human condition in a methodical way, by employing scientific principles in the analysis of society.

The Enlightenment thinkers upheld *reason* as the criterion by which to assess social institutions and their suitability for human nature and needs. Human beings, they maintained, are essentially rational. Hence, by criticizing and changing repressive social institutions, humans could widen the boundaries of freedom and thus actualize their creative powers and perfect themselves. The philosophers of the Enlightenment were therefore *critical* as well as scientific. Their central premises—the rationality and perfectibility of humanity—eventually inspired the French revolutionaries; and soon after the Revolution, influential European thinkers, attributing the causes of the violent upheaval to Enlightenment ideas, sought to repudiate them.

The response to the Enlightenment and to both the French and the Industrial Revolutions is treated by historians under the headings of Romanticism and the Conservative Reaction. This reaction constitutes an important stage in the development of social theory. For it was the Romantic-Conservatives who rejected the mechanistic metaphors of the Enlightenment and who replaced them with an organic conception of society and history. The response to the Industrial Revolution also gave rise to Positive Philosophy, the theories of Saint-Simon and Comte, the official founders of sociology.

Later in the nineteenth century it was Karl Marx who coined the term "capitalism" to describe the new type of society that had emerged as a product of the Industrial Revolution. Marx, as the severest critic of the capitalist system, called attention to its alienating character. In presenting his critique of the system, Marx developed a highly fruitful historical-sociological approach to the study of society. Marx's contribution to sociological thinking stands out in the context of the late nineteenth century as possessing extraordinary intellectual significance. That is true, I believe, not only because of his own ideas, but also because of the widespread response his ideas provoked, a response that accounts, in a large measure, for the character of Western sociology. My discussion of Marx is therefore followed by the intense debate with his "ghost," the Marxian legacy.

In a series of chapters I present the ideas of several key participants in the debate—Weber, Pareto, Mosca, Michels, Durkheim, and Mannheim. Pareto, Mosca, and Michels—the so-called Neo-Machiavellians or Elite-Theorists—sought to repudiate the Marxian legacy; Mannheim actively employed Marxian concepts; and Durkheim developed his own approach as a kind of mediation between Comte and Marx by elaborating the ideas of their common intellectual ancestor, Saint-Simon.

As for Max Weber, who must be regarded as the greatest social scientist of the twentieth century, I show that his engagement with Marx, whom he describes as a "great thinker," is more complex than is widely assumed. It is not Marx whom Weber criticizes, but the Marxists after Marx, some of whom fostered a mechanistic and misleading view of Marx's ideas. Indeed, I document the proposition that Weber converges with Marx both substantively and methodologically, and that much of Weber's work may be understood as complementary to Marx's—an exploration of what Marx called the cultural or ideological "superstructure."

I trust, therefore, that this abridged version of my *Ideology and the Development of Sociological Theory* succeeds in preserving the most valid insights of these classical thinkers.

CHAPTER 1

The Enlightenment: Philosophical Foundations

The term "Enlightenment" refers to the intellectual movement that developed within the hundred-year span beginning with the English Revolution and culminating in the French Revolution.[1] Montesquieu was born in 1689 and Holbach died in 1789. The movement's leading representatives were religious skeptics, political reformers, cultural critics, historians, and social theorists who exercised considerable influence from Edinburgh to Naples, Paris to Berlin, Boston to Philadelphia. Although all these men were committed to the rational pursuit of truth, they also had their philosophical and political differences. In spite of the merciless criticism levelled against Christian dogma and myth, a few of these thinkers held tenaciously to the vestiges of their former religious beliefs. Others embraced materialism and atheism. Some, a distinct minority, remained loyal to dynastic authority, while radicals developed democratic ideas. The British thinkers were relatively content with their social and political institutions. The Germans were almost entirely unpolitical. In sharp contrast to both the British and the Germans, however, it was the French *Philosophes* who most vehemently criticized both church and state, campaigning unrelentingly for the basic freedoms—freedom from arbitrary power, freedom of speech, freedom of trade, freedom to realize one's talents. It was in eighteenth-century France that the conflict of the Enlightenment with the Establishment became the most intense and dramatic. Typically, the French *Philosophe* was most uncompromising in his opposition to the old regime. He tore it down intellectually, thus paving the way for its actual destruction by the revolution of 1789.

The Enlightenment, of course, had its prehistory, its roots in the past. Several centuries earlier a secular mode of thought had been slowly developing. In the four hundred years between 1300 and 1700 social forces first weakened and then shattered whatever unity western Christendom had possessed. Those social forces may be summarized with the catch phrase, "Protestantism, science, and capitalism." We must remember, however, that medieval science was teleological; Its purpose was to attain knowledge for the sake of God. The purpose of science was to discover God's intentions for his creation. Even the most rational of medieval thinkers conceded that there were sacred areas into which they must not venture, spheres in which revelation, faith, tradition, and ecclesiastical authority offered the answers and gave the orders. Scientific curiosity as applied to those spheres was an unwelcome intrusion into holy ground. It was this inviolable domain of the *sacred* that distinguished the Middle Ages at its most scientific and skeptical from the later ages of criticism. The medieval mind was dominated by the Church, literally, emotionally, and intellectually. "A Revolution was necessary," wrote Rousseau, "to bring men back to common sense."[2]

In contrast to the medieval era, the men of the Enlightenment regarded all aspects of human life and works as subject to critical examination—the various sciences, religious beliefs, metaphysics, aesthetics, education, and so on. Self-examination, a scrutiny of their own actions and their own society, was an essential function of thought. By gaining an understanding of the main forces and tendencies of their epoch, human beings could determine their direction and control their consequences. Through reason and science, humanity could attain ever greater degrees of freedom and, hence, ever greater degrees of perfection. Intellectual progress, an idea permeating the thinking of that era, would serve to further humanity's general progress.

The *Philosophes* waged an unceasing war against superstition, bigotry, and intolerance; they fought against censorship and demanded freedom of thought. They attacked the privileges of the feudal classes and their restraints upon the commercial and industrial classes. It was the Enlightenment faith in science and education that provided so powerful an impetus to their work, making them humanitarian, optimistic, and confident. Philosophy was no longer merely a matter of abstract thinking. It acquired the practical function of asking critical questions about existing institutions and demanding that the unreasonable ones, those contrary to human nature, be changed. All social obstacles to human perfectibility were to be progressively eliminated. Enlightenment thinking, then, had a *negative-critical* as well as a positive side.

Unlike the rationalists of the seventeenth century for whom explanation was a matter of strict deduction, the *Philosophes* constructed their ideal of explanation on the model of the contemporary natural sciences. They turned not to Descartes but primarily to Newton whose investigations rested on the data of experience and observation. Newton's empirical method was based on the assumption of universal order and law in the material world. Facts appear to fall into patterns, exhibiting definite regularities and relationships. Order is immanent in the universe, Newton believed, and is discovered not by abstract reasoning alone, but by observation. That became the methodological premise of eighteenth-century thought, and it is this premise that distinguishes it from that of the seventeenth-century continental philosophers (e.g., Descartes, Leibniz, and Spinoza). Condillac, for example, in his *Treatise on Systems,* explicitly defends the empirical method and criticizes the great rationalists of the seventeenth century for having failed to adhere to it. The phenomena of the real world were, for all practical purposes, ignored by the seventeenth-century system builders. Ideas and concepts were elevated to the status of dogma. Thus Condillac argues the necessity of a new method that unites the empirical with the rational. One must study the phenomena themselves if their forms and connections are to be known. Condillac, d'Alembert, and others now call for this new method as a prerequisite to intellectual progress. The logic of this method was indeed new, for it was neither the logic of the medieval scholastic nor even of the purely mathematical concept; it was rather the "logic" of the facts.

Employing Galileo's discovery that falling bodies accelerate at a constant rate, and Kepler's observation that there exists a fixed relationship between the distance of a planet from the sun and the speed of its revolution, Newton arrived at the law that the sun attracted planets to itself at a rate directly proportional to their mass and inversely proportional to the square of the distance between them. Eventually, he was able to demonstrate that all bodies of the universe took their positions and movement through the force of gravitation. Moreover, the force that held the planets in orbit also made objects fall to the ground. The law was operative throughout the universe. The finite universe had become an infinite machine eternally moving by its own power and mechanisms. External causation accounted for its operation, which was apparently devoid of purpose or meaning. Space, time, mass, motion, and force were the essential elements of this mechanical universe that could be comprehended in its entirety by applying the laws of science and mathematics. This conception had an incalculable impact on the intellectuals of the Enlightenment. Here was a magnificent triumph of reason *and* observation, the new method that takes observed facts and advances an interpretation that accounts for what is observed, so that if the interpretation is correct, it can guide observers in the quest for new facts.

What is new and original about Enlightenment thought, therefore, is the whole-hearted adoption of the methodological pattern of Newton's physics, and that immediately with its adoption it was generalized and employed in realms other than the mathematical and physical. It became an indispensable tool in the study of all phenomena. "However much individual thinkers and schools differ in their results," writes Cassirer, "they agree in this epistemological premise. Voltaire's *Treatise on Metaphysics,* d'Alembert's *Preliminary Discourse,* and Kant's *Inquiry Concerning the Principles of Natural Theology and Morality* all concur on this point."[3] Here again this may be contrasted with the seventeenth-century rationalists' understanding of the term "reason." For Descartes, Spinoza, and Leibniz, to select the most typical thinkers of that period, reason was the realm of "eternal verities"—truth held in common by man and God. That is not the view of the eighteenth century, which, Cassirer maintains

> takes reason in a different and more modest sense. It is no longer the sum total of "innate ideas" given prior to all experience, which reveal the absolute essence of things. Reason is now looked upon rather as an acquisition than as a heritage. It is not the treasury of the mind in which the truth like a minted coin lies stored; it is rather the original intellectual force which guides the discovery and determination of truth…. The whole eighteenth century understands reason in this sense; not as a sound body of knowledge, principles, and truths, but as a kind of energy, a force which is fully comprehensible only in its agency and effects.[4]

Reason bows neither to the merely factual, the simple data of experience, nor to the "evidence" of revelation, tradition, or authority. Reason together with observation is a facility for the acquisition of truth. Even the authors of the *Encyclopedia* viewed its function from this standpoint, not merely to provide knowledge and information but also and primarily to change the traditional mode of thinking. The change did indeed become increasingly manifest, and analysis was now applied to psychological and even socio-logical phenomena. In these realms, too, it had become clear that reason is a powerful instrument when employed in that special method—analysis into separate elements as well as synthetic reconstruction.

The eighteenth-century thinkers were aware of the two philosophical and intellectual tendencies of the previous century that had remained rela-tively separate from each other and thus without any significant reciprocal influence: rational philosophy and empirical philosophy. Descartes had a fundamental influence in founding the first movement, while Galileo used experimentation and Bacon explained its particular virtues. One way, then, of viewing the special contribution of the Enlightenment is to see its sustained effort at bringing together these distinct philosophical approaches into one unified methodology. The *Philosophes* believed that they had synthesized the best elements of both philosophical movements. Empirical philosophy had a very profound impact upon the *Philosophes'* thinking and from that standpoint the influence of John Locke, the great exponent of empiricism, was almost as great as that of Newton.

In his famous *Essay Concerning Human Understanding*, Locke asserted in opposition to certain of his contemporaries, that ideas are not innate in the human mind. Quite the contrary, at birth the mind is a *tabula rasa*—that is in a blank and empty state; only through experience do ideas enter the mind. The function of the mind is to collect the impressions and material provided by the senses. In this view, the role of the mind is essentially a passive one, with little or no creative or organizing function. Clearly, this lent great support to the empirical and experimental methods: Knowledge could be increased only by extending the experiences of the senses. Moreover, Locke further supported the scientists' method of focusing on measurable qualities, and ignoring the other aspects of the things they were investigat-ing, by advancing a classification of the qualities of matter into primary and secondary: Extension, number, and motion could be directly and immedi-ately experienced. On the other hand, colour and sound had no existence outside of the observer's mind. Subsequently, Locke's epistemology led to idealism and skepticism among English philosophers and to materialism among the French.

In England, Bishop Berkeley, for example, argued that Locke's distinction between "primary" and "secondary" was a dubious and tenuous one; neither of these qualities had any existence apart from the perceiver's mind. This was tantamount to saying that matter does not exist—or at least that there was no way of proving the existence of matter. Indeed, Berkeley insisted that only spirit exists and that the spirit is God. Thus, spirit, the subject of religion, was defended by attacking matter, the subject of science. A further step was taken by David Hume: The mind could know nothing outside itself; all human knowledge of the external world is therefore impossible. Hume's work will be discussed in a later context since it was at this point that Immanuel Kant began his own philosophical system.

Among many French philosophers, in contrast, Locke's ideas were translated into scientific materialism—a development probably related to the rigid and capricious absolutism in France and its support of the Church. Materialism appeared as an effective ideological weapon against Church dogma. Condillac expounded and elaborated Locke's theory of the origin of knowledge. The most thoroughgoing in this respect was Holbach, who rejected all spiritual causes and reduced consciousness and thought to the movement of molecules within the material body. While Helvetius, Holbach, and La Mettrie became exponents of materialism, Condillac, though accepting Locke's theory in most of its essentials, introduced important modifications whose implications Kant was later to develop even further. If Locke's theory implied a passive role on the part of the observer—merely receiving sensory impressions, with the mind playing no active role in their organization—Condillac now argues that once the power of thought and reasoning is awakened in man, he is no longer passive, and no longer merely adapts himself to the existing order. Now thought is able to advance even against social reality. Condillac thus assigned a decisive role to judgment and reason even in the simplest act of perception; this was true whether one was perceiving the natural world or the social world. The senses in themselves could never produce the world as we know it in our consciousness; the cooperation of the mind is an absolute necessity.

It should be clear, then, why the Enlightenment is a most logical point of departure if one is interested in the origins of sociological theory. It is in that period that one may see, more consistently than before, the emergence of the scientific method. Reason in itself will not yield a knowledge of reality, neither will observation and experimentation alone yield such knowledge.

Knowledge of reality, whether natural or social, depends on the unity of reason and observation in the scientific method. The Enlightenment thinkers were as interested in society and history as they were in nature, and these were treated as an indivisible unity. By studying nature—including the nature of man—one could learn not only what *is*, but also what is *possible*; likewise, by studying society and history, one could learn not only about the workings of the existing factual order, but about its inherent possibilities. These thinkers were "negative" in that they were critical of the existing order which, in their view, stifled the human potential and did not allow the possible to emerge from the "is." The existing factual order was studied scientifically to learn how to transcend it. These premises, as will be seen, were either accepted, modified, or rejected in the subsequent development of *sociological* thought. In these terms, early sociology developed as a reaction to the Enlightenment.

NOTES

1.   My interpretation of this intellectual movement has been heavily influenced by two studies in particular: Ernst Cassirer, *The Philosophy of the Enlightenment*, trans. Fritz C. A. Koelln and James P. Pettegrove (Princeton, N.J.: Princeton University Press, 1951), and Peter Gay, *The Enlightenment: An Interpretation* (New York: Alfred A. Knopf, 1976).

2.   *Discours sur les sciences et les arts*, in *Ouevres*, Vol. III, p. 6, cited in Gay, *The Enlightenment*, p. 208.

3.   See Cassirer, *The Philosophy of the Enlightenment*, p. 12.

4.   Ibid, p. 13.

CHAPTER 2

Mary Wollstonecraft (1759–1797)

A true child of the Enlightenment, Mary Wollstonecraft was profoundly influenced by the outstanding thinkers of that movement, notably by Rousseau whose writing she much admired and yet criticized for his attitude toward the education of women. In his *Émile*, Rousseau proposed an educational program for women which, in Wollstonecraft's judgment, was founded not on reason but on age-old prejudices. It was in response to the views of Rousseau and to those of several British writers that Wollstonecraft composed her major work, *Vindication of the Rights of Woman* (1792).

In an earlier work she had defended the first phase of the French Revolution as the practical application of Enlightenment principles.[1] Edmund Burke, in his *Reflections on the Revolution in France*, had condemned the events in France as threatening to break up the established social order throughout Europe, an order embodying, in his view, the sum of political wisdom. Wollstonecraft replied to Burke in her *Vindication of the Rights of Men*.

Burke, as his political record demonstrated, was no out-and-out reactionary. He supported the American claim to independence, abhorred slavery, condemned the harshness of the penal system, and threw his weight behind the reforms of the British colonial administration of India. In his *Reflections on the Revolution in France*, however, Burke maintained that the laws of inheritance and inequalities of rank were the chief elements of a civilized society. This, together with his attitude toward the poor, aroused Wollstonecraft's greatest indignation. Burke, advocating what he called "the principles of natural subordination," wrote:

They [the poor] must respect that property which they cannot partake. They must labour to obtain what by labour can be obtained; and when they find, as they commonly do, the success disproportioned to the endeavour, they must be taught their final consolation in the final proportions of eternal justice.[2]

In Wollstonecraft's view, such an attitude was an affront to both humanity and God:

This is contemptible, hard-hearted sophistry, in the specious form of humility, and submission to the will of heaven. It is, Sir, possible to render the poor happier in this world, without depriving them of the consolation which you gratuitously grant them in the next. They have a right to more comfort than they, at present, enjoy; and more comfort might be afforded them, without encroaching on the pleasure of the rich; not now waiting to enquire whether the rich have any right to exclusive pleasures.[3]

But it was Burke's views of women that Mary Wollstonecraft found to be especially repugnant. In his *A Philosophical Enquiry into the Sublime and Beautiful* (1757), Burke ascribed women's beauty to their "littleness and weakness," which "clearly proved that one half of the human species, at least, have not souls."[4] For Mary Wollstonecraft, this concept of beauty was far from sublime, implying, as it did, that women should not cultivate such "manly" virtues as might interfere with the pleasurable sensations women were presumably created to inspire. In his attitude towards women, Burke had separated love from respect, making them antagonistic principles. It is this attitude that Wollstonecraft assailed in her major work on the rights of woman. There she applied to the status of women the same Enlightenment principles she had earlier affirmed as self-evident in her *Vindication of the Rights of Men*:

that there are rights which men inherit at their birth, as rational creatures, who were raised above the brute creation by their improvable faculties; and that, in receiving these, not from their forefathers but, from God, prescription can never undermine natural rights.[5]

From the general injustices of the old regime, she turned her attention to the specific wrongs perpetrated against the female half of the species.

Doubtless, Mary Wollstonecraft's own childhood experiences contributed to her acute awareness of the plight of women. As the eldest daughter of a drunken, brutish father and a weak but harsh mother, she was made painfully aware in her early years of the "wrongs of women."[6] And it appears that her experiences were not untypical of the condition of women in the eighteenth century. As Margaret Tims has remarked, "The uncouth, overbearing father was evidently a commonplace character and he crops up in much of the literature of the day."[7]

The outstanding advances in eighteenth-century philosophy and science had left the status of women untouched, and Wollstonecraft recognized that this was partly due to the general submission of women to the prevalent view of them propounded by men. Indeed, these deeply rooted, antiwoman prejudices could be traced back to the Bible and to classical Greece. Erroneous and debilitating conceptions of women could be eliminated, Wollstonecraft believed, by the right kind of education. Education was the foundation on which women's rights could be established. This was not an entirely new idea, since several Enlightenment thinkers had already made similar proposals.

Baron d'Holbach defended women's rights in his *Système Sociale* (1773), and Condorcet provided for the education of girls as well as boys in his first "memoir on public instruction" in 1790. By and large, however, the men of the French Revolution ignored the rights of women. In England, it was Catherine Macauley, the author of several significant works including a *History of England*, who anticipated and most directly influenced Wollstonecraft's *Rights of Woman*. She had written a lengthy review of Macauley's *Letters on Education* (1790) in the *Analytical Review*, and most of the principles expounded in the *Rights of Woman* are to be found in Macauley's work.

VINDICATION OF THE RIGHTS OF WOMAN

Mary Wollstonecraft's main argument in her rebuttal of Rousseau is that women deserve social equality with men and should be given the education necessary to achieve it. The woman who strengthens her body and develops her mind will become the friend, and not the humble dependent, of her husband. If women appear to be inferior, that is only because they are indoctrinated from infancy with so-called feminine virtues: gentleness, passivity, submission, a spaniel-like affection for fathers, brothers, and husbands. But just give women the opportunity to unfold and sharpen their physical and mental faculties, and then we shall see where they stand in the scale of excellence. That woman is essentially inferior to man cannot be demonstrated so long as she is held in a state of subjugation. "I will allow," wrote Wollstonecraft,

> that bodily strength seems to give man a natural superiority over woman; and this is the only solid basis on which the superiority of the sex can be built. But I still insist that not only the virtue but the *knowledge* of the two sexes should be the same in nature, if not in degree, and that women, considered not only as moral but rational creatures, ought to endeavor to acquire human virtues (or perfections) by the *same* means as men, instead of being educated like a fanciful kind of *half* being—one of Rousseau's wild chimeras.[8]

When Rousseau denies to woman the same rigorous physical and intellectual education he proposes for man, the effect is to perpetuate not a natural but an artificial inferiority. If, therefore, mothers wish to give their daughters a true dignity of character, they should proceed on a plan diametrically opposed to that of Rousseau. Mothers should recognize that their daughters are made even weaker than nature intended when they are condemned to lead a sedentary life while boys run, jump, climb, and frolic in the open air. "As for Rousseau's remarks, which have since been echoed by several writers, that they [girls] have naturally, that is, from their birth, independent of education, a fondness for dolls, dressing and talking, they are so puerile as not to merit a serious refutation" (p. 128).

We need to remind ourselves that in Wollstonecraft's time the "civil death" of women was written into law. The common law of England ruled that whatever property a woman owned before marriage or might receive thereafter became automatically her husband's. This is how William Blackstone, the distinguished professor of law at Oxford, interpreted the legal status of married women:

> By marriage the husband and wife are one person in law; that is, the very being or legal existence of the woman is suspended during the marriage or at least is incorporated and consolidated into that of her husband; under whose wing, protection and cover, she performs everything.[9]

The wealthy woman, then, was no less subordinate than the poor.

Mary Wollstonecraft had a vision of a reformed society in which the subjection of women would disappear together with other basic social inequalities:

> We shall not see women affectionate till more equality be established in society, till ranks are confounded and women freed. (p. 315)

And yet, as we shall see, her proposals for the emancipation of women presuppose the perpetuation of certain social inequalities. A careful reading of the *Vindication* reveals that Wollstonecraft directs her argument to the middle-class woman, effectively excluding both the aristocratic and the poor woman from her audience. Aristocratic women are incapable of improvement by means of education. They are "weak, artificial beings" who "undermine the very foundation of virtue, and spread corruption through the whole mass of society! As a class of mankind they have the strongest claim to pity; the education of the rich tends to render them vain and helpless.... They only live to amuse themselves, and by the same law which in nature invariably produces certain effects, they soon only afford barren amusement" (p. 81).

And although Wollstonecraft exhibits a sincere and profound compassion for the poor, she seems to believe that the oppressive routine of domestic drudgery makes it virtually impossible for the impoverished woman to emancipate herself through education. Moreover, it is worth noting that Wollstonecraft does not envision the elimination of a servant class in her more egalitarian society. Indeed, for Wollstonecraft, the middle-class woman's education and emancipation is unattainable without the existence of servants:

> To render the poor virtuous they must be employed, and women in the middle ranks [i.e., class] of life, did they not ape the fashions of nobility, without catching their ease, might employ them, whilst they themselves managed their families, instructed their children, and exercised their own minds. (p. 170)

Wollstonecraft contemplates with pleasure the emancipated woman,

> nursing her children, and discharging the duties of her station *with perhaps merely a servant-maid to take off her hands the servile part of the household business.* (pp. 254–55, italics added)

For Wollstonecraft, a woman was to be educated not only in her own interest, but especially in the interest of creating more enlightened mothers and wives. Speaking of women in general, she affirms again and again, that women's

> first duty is to themselves as rational creatures, and the next, in point of importance, as citizens, is that, which includes so many, of a mother. The rank in life which dispenses with their fulfilling their duty, necessarily degrades them by making them mere dolls. (pp. 257–58)

And in the same vein,

> As the care of children in their infancy is one of the grand duties annexed to the female character by nature, this duty would afford many forcible arguments for strengthening the female understanding, if it were properly considered. (p. 265)
>
> To be a good mother, a woman must have sense, and that independence of mind which few women possess who are taught to depend entirely on their husbands. Meek wives are, in general, foolish mothers. (p. 266)

And in this important respect she agreed with Rousseau. A woman's

> parental affection, indeed, scarcely deserves the name, when it does not lead her to suckle her children, because the discharge of this duty is equally calculated to inspire maternal and filial affection … ; and what sympathy does a mother exercise who sends her babe to a nurse, and only takes it from a nurse to send it to school? (p. 266)

Mary Wollstonecraft was also a pioneer in calling for universal suffrage:

> I really think that women ought to have representatives instead of being arbitrarily governed without having any direct share allowed them in the deliberations of government. (p. 260)

In her discussion of national education, she was also among the first to call for public schools in which boys and girls would be educated together. The schools for the younger children, ages five to nine, would be absolutely free and open to all social classes. But just as Wollstonecraft's proposal for the emancipation of woman retains a servant class, her proposals for national education tend to perpetuate and reinforce social-class distinctions. "After the age of nine," she wrote,

> girls and boys, intended for domestic employments, or mechanical trades, ought to be removed to other schools, and receive instruction in some measure appropriate to the destination of each individual.…
>
> The young people of superior abilities, *or fortune*, might now be taught, in another school, the dead and living languages, the elements of science, and continue the study of history and politics, on a more extensive scale. (p. 287, italics added)

As Miriam Brody has observed, "not all these visions of a reformed society are reconcilable with Wollstonecraft's egalitarian principles. And she has not attempted to make them so."[10]

As we reflect on the *Vindication* taken in its entirety, we can see that Wollstonecraft's response to Rousseau was effective in at least one crucial respect. For she certainly succeeded in challenging his central thesis that woman's nature made her unfit for intellectual pursuits. Indeed, it is surprising that Rousseau, who so clearly recognized the role of indoctrination in making men into warriors ("man becomes a citizen before he becomes a soldier"), failed, somehow, to recognize the role of education and upbringing in the shaping of a woman's mind and conception of self.

Wollstonecraft believed that women are capable of achieving intellectual equality with men and that once they have done so, they should acquire political equality as well. She demanded honourable vocations for women, but she also always insisted that women should direct most of their energy to their tasks as wives and mothers. In her words, "whatever tends to incapacitate the maternal character takes woman out of her sphere" (p. 298).

Critics have noted numerous faults of style and organization in the *Vindication*,[11] and we have noted Wollstonecraft's failure to reconcile her egalitarian vision of a future society with the class distinctions she left intact in her proposals for woman's emancipation. In spite of these shortcomings, however, the *Vindication* has to be considered a major pioneering achievement, alerting men and women alike to the plight of oppressed womankind.[12]

NOTES

1. As the Revolution ran its course, however, she was shocked and horrified that so many men and women had been guillotined merely because they were members of the nobility. She now developed serious doubts that human perfectibility could prevail against human viciousness.

2. Quoted in Margaret Tims, *Mary Wollstonecraft: A Social Pioneer* (London: Millington Books, 1976), p. 117.

3. Ibid., p. 117.

4. Janet M. Todd, *A Wollstonecraft Anthology* (Bloomington: Indiana University Press, 1977), p. 64.

5. Ibid., p. 117.

6. This is the title of a largely autobiographical novel, exploring the parallels between domestic and political life. See Mary Wollstonecraft, *Mary and The Wrongs of Woman*, edited with an introduction by Gary Kelly (Oxford: Oxford University Press, 1976).

7. Tims, *Mary Wollstonecraft*, p. 122.

8. Mary Wollstonecraft, *Vindication of the Rights of Woman*, edited with an introduction by Miriam Brody (Middlesex, England: Penguin Books, 1986), p. 123, italics in original. (Hereafter all page references to this work are indicated in parentheses immediately following the quoted passage.)

9. *Commentaries on the Laws of England* (New York, 1847), vol. I, p. 441.

10. See Miriam Brody's exceptionally thoughtful introduction to Wollstonecraft's *Vindication of the Rights of Woman*, p. 44.

11. Miriam Brody's criticism is fairly typical: Wollstonecraft's "prose is an imitation, and not a particularly felicitous one, of the rounded sentences of eighteenth-century prose; one comes all too often, panting to the end of hopelessly long sentences, a little unsure of what the subject was.... There are many digressions in the text, with the argument turning suddenly from one subject to another." See ibid., p. 41.

12. In addition to the secondary sources already cited, the reader might wish to consult Ralph M. Wardle, *Mary Wollstonecraft: A Critical Biography* (Lawrence: University of Kansas Press, 1951), and Claire Tomalin, *The Life and Death of Mary Wollstonecraft* (London: Weidenfeld and Nicolson, 1974).

CHAPTER 3

The Romantic-Conservative Reaction

The philosophy of the Enlightenment, as we have seen, was rooted in the thought of the seventeenth century. The two main philosophical currents of that century —rationalism and empiricism—were synthesized rather successfully by the *Philosophes*, who expressed great confidence in reason and observation as a means of solving human problems. The universe was governed by immutable laws, and man and society could be made better by ordering the social and political environment according to those discoverable laws. These ideas became the foundation of the intellectual movements of the nineteenth century as well, but they were modified considerably by Romantic and Conservative thinkers. They turned away from what they considered to be the naive optimism and rationalism of the eighteenth century; they did so not only by recognizing the irrational factors in human conduct but also by assigning them positive value. Tradition, imagination, feeling, and religion were now regarded as natural and positive. Generally deploring the disorganizing consequences of the French Revolution for Europe, the Romantic and Conservative thinkers attributed those consequences to the folly of the revolutionaries, who had uncritically accepted Enlightenment assumptions and had attempted to reorder society according to rational principles alone. In reaction to the eighteenth-century exaltation of reason, then, the nineteenth century extolled instead emotion and imagination, leading to a great revival of religion, poetry, and art. In addition, *the group, the community,* and *the nation* now became important concepts. Historic memories and loyalties were viewed as binding the individual to a *nation*, a category now elevated to a position of supreme importance. Gone was the cosmopolitanism of the Enlightenment. Increasingly, the nineteenth century turned to the investigation of the origins of existing institutions rather than to their transformation according to rational principles. An historical attitude emerged in which more than ever before institutions were regarded as the product of slow organic development and not of deliberate rational, calculated action.

Although the Romantic movement was in evidence throughout Europe, its form varied from one country to another. In England, and especially in Germany, the movement reflected a strong national reaction to the radicalism of the Enlightenment as expressed in the Revolution and against Napoleonic expansionism. In general, the Enlightenment conception of a rational, mechanistic universe was now rejected. In every field—literature, art, music, philosophy, and religion—an effort was made to free the emotions and imagination from the austere rules and conventions imposed during the eighteenth century. In religion, the importance of inner experience was restored; in philosophy, the individual mind was assigned a creative role in shaping the world. It is the philosophical movement, in particular, that is most directly pertinent to our discussion of social theory.

This movement, which began with the work of Rousseau and Hume and was further developed in the philosophy of Immanuel Kant, expressed a shift in emphasis from the mechanistic universe of Newton to the creative character of the personality, having as its intention the liberation of the mind from purely rationalistic and empirical thinking. Rousseau, though an Enlightenment thinker, departed somewhat from the "typical" standpoint; he was less inclined than his contemporaries to counsel the reconstruction of society according to abstract rational principles alone. Inner moral will, conscience, and convictions are also important if man is to free himself.

The most dramatic break with the Enlightenment, however, was expressed in the work of David Hume.[1] His critical examination of its leading assumptions served to undermine the prevailing faith in the universe as a network of cause-effect relationships. These are far from being immanent in the universe; instead, he argued, "causality" is simply an idea, a customary way of thinking. Because phenomenon B follows phenomenon A, one assumed that B is the effect of A. Hume thus assigned a creative role to the mind by insisting that the mechanistic conception is merely a way of thinking whose relationship to the real world is an open question. In that way, Hume along with other thinkers, notably Leibniz—who accepted the Newtonian conception but saw in it personal, idealistic, and teleological elements—laid the groundwork for Kant's epoch-making philosophy.

To appreciate the importance of Kant's new epistemology, we need to understand that he was arguing against the theory of knowledge advocated by John Locke and his followers. Locke likened the human mind to a dark room wholly shut off from light except through a single opening.[2] He called that hypothetical construct a *tabula rasa*, a blank or empty slate. At birth the mind contains nothing. Then as the infant begins to experience sensations of the outside world, the mind begins to acquire knowledge. The *tabula rasa* is illuminated by means of sensory experience, which conveys a faithful and complete representation of things as they actually exist outside the mind. It is as if the mind were a camera producing photographs of the outside world. For that reason, Locke's theory has been called "empiricism"—that is, a theory that all knowledge originates in sensory experience. It has also been called a photographic or copy theory of knowledge.

For Locke, the mind is wholly *passive* in receiving sensory impressions; it is like a receptacle or mirror. Locke allows the mind no creative role in selecting, modifying, or organizing the materials it receives. His conception of what the mind is capable of is quite mechanical:

1. It combines simple ideas into complex ones.
2. It sets ideas side by side without, however, uniting them.
3. It separates an idea from all the others accompanying it in reality.

The third process is called *abstraction*, which is how all general ideas are made. The three processes are analogous to human powers in the material world, where men combine things, set them side by side, and separate them. The mind, thus working like a mechanical instrument, arrives at the concepts of "infinity" by adding space to space, and "eternity," by adding stretches of time.

In contrast to Locke, Kant maintained that the mind is an active and creative entity that always plays a role in sensory experience.[3] Kant argued that there exist certain universal and necessary elements in all knowledge, the origin of which is to be found in the nature of human thinking and *not* in the objects of experience themselves. He called those elements "a prioris" because they are inherent in the mind; he called his theory of knowledge "transcendental logic" because those elements are a necessary factor in all experience.

Hume was right, Kant believed, to say that cause, effect, and so on are somehow added, and are not immediately given by sensory experience; but Hume had not seen the a priori origin of the added ideas. For Kant, the very possibility of experience presupposes that it will occur in relation to other experiences—before, after, together, and so forth. Sequence, coexistence, and other such processes are what the mind, by its very nature, demands. To support his argument, Kant asked this key question: What elements are *not* objects of perception but are nevertheless necessary for perception? His answer was *space* and *time*. All objects of experience appear in space and time; they are "a prioris," or organizing principles of the mind that are inherent in it. It followed that there is an unavoidably subjective element in all experience, and that knowledge of the world as it exists independently of a knowing subject is impossible. The mind, far from "photographing," *interprets* according to its own nature and laws.

In that way Kant tried to free the mind from its dependence on solely external sources for knowledge and to give a renewed validity to truth derived from the spiritual realm—religion, morality, and art. The *Philosophes* had regarded "knowledge" derived from those realms as inferior to that provided by science; only science could provide a true conception of nature and society—that is, a conception of the world as it actually is. For Kant, the knowledge derived from both realms, the spiritual as well as the scientific, had the same validity. If the concepts "causality" and "necessity" are also the product of the creative activity of the mind, why should scientific knowledge have greater validity than nonscientific knowledge? By demonstrating the limitations of scientific knowledge, Kant intended to restore the validity of faith and intuition. And, indeed, in sharp contrast to the Enlightenment, the Romantic thinkers regarded faith and intuition as essential for an understanding of nature and society.

If it was Kant who challenged the general methodological assumptions of the *Philosophes*, it was Edmund Burke who criticized their sociological assumptions. Burke expressed the growing national and conservative reaction to both the principles of the Enlightenment and the French Revolution. Burke's views, as well as those of Hegel, provide an important background for an understanding of the intellectual and historical context in which the founders of sociology, Saint-Simon and Comte, developed their own ideas. Burke's critical reflections contributed greatly, not only in England but also on the continent, to the formation of a conservative political and social philosophy. Although he criticized and condemned the French revolutionary leaders, he had a different view of the American Revolution. The American colonists were attempting to preserve the organic character of society by struggling to retain their ancient rights and privileges; in effect, it was George III who was undermining the organic character by attempting to deprive them of the privileges. Society is an "organism," but its separate organs are not necessarily perfectly coordinated as they are in a natural organism. In the social organism some parts may change more rapidly than others. When that occurs, reforms are necessary to bring the parts into harmony again. Reforms, not revolution. That Burke favored reforms is clear from his stand with respect to British rule in India and Ireland. Reforms were necessary to bring the state into harmony with the other social conditions. But there should be no sudden breaks with the past as had been the case in France.

In advancing his *organic* conception of society, Burke was explicitly repudiating the abstract rational conception of the *Philosophes*—namely, that there were general natural laws and natural rights that could be discovered by the mind, and that the laws men make should conform with the ideal principles as nearly as possible. In their application of that doctrine, Burke argued, the revolutionaries had treated society as a machine, thinking they could simply pluck out the obsolete parts and replace them with new ones. They therefore discarded old and established institutions, which had developed through time and which were integral parts of the social order and tried to replace those institutions on the basis of some abstract formula. The individual was proclaimed more important than the nation or state, the element more important than the whole; the state, far from being conceived as organically related to the rest of the social order, was treated as a mere contractual relationship. The implications were clear: If the state is a mere contract, then it can, and indeed should, be dissolved as soon as the contracting parties decide it no longer satisfies their interests.

In his *Reflections on the Revolution in France*, Burke presents a point-for-point rebuttal of the rationalistic position.[4] The individual has no abstract rights. On the contrary, he has only those rights and privileges that prevail in a given community and which he acquires by virtue of having been born there. Rights and privileges develop slowly and organically; they are historical in character, not abstract. A community does not exist merely in the present; it is an endless chain of generations, each one inheriting from its predecessors and each individual being but one link. The generation of the Revolution therefore had no right to destroy customs and institutions that belonged not solely to them but to past generations and even future generations. Twenty-six million Frenchmen had no right to regard themselves as having sovereign authority over what belonged equally to the past and the future. Each generation should merely add to what the dead have achieved and left behind and pass on the total to its heirs.

As for the State, it is no mere contract made by individuals for the attainment of limited ends and therefore to be dissolved when the ends are attained or the agreement breached. Quite the contrary, the State is a higher organic unity, an integral part of the national community. The State, Burke wrote, "is a partnership in all science; a partnership in all art; a partnership in every virtue, and in all perfection. As the ends of such a partnership cannot be obtained in many generations, it becomes a partnership not only between those who are living, but between those who are dead and those who are to be born."[5] The State and the Nation are organisms and hence the product of a long process of growth; they are not deliberate calculated inventions out of whole cloth. Moreover, it is not calculated interest nor rational convictions that hold nations and societies together, but certain nonrational factors. Not only material interests but spiritual ties and sentiments bind the members of a community together. Such ties may be as "light as air" but they are "as strong as links of iron."[6] Burke had thus formulated his conservative reflections on the Revolution.

Burke's philosophy embodied within it a new conception of society, which now alerted social thinkers to a variety of factors the Enlightenment had ignored. Burke had advanced an historical, developmental, organic view of society and, together with his emphasis on the nonrational elements in human conduct, presented an important perspective from which to view the structure of a society and the process by which it changed. Burke's historical and conservative conception of the state and nation was given a more explicitly philosophical foundation by the German philosopher, Georg Wilhelm Friedrich Hegel.

HEGEL'S HISTORICAL SYNTHESIS

For Hegel, the Romantic-Conservative conception of "historical develop-ment" and the Enlightenment emphasis on reason were each in their own way very important ideas. He therefore attempted to bring them together in one philosophical synthesis. Reason, he argued, is not merely a faculty existing in the individual by which he might measure customs and insti-tutions; reason is inherent in the process of development itself. That is the meaning of his celebrated notion that "what is rational is real" and "what is real is rational." Reason is not, as the *Philosophes* had regarded it, a mere abstraction from the real; it is an immanent force which determines the structure and development of the universe. In that way Hegel transforms reason into a great cosmic force that he variously calls the Idea, the Spirit, the Absolute, or finally, God. The Idea is not an unchanging essence but is continually developing and becoming. Moreover, it is an impersonal, logical, and cosmic process which unites the social as well as the natural realm; all customs, habits, institutions, and conceptions are united into one dynamic and organic whole.

The historical process is a manifestation of the progressive unfolding of Reason in the various social and cultural institutions; that development follows a form not dissimilar to the way human thought develops. The cosmic reason objectifies itself in institutions by the process of fusion of contradictions; fusion produces new contradictions, which in turn are brought together in a new synthesis, and so on, to infinity. In other words, each thesis engenders its own antithesis; both are then resolved in a syn-thesis, which in turn becomes a new thesis. If the cosmic reason is to be distinguished in any way from individual reason, it is by the greater or more complete unfolding of the former's inherent potentialities. The individual mind can comprehend only aspects of reality; the acorn, however, becomes what it can become; it unfolds into an oak tree.

In the human realm, the nation stands higher than all other institutions, for it is the vehicle through which the cosmic reason realizes its destiny. That becomes clear from Hegel's philosophy of history in which he divides history into a series of succeeding epochs, each of which expresses a partic-ular phase in the development of the World Spirit. When a nation is still in its ascending phase, it embodies not the whole of cosmic reason, but only a particular phase of its ultimate fulfillment. A nation is an individualized expression of the World Spirit and is therefore the medium through which the spirit achieves self-consciousness. In his *Philosophy of History*, one learns, much to one's astonishment, that Hegel concludes the process with the Spirit ultimately having reified itself in the Prussian state, the highest expression of the Cosmic Reason on earth. A surprising conclusion indeed! One can see, then, two distinct and opposing tendencies in Hegel's thought. On the one hand, it led explicitly to the ideological defence of the Prussian state and of German society at the time; many concluded that what is, is rational and therefore necessary and unavoidable. In those terms Hegel's philosophy became definitely conservative in its influence. But on the other hand, there was the emphasis on constant change, a dynamic and dialectical development that would continue ceaselessly and inexorably.

To perceive more clearly the two tendencies in Hegel's thought, it will be instructive to examine more closely his conception of dialectical development.[7] On the one side, one can see the emphasis on slow, organic growth determined by immanent rational laws. Between phases, however, as in the transition from the acorn to the oak tree, there is a kind of "dialectical leap" from one quality (acorn) to another (oak tree). That takes place when the quantitative accumulation of slow organic change reaches a nodal point at which an increment produces a *qualitative* change. This process may also be described as the "negation of the negation." The acorn in this example was itself a negation of the previous form (the seed), in which the acorn was inherent. With the continuation of the quantitative changes it, too, is negated by the new and potential form within it—the oak tree. Contained already within the seed is the chain of opposing forces which, if the seed is to develop, must continue to negate one another until its full potential is actualized. Each thing or form contains its own negation, and each is a unity of opposites. When a particular thing is "negated," it is superseded by a new force, which continues to develop until it, too, engenders its own negation. That is precisely what "development" means—changing according to the immanent pattern of a given thing. Negation, then, is not synonymous with outright destruction. The seed, or acorn, or even the tree, is not *negated* when it is destroyed—for example, by crushing the seed. Negation occurs only when the initial form is transcended by new qualities inherent in the first, and when the new qualities in their subsequent development actualize the full potential of the initial form.

Things strive to attain *actually* what they always were *potentially*, Hegel is saying, in his own formulation of an essentially Aristotelian notion. In natural organisms, this takes place in a "direct, unopposed, unhindered manner." Why? Because between "the Idea and its realization—the essential constitution of the original germ and the conformity to it of the existence derived from it—no disturbing influence can intrude."[8] In nature, typically, essence is actualized in existence as an undisturbed process, harmoniously. The opposite, however, is true in relation to Spirit, or the human, sociocultural realm: "the realization of *its* Ideal is mediated by consciousness and will.… Thus Spirit is at war with itself; it has to overcome itself as its most formidable obstacle. That development which in the sphere of Nature is a peaceful growth, is in that of Spirit, a severe, a mighty conflict with itself. What Spirit really strives for is the realization of its Ideal being; but in doing so, it hides that goal from its own vision, and is proud and well satisfied in this alienation from it." The development of the sociocultural sphere, therefore, "does not present the harmless tranquility of mere growth, as does that of organic life, but a stern reluctant working against itself."[9]

In metaphysical terms, Hegel is saying that the dialectical development in the social realm is a process characterized by conflict; if development means that each succeeding phase is a step forward or "higher" than the preceding phase, then progressive development is conflictive. It is easy to see some of the radical implications of this philosophy, particularly those which Marx later found so appealing. For in the cultural realm, Hegel had emphasized that development toward freedom, far from being a natural and mindless process, was contingent upon consciousness and will. "Universal history … shows the development of the consciousness of Freedom on the part of the Spirit, and the consequent realization of that Freedom. This development implies a gradation—a series of increasingly adequate expressions or manifestations of Freedom, which result from its Idea."[10]

Yet, this philosophy, as we have seen, had its conspicuously conservative side. Much like Burke, Hegel argued that it is not the individual, nor even the family, but the State that is the embodiment of Law. The State is the highest order to which all others must subordinate themselves. Real World History, for Hegel, begins with the State; its Right and Law supersede all prehistorical forms—family, community, and so on—with their right and law. But in the final analysis, it is not just any state or nation, but the German state which embodies the true, the eternal wisdom of the Spirit—of God. Thus Hegel concludes: "We have now arrived at the third period of the German World, and thus enter upon the period of Spirit conscious that is free, inasmuch as it wills the True, the Eternal—that which is in and for itself Universal."[11]

As will be seen later in a discussion of Marx's intellectual origins, he adopted some of the negative-critical or radical aspects of Hegel's thought but rejected the others. Marx's theory is of a completely different order and cannot be adequately comprehended as an extension of any of Hegel's themes. But before that can be taken up, other aspects of the Conservative Reaction to the Enlightenment and the Revolution must be explored.

CONSERVATIVE PHILOSOPHY AND SOCIOLOGY: A SUMMARY

We have seen how the principles of the Enlightenment, as they became manifest in the Revolution, engendered a conservative philosophical reaction. That reaction, in turn, engendered a new interest in *social order* and various related problems and concepts.

Conservatives, like Burke, Hegel, Bonald, and Maistre, are so called because they desired quite literally to conserve and maintain the prevailing order. Moreover, some of them, as we have seen, sought not so much to conserve the existing order as to regress to a *status quo ante*. The disorder, anarchy, and radical changes those thinkers observed after the Revolution led them to generate concepts that relate to aspects of order and stability: tradition, authority, status, cohesion, adjustment, function, norm, symbol, ritual. As compared with the eighteenth century, the conservative concepts constituted a definite shift of interest from the individual to the group, from criticism of the existing order to its defence, and from social change to social stability.[12]

From the conservative standpoint, the social changes following in the wake of the Revolution had undermined and destroyed fundamental social institutions and had resulted in the loss of political stability. The conservatives traced those results to certain preceding events and processes in European history that had led, they believed, to the progressive weakening of the medieval order and hence to the upheaval of the Revolution. Quite precisely, they singled out Protestantism, capitalism, and science as the major forces. Those processes, furthermore, which were hailed as progressive by their liberal and radical contemporaries, were leading even now to an increasing atomization of peoples. Large "masses" now appeared, presumably unanchored in any stable social groups; widespread insecurity, frustration, and alienation became evident; and, finally, a monolithic secular power had emerged that was dependent for its existence on the mass of rootless individuals.

The conservatives had idealized the medieval order, and from that standpoint the modern era was very wanting indeed. As an antidote to the principles of the *Philosophes*, and as a critique of post-Revolutionary "*disorder*," the conservatives advanced a number of propositions about society:

1. It is an organic unity with internal laws of development and deep roots in the past, not simply a mechanical aggregate of individual elements. The conservatives were "social realists" in the sense that they firmly believed that society is a reality greater than the individuals who comprise it. That was in direct opposition to the social nominalism of the Enlightenment, the view that only individuals exist and that society is simply the name one gives to those individuals in their interrelationships.
2. Society antedates the individual and is ethically superior to him. Man has no existence outside of a social group or context, and he becomes human only by participating in society. Far from individuals constituting society, it is society that creates the individual by means of moral education, to employ Durkheim's term.
3. The individual is an abstraction and not the basic element of a society. Society is composed of relationships and institutions; individuals are simply members of society who fulfill certain statuses and roles—father, son, priest, and so on.
4. The parts of a society are interdependent and interrelated. Customs, beliefs, and institutions are organically intertwined so that changing or remaking one part will undermine the complex relationships maintaining the stability of society as a whole.
5. Man has constant and unalterable needs, which every society and each of its institutions serve to fulfill. Institutions are thus positive agencies by which basic human needs are met. If those agencies are disturbed or disrupted, suffering and disorder will result.

6. The various customs and institutions of a society are positively functional; they either fulfill human needs directly or indirectly by serving other indispensable institutions. Even prejudice is viewed in those terms; it tends to unify certain groups and also increases their sense of security.

7. The existence and maintenance of small groups is essential to society. The family, neighbourhood, province, religious groups, occupational groups—those are the basic units of a society, the basic supports of people's lives.

8. The conservatives also conceived of "social organization." The Revolution, as they saw it, had led not to a higher form of organization, but to social and moral disintegration. They wanted to preserve the older religious forms, Catholicism not Protestantism, and sought to restore the religious unity of medieval Europe. Protestantism, in teaching the importance of individual faith, had undermined the spiritual unity of society. And, as we have seen in the case of Bonald, the disorganizing consequences of urbanism, industry, and commerce were recognized.

9. The conservatives insisted, in addition, on the essential importance and positive value of the nonrational aspects of human existence. Man needs ritual, ceremony, and worship. The *Philosophes*, in their merciless criticism of those activities as irrational vestiges of the past, had weakened the sacred supports of society.

10. Status and hierarchy were also treated as essential to society. The conservatives feared that equality would destroy the "natural" and time-honoured agencies by which values were passed on from one generation to another. Hierarchy was necessary in the family, the Church, and the States, without which social stability was impossible.

Those are some of the major sociological tenets of the conservative legacy—a legacy that greatly influenced such thinkers as Saint-Simon, Comte, and, later, Durkheim. Those thinkers attempted to take conservative ideas and concepts out of their theological-reactionary context and to make them part and parcel of a scientific sociology. To see the beginnings of that attempt, the work of Comte, one of the founders of modern sociology, has to be considered.

NOTES

1. See V.C. Chapell, ed., *The Philosophy of David Hume* (New York: Modern Library, 1963).

2. John Locke, "An Essay Concerning Human Understanding," in *The English Philosophers from Bacon to Mill*, ed. Edwin A. Burtt (New York: Modern Library, 1939 and 1967).

3. Carl J. Friedrich, ed., *The Philosophy of Kant: Immanuel Kant's Moral and Political Writings* (New York: Modern Library, 1949 and 1977).

4. Edmund Burke, *Reflections on the Revolution in France* (New York: E. P. Dutton, 1960).

5. Ibid., p. 117.

6. Ibid., p. 219.

7. See G. W. F. Hegel, *Science of Logic*, trans. W. H. Johnston and L. G. Struthers (New York: Macmillan, 1951), Vol. 1. pp. 147–70.

8. G. W. F. Hegel, *The Philosophy of History* (New York: Dover Publications, 1956), p. 55.

9. Ibid., p. 55.

10. Ibid., p. 63.

11. Ibid., p. 412.

12. In the present discussion, I have drawn upon a number of points made by Robert A. Nisbet in his article entitled "Conservatism and Sociology," *American Journal of Sociology* (September 1952).

CHAPTER 4

Auguste Comte (1798–1857)

The term "positive," as Comte employed it in his positive philosophy, was explicitly polemical, intended as an ideological weapon with which to combat the philosophical legacy of the Enlightenment and the Revolution. The critical and destructive principles of *negative* philosophy were to be discredited and repudiated so that they could be replaced by the affirmative and constructive principles of *positive* philosophy. Actually, this counterattack also took place in Germany, where positivists attempted to challenge the radical tendency in Hegel's thought. Their most fundamental objection to Hegel's negative philosophy was that it

> "negates" things as they are. The matters of fact that make up the given state of affairs, when viewed in the light of reason, become negative, limited, transitory—they become perishing forms within a comprehensive process that leads beyond them. The Hegelian dialectic was seen as the prototype of all destructive negations of the given, for in it every immediately given form passes into its opposite and attains its true content only by so doing. This kind of philosophy, the critics said, denies to the given the dignity of the real; it contains the principle of revolution.[1]

In the present discussion, attention will be confined to France where Comte fought against the heritage of the *Philosophes* and in the process formed his own philosophy.

Comte saw a "deplorable state of anarchy" in his time, and he believed that his "social physics," bearing directly upon the "principal needs and grievances of society," would help bring order out of chaos.[2] He hoped to call this "science" to the attention of statesmen who "profess to devote themselves to the task of resolving the alarming revolutionary constitution of modern societies" (p. 2). Social and moral anarchy are the result of intellectual anarchy, itself a consequence of the fact that, on the one hand, theological-metaphysical philosophy has declined and, on the other, positive philosophy has not yet reached the point where it can provide an intellectual basis for a new organization and thus deliver society from the peril of dissolution.

Order and progress, which the ancients thought irreconcilable, must be united once and for all. Comte considered it the great misfortune of his time that the two principles were regarded as contradictory and were represented by opposing political parties. What he called the retrograde party was for order, whereas the anarchical party was for progress. The principle of order was derived from the Catholic-feudal, or theological, state of social philosophy, whose exponents were Bonald, Maistre, and others. The principle of progress, on the other hand, was derived from the critical tendencies of the Reformation and the Enlightenment. Existing social classes, much to Comte's chagrin, tended to polarize and to support either one or the other—hence, conflict, disorder, and anarchy. In every crisis, the retrograde party argued that the problem was due to the destruction of the older order and therefore demanded its complete restoration; the anarchical party, in contrast, argued that the trouble stemmed from the fact that the destruction of the old order was incomplete, and, therefore, that the revolution must continue.

Comte, like Saint-Simon, appreciated certain aspects of the feudal-theological order and did not reject it altogether. True, it had become "pernicious" by outliving its usefulness, but it had facilitated the development of modern society. Because, however, it can no longer hold its own before the natural progress of scientific intelligence and other social changes, the theological polity can never again become the basis of social order. Thus, Comte, unlike Bonald, believed it was impossible to restore the old order. The decline of the old is not temporary; neither is it the work of Providence. Somehow, Comte argues, a synthesis of the opposing ideas, order and progress, must be achieved, because only through intellectual unity and harmony can social unity be restored.

Science and industry were the main causes of the decline of the feudal-theological order, and the rise of the scientific spirit now precludes the restoration of that order; likewise with the industrial spirit, which now prevents the recurrence of the feudal-military spirit. Moreover, the new spirit is so strong that the spokesmen for the theological are themselves infected with it. Maistre, for example, tried to justify the restoration on the grounds of *reason* rather than divine right, thereby showing he was a child of his times. Also, the spokesmen for this school are not unified; torn as they are by sects, they have even accepted many basic principles that are antagonistic to their theological spirit—for example, subordinating the spiritual to the temporal authority. If, finally, they could succeed even temporarily in restoring the old order, the crisis would break out all over again—but even more violently than before because the same disintegrating forces would constantly be at work within it. So much for the theological stage and any hopes for restoring it. What about the metaphysical?

The principles of the "metaphysicians," Comte's term for the Enlightenment thinkers, were essentially critical and revolutionary. They contributed to progress but only in a negative sense. The metaphysical stage was necessary because it broke up the old system and paved the way for the next stage—the positive one that would put an end to the revolutionary period by the formation of a social order uniting the principles of order *and* progress. The metaphysical stage, necessary but provisional, "must be dangerously active till the new political organization which is to succeed it is ready to put an end to its agitation" (p. 9). The metaphysical spirit was necessary to direct the struggle and organize the maximum energy for the overthrow of the great ancient system. But, it, too, has outlived its usefulness and has become obstructive. Comte is especially indignant at the metaphysical view that represents "all government as being the enemy of society, and the duty of society to keep up a perpetual suspicion and vigilance, restricting the activity of the government more and more, in order to guard against its encroachments" (p. 11). Liberty of conscience is a dogma which *had* value as a weapon against theological dogmatism but is no longer useful because it can never be a positive organic principle—that is, the basis for the reorganization of society. The various demands for liberty are strictly "negative" principles. Just as astronomers, physicists, and chemists would not allow laymen to question or interfere with their operations, so in social physics (the term "sociology" does not yet appear at this stage of his discussion), the scientific experts should not yield to the incompetent. Social reorganization requires intellectual reorganization, and that is impossible so long as individuals have the right of inquiry on subjects above their qualifications. Comte insists that unity and unanimity will be essential in the new organic society. Social order, he writes, "must ever be incompatible with a perpetual discussion of the foundations of society" (p. 13).

Equality is another dogma: It has limited historical value as a weapon, but must not be turned into an absolute. It is an anarchic principle and hostile to order, as is the dogma of the "sovereignty of the people," which condemns the superior to dependence on the masses and opposes reorganization on different principles.

Comte also finds particularly objectionable Rousseau's "metaphysical notion of a supposed state of nature" and his representation of "civilization as an ever growing degeneracy from the primitive ideal type" (p. 16). Rousseau's presupposition that one can ask questions about the suitability of social systems for the nature of individuals was for Comte presumptuous and dangerous. He therefore dismisses Rousseau's conception as nothing more than the "metaphysical form of the theological dogma of the degradation of the human race by original sin" (p. 16). The disciples of the metaphysical school are also inconsistent if not hypocritical; for once in power they change their conduct and adopt many retrograde principles: war, centralization, natural religion, and so on.

Social crisis will continue so long as the two conflicting doctrines, the theological and the metaphysical, prevail. No order is possible until both are superseded by the positive state, which will be more *organic* than the theological and more *progressive* than the metaphysical. But one must not rush to bring about the new order. Rather, the people must wait patiently for the new system to emerge, and when the right conditions arise, society will submit to the rules that will assure its preservation. The new society will not arise so long as the theological and metaphysical spirits prevail, for they are mutually contradictory and cannot survive together indefinitely in one system. All contradictions must be banished from the new order. England's constitutional monarchy is based on contradictory principles, and therefore, predicts Comte, its "inevitable end cannot be very far off" (p. 22).

Comte despised intellectual anarchy and regarded it as the main cause of moral disunity. He had disdain for those laymen who expressed themselves about complex social and political issues as if such issues were not dependent on education and training. True moral order, Comte believed, "is incompatible with the existing vagabond liberty of individual minds if such license were to last; for the great social rules which should become customary cannot be abandoned to the blind and arbitrary decision of an incompetent public without losing all their efficacy" (p. 25). Comte feared and disliked social criticism and its disorganizing results. Criticism of the traditional patriarchal family, for example, had led to the legalization of divorce, and hence to personal and domestic disorder. Questioning and criticizing time-honoured institutions is destructive and threatens to undermine all social life. No important social duties should be questioned or discussed until such time as the discussion is directed by "true" positive principles. Such principles will provide a basis for intellectual unity; lacking such unity, society also lacks a moral authority and degenerates into a state of terror, anarchy, and corruption.

Comte also feared the contemporary emphasis on "material" considerations and regarded it as fatal to progress. That emphasis had revolutionary implications, dangerously annulling the resignation and submissiveness of the lower classes that he so strongly desired. The source of social evils is not to be sought in basic economic and political institutions but in ideas and manners. "When all political evils," he writes, "are imputed to institutions instead of to ideas and social manners, which are now the real seat of the mischief; the remedy is vainly sought in changes, each more serious than the last, in institutions and existing powers" (p. 31). Private property, to be sure, brings with it certain evils, but "it is equally evident that the remedy must arise from opinions, customs, and manners, and that political regulations can have no radical efficacy" (p. 32). The point, then, is not to tamper with, or change, existing institutions but rather to bring about a moral reorganization—a euphemism for the acquiescence of the lower classes to their social condition. There will be neither order nor progress so long as men fail to recognize that their suffering is not of a physical but "of a moral nature."

THE ADVENT OF POSITIVE PHILOSOPHY

Comte had great confidence in the ascendancy of the positive doctrine. Its "perfect logical coherence" and its social function assured success, because this doctrine "will impart a homogeneous and rational character to the desultory politics of our day, and it will … establish a general harmony in the entire system of social ideas" (p. 35). Positive philosophy, he believed, is undoubtedly superior to its predecessors. For, while the metaphysical school condemned all periods prior to the Revolution, and the retrograde school disparaged the whole of the modern era, only the positive principle is able to recognize "the fundamental law of continuous human development, representing the existing evolution as the necessary result of the gradual series of former transformations, by simply extending to social phenomena the spirit which governs the treatment of all other natural phenomena" (p. 36). And towards what end is the positive science to be developed? "It is plain that true science has no other aim than the establishment of intellectual order, which is the basis of every other order" (p. 36).

We must let Comte speak for himself to demonstrate the degree to which he advanced his positive doctrine with one purpose in mind—to avert revolution and to achieve the resignation of the "multitude" to the conditions of the existing order. He explicitly pushes to the extreme some of the conclusions which were only implicit in Saint-Simon's work and purges from that work every last critical element that might have remained:

> It is only by the positive polity that the revolutionary spirit can be restrained, because by it alone can the influence of the critical doctrine be justly estimated and circumscribed.… Under the rule of the positive spirit, again, all the difficult and delicate questions which now keep up a perpetual irritation in the bosom of society, and which can never be settled while mere political solutions are proposed, will be scientifically estimated, to the great furtherance of social peace.… At the same time, it [the positive polity] will be teaching society that, in the present state of their ideas, no political change can be of supreme importance, while the perturbation attending change is supremely mischievous, in the way both of immediate hindrance, and of diverting attention from the true need and procedure.… Again, the positive spirit tends to consolidate order, by the rational development of a wise resignation to incurable political evils.… A true resignation—that is, a permanent disposition to endure, steadily, and without hope of compensation, all inevitable evils—can proceed only from a deep sense of the connection of all kinds of natural phenomena with invariable laws. If there are (as I doubt not there are) political evils which, like some personal sufferings, cannot be remedied by science, science at least proves to us that they are incurable, so as to calm our restlessness under pain by the conviction that is by natural laws that they

are rendered insurmountable. Human nature suffers in its relations with the astronomical world, and the physical, chemical, and biological, as well as the political. How is it that we turbulently resist in the last case, while, in the others we are calm and resigned …? Finally, the positive philosophy befriends public order by bringing back men's understanding to a normal state through the influence of its method alone, before it has had time to establish any social theory. It dissipates disorder at once by imposing a series of indisputable scientific conditions on the study of political questions. By including social science in the scientific hierarchy, the positive spirit admits to success in this study only well-prepared and disciplined minds, so trained in the preceding departments of knowledge as to be fit for the complex problems of the last. The long and difficult preliminary elaboration must disgust and deter vulgar and ill prepared minds, and subdue the most rebellious. (pp. 37–38)

The positive conception of progress is superior to all others, and especially superior to the revolutionary view in which progress consists of the continuous extension of freedom, and the "gradual expansion of human powers. Now, even in the restricted and negative sense in which this is true—that of the perpetual diminution of obstacles—the positive philosophy is incontestably superior: for true liberty is nothing else than a rational submission to the preponderance of the laws of nature …" (p. 39). The scientific elite will be the final authority of what those are and will indicate the degree to which the lot of the lower classes may be slowly improved. In that way the positive doctrine will provide a so-called constructive alternative to the insurrectionary solution advocated by the revolutionary school. Basic economic and political institutions are not to be changed, for history has shown that such change avails nothing. The class structure should remain as it is; and class conflict presumably will be reduced, even eliminated, through the moral reconciliation of the classes. That will be facilitated by imposing a moral authority between the working classes and the leaders of society.

Those who identify with the theological-retrograde school probably will not support the positive doctrine because they are not interested in just any order but in their unique one. The "stationary school," the defenders of the status quo, on the other hand, may be won over when they recognize that it will further their interests. But Comte's real target is the revolutionary school whose "doctrines will be absorbed by the new philosophy, while all its anarchical tendencies will be extinguished" (p. 41). The present generation of scientists, however, is too much infected with revolutionary principles to adopt the positive view. Therefore the chance of winning over the scientists will depend on the younger generation who will be given a really thorough positive education. In all cases, "progress" will depend on "an intellectual, and then a moral reorganization [which] must precede and direct the political" (p. 42).

THE POSITIVE METHOD IN ITS APPLICATION TO SOCIAL PHENOMENA

For Comte, what distinguishes the scientific spirit is its steady subordination of imagination to observation, of reason to "facts." That is quite different from the eighteenth-century conception in which reasoning and observing are coordinate functions of the scientific method. In Comte's view, prediction, or "prevision" as he calls it, will facilitate social control, a primary and even exclusive aim of his positive doctrine. In those terms, "to predict in order to control," becomes a totalitarian slogan in his hands. That becomes even clearer in his "scientific" conception of society.

Order and progress are the static and dynamic aspects of a society. Order refers to the harmony that prevails among the various conditions of existence, whereas progress refers to the society's orderly development according to natural social laws. Thus the two principles, previously mutually antagonistic, are reconciled. It is natural and normal for the elements of the social system, the institutions of society, to be interdependent and interrelated. Therefore, even for analytical purposes, social elements should not be contemplated separately as if they had an independent existence. All the parts of the system make up a harmonious whole, which, by definition, is divested of all conflictive, contradictory, and antagonistic elements. He enunciates as a scientific principle "that there must always be a spontaneous harmony between the whole and the parts of the social system," (p. 65) and he insists that harmony will establish itself through radical consensus, the only condition proper to the social organism. Emphasis is always on adjustment to the "natural" social laws, quite deliberately opposed to Enlightenment principles where the emphasis is on changing the social system to allow for the infinite perfection of the human individual. Again and again Comte stresses that the scientific method requires that society be studied as a whole and not separated into its component parts. It is as if he fears that the logical analysis of a society's institutions will inevitably lead to its actual dissolution; an analytical view of society, in which relationships are critically scrutinized, will revive the very same critical, negative, and revolutionary philosophy that positivism was to replace once and for all.

Social dynamics refers to the study of the patterns of evolutionary progress in which the sequences of development are necessary and inevitable. Social dynamics, then, is really "dynamic order" proceeding according to natural, orderly, and necessary laws. For "unless the movement was determined by those laws, it would occasion the entire destruction of the social system" (p. 72). Amelioration accompanies development but it is not unlimited. "The chimerical notion of unlimited perfectibility is thus as once excluded" (p. 73). The tendency toward improvement is spontaneous, and therefore does not require any special political action directed toward change. The latter is in effect "superfluous," because each stage is as perfect as it can be. Not only political action but human action in general is very limited in its effects and subject to the constriction of natural laws. Can those laws nevertheless be modified in any way? The human race could perhaps accelerate or retard certain tendencies but never change the nature of those tendencies. It certainly cannot reverse certain orders of development nor can it skip stages. The importance of human action, in general, and political action, in particular, has been greatly exaggerated.

As for other aspects of Comte's method, he emphasized such techniques as observation, experiment, and comparison. And in spite of the transparent ideological elements of his methodology, he does manage to grasp some of the principles of scientific method—which always remains subordinated, however, to the construction of his hierarchical, organic, authoritarian society. Observation is impossible without theory, first to direct it and then to interpret what is observed. Facts cannot speak for themselves, for "though we are steeped to the lips in them, we can make no use of them, nor even be aware of them, for want of speculative guidance in examining them" (p. 81). Facts must be attached at least by a tentative hypothesis to the laws of social development. But for Comte, as we have seen, those laws as well as all his other assumptions and concepts about society were in the first instance inspired by their ideological function. The whole apparatus of his positive doctrine is ideological in the strictest sense of that term, and science never achieves very much autonomy in his doctrinaire and totalitarian system. He remained blind throughout his work to the ideal of freedom even as it related to science and apparently failed to see how many aspects of society he had dogmatically closed off from the view of science by means of his doctrinaire pronouncements.

As Comte proceeds in his exposition of social statics, he considers the individual, the family, and society, "the last comprehending in a scientific sense, the whole of the human species, and chiefly, the *whole of the white race*" (p. 105, italics added). Not the individual but the family is the true social unit, because the family is the school of social life. Man is a social being whose social nature is formed in the family context. But those assertions and the like are always made with a specific ideological intention in mind. The subordination of woman is natural and will continue in the "new" society: The female sex is in a state of perpetual infancy. "Sociology will prove that the equality of the sexes, of which so much is said, is incompatible with all social existence" (p. 112). Thus Comte argues the organic inferiority of woman and attempts to provide a "scientific" rationale for the same state of affairs that the theological school regarded as determined by Providence.

Generally, "providential wisdom," though in a secularized form, dominates Comte's conception of society and its development. The changes brought about by the inherent wisdom of the spontaneous evolutionary process are always "superior to any that the most eminent reformers would have ventured to conceive of before hand" (p. 114). Nevertheless, there are developments which, though natural, can threaten the very existence of society. Comte views the division of labour, growing increasingly complex, in that light. It seems to be an inexorable process, the very principle of society's development; but at the same time, as the division of labour is extended, it seems to decompose and fragment society. Thus government is assigned the role "to guard against and restrain the fundamental dispersion of ideas, sentiments, and ideals, which is the inevitable result of the very principle of human development, and which, if left to itself, would put a stop to social progression in all important respects" (p. 119). Every element and institution of the society, including government, must serve to further stability, solidarity, and order. Society is everything in Comte's scheme—the individual, nothing. Each must subordinate himself, but that has its rewards because "there can be no one who, in his secret mind, has not often felt, more or less vividly, how sweet it is to obey when he can have the rare privilege of cosigning the burdensome responsibility of his general self-conduct to wise and trustworthy guidance" (p. 122).

This review of Comte's work should suffice to show how much of it was explicitly justificatory and apologetic for his "best of all possible worlds." Despite the lip service paid to "science," virtually every assertion he makes is based not on experience, observation, and reasoning, but on values and sentiments. He refused to see that the human being is not merely an object but an active subject; that he *determines* and is not merely determined; that he can change society according to goals, "something which positivism must deny, for goals, in their very nature, are something that have not as yet been experienced."[3]

In his later work, *Politique Positive* (1851–54), the religious and sentimental factor finally prevailed and Comte unabashedly proclaimed himself pope of the new positive religion—an ironic turn of events for the ardent defender of positive science. Little wonder, then, that J. S. Mill described Comte's later views as "the most complete system of spiritual and temporal despotism that ever issued from the brain of any human being—except, perhaps, Ignatius Loyola."[4]

Despite Comte's philosophic efforts, the peoples of Europe failed to achieve an organic, integrated, conflict-free civilization. It was Karl Marx who was to draw the most radical conclusions from that failure.

NOTES

1. Herbert Marcuse, *Reason and Revolution* (Boston: Beacon Press, 1960), p. 325. For a full discussion of the positive reaction, see pp. 323–74.

2. The present discussion of Comte is based on the second volume of Harriet Martineau's translation and condensation of his *Cours de Philosophie Positive*. It appeared in English as *The Positive Philosophy*, 2 vols. (London: Routledge and Kegan Paul, 1893). Martineau's rendition so impressed Comte that he recommended it over

the original and as a result her version was retranslated into French. (Hereafter all page references to this work will be indicated in parentheses immediately following the quoted passage.)

3.   See Frank Hartung, "The Social Function of Positivism," *Philosophy of Science*, Vol. 12, no. 2 (April 1945), pp. 120–33.

4.   Quoted in F.M.H. Markham, *Henri Comte de Saint-Simon* (Oxford: Basil Blackwell, 1952), p. xviii.

CHAPTER 5

The Philosophical Orientations of Karl Marx (1818–1883)

Comte's positive philosophy, as we have seen, was a conscious attempt to discredit and repudiate what he had termed "negative" philosophy. The negative-critical philosophy that emerged and took shape with the Enlightenment had proved itself a formidable weapon in the hands of the rising bourgeoisie in its struggle against the older classes of the theological-feudal order. Ultimately, that struggle resulted in the French Revolution and the dissolution of the old order. In those terms, negative philosophy, even for Comte, had fulfilled a useful historical function. Now, however, with the establishment of the bourgeois order, Comte believed negative philosophy, the legacy of the Enlightenment, had outlived its usefulness. Now, when the major task had become consolidation of the new bourgeois-industrial order and creation of a truly organic and integrated society, negative philosophy led only to divisiveness, conflict, and disorder. It stirred the imagination and hopes of the proletariat and encouraged class conflict. The proletarians, instead of finding their place in the new organic society and adjusting peacefully to it, as Comte desired, were being agitated to struggle for the transformation of the existing society.

Each stage in the evolution of the new organic society was viewed by Comte as a necessary one; therefore, the working class must adjust to the present stage. Improvement would come about organically as the society progressed harmoniously from stage to stage. Revolution—that is, a total transformation of the social system—was out of the question. Revolution could have only negative consequences; it would only shatter the existing order without bringing in its wake any fundamental change in the condition of the vast majority of the people. Progress was best assured not by criticism, class conflict, and revolutionary activity, but by reconciling the conflicting tendencies and classes; by educating all classes of society—and especially the lower classes—to take their proper place in the new, hierarchically organized society and to resign themselves to their condition. This is what the new positive science taught and this was to be its chief function: to achieve an organic and conflict-free social order.

If with Comte, then, there is a complete renunciation of the legacy of the Enlightenment (and the French Revolution), with Marx we return full circle to a whole-hearted reaffirmation of that legacy. Marx restores, and skilfully employs, the very philosophical premises Comte so intensely detested.

First among those premises was the perfectibility of man. Marx had a conception of "natural man"—the individual human being, his needs, and his potential for development—not unlike that of Rousseau and, more generally, of the Enlightenment thinkers. Although Marx's conception is expressed most explicitly in his early writings, it remains throughout his life the basis of his analysis and criticism of the capitalist system, and of his hopes for the attainment of a truly *human* society.

Man, Marx believed, is infinitely perfectible. Man's *essential* powers—his latent and potential human powers—are unlimited in their capacity for development. If man is now no more than a labouring beast, he need not remain in that condition; he can attain the highest forms of creativity, thought, and action. This is the underlying conception by which Marx assessed and evaluated social systems. Man's latent creative powers were stifled and repressed under the social conditions of all class societies. The existing system, capitalism, was not only preventing the fulfillment of his potential, it was depriving him of his animal needs—fresh air, food, sex, and so on. Hunger, for example, was a condition of deprivation imposed by other men. Marx thus condemned the capitalist system for its effect on individual human beings. That view finds it clearest and most consistent expression in one of Marx's early philosophical works, *Economic and Philosophic Manuscripts of 1844*, to which we now turn.

It offended Marx's conception of man that the capitalist-industrial system had reduced him to an *animal laborans*, "a beast reduced to the strictest bodily needs."[1] The workers' "needs" were now at the "barest and most miserable level of physical subsistence" and their activity for the better part of their waking day was a tedious and repetitive mechanical movement.

The lowest possible level of life and activity had become the general standard—one in which men were deprived not only of their human needs but of their animal needs as well:

> Even the need for fresh air ceases for the worker. Man returns to living in a cave, which is now, however, contaminated with the mephitic breath of plague given off by civilization, and which he continues to occupy only *precariously*, it being for him an alien habitation which can be withdrawn from him any day—a place from, if he does not pay, he can be thrown out any day. For this mortuary he has to *pay*. A dwelling in the *light*, which Prometheus in Aeschylus designated as one of the greatest boons, by means of which he made the savage into a human being, ceases to exist for the worker. Light, air, etc.—the simplest *animal* cleanliness—ceases to be a need for man. *Dirt*—this stagnation and putrefaction of man—the *sewage* of civilization (speaking quite literally)—comes to be the *element of life* for him. Utter, unnatural neglect, putrefied nature, comes to be his *life-element*. None of his senses exist any longer, and not only in his human fashion, but in an *inhuman* fashion, and therefore, not even in an animal fashion. (p. 117)

Clearly, Marx had an image of man as he could be and hence ought to be, and what he saw and described was a far cry from that image. For instead of developing his essential human powers, man was being debased and deformed and thus becoming something less than animal.

In these philosophical writings, the dehumanization of man was viewed by Marx as a consequence of *alienation*. That idea, though Hegelian in origin, was fundamentally transformed in Marx's hands. Alienation for Hegel, like his other constructs, was exclusively a phenomenon of the mind. With the Young- or Left-Hegelians, the concept was significantly altered but remained primarily a philosophical notion—that is, a condition in which man's own powers appear as independent forces or entities controlling his actions.

One of the Left-Hegelians, Ludwig Feuerbach, had elaborated the Enlightenment view of religion as an "illusion." For the French *Philosophes*, "God" was simply a symbolic expression of humanity's yearnings for perfection. Feuerbach, in a book called, *The Essence of Christianity*, presented a view of religion quite similar to that of the Enlightenment. God, he maintained, is a creation of the human imagination. The Divine is a symbolic expression of humanity's unfulfilled promises and aspirations. Humans unconsciously project their ideals unto hypothetical beings, which they then treat as sacred and divine. They thus come to worship the product of their own minds.

When Marx was a young university student, such atheistic ideas were quite fashionable in radical circles. He found them convincing as far as they went. In his judgment, however, they did not go far enough. Existing theories remained on the psychological level and ignored what he regarded as the key sociological question: *Why* do people project the best part of themselves unto the cosmos? What are the social conditions that prompt people to externalize their own powers and values and to attribute them to hypothetical, superhuman beings? Marx's reply was, in a word, that religion is the product of *social alienation*. That meant that, historically, humanity has been divided against itself by the social-class cleavages of society. It is the domination, oppression, and exploitation of man by man that has given rise to religion. Religious ideas are an expression of human suffering and a protest against it as well. In the words of the young Marx:

> Religion is the sigh of the oppressed creature, the sentiment of a heartless world, and the soul of soulless conditions. It is the opium of the people.
>
> The abolition of religion as the *illusory* happiness of men, is a demand for their real happiness. The call to abandon their illusions about their conditions is a call to abandon a condition which requires illusions.[2]

Reflecting on the degraded condition of the industrial proletariat and other oppressed classes, Marx concluded that, by itself, a demonstration of the illusory character of religion was not likely to have liberating effects. So long as oppression and sharp inequalities prevail, people will continue to create comforting illusions. The main task, therefore, is to change the social order and to eliminate the circumstances that require illusions. For Marx, it was industrial capitalism in particular which imposed great suffering on the majority of the people, diminishing their humanity and distorting their self-understanding. Religion is an "opium" because it so often leads people to seek meaning and happiness not in the human world but in the divine hereafter.

In that light we can more readily grasp Marx's meaning when he writes that religious criticism has plucked the imaginary flowers from the chain, not in order that man shall bear the chain without … consolation but so that he shall cast off the chain and pluck the living flower. The criticism of religion disillusions man so that he will think, act and fashion his reality as a man who has lost his illusions and regained his reason.…[3]

It is only through the rational reconstruction of society, so that it may meet the human needs of each and every member, that alienation can be overcome.

There are several senses in which Marx employed the term *alienation*, and the meanings he assigned to the concept may best be grasped from the two German words he used to describe the phenomenon he had in mind: (1) *entäussern* (verb) or, in its noun form, *Entäusserung*, and (2) *entfremden* (verb) and *Entfremdung* (noun). The first of these means "to part with," "to give up," "to deprive one's self of," and "to divest one's self of," and, as noted by the translator of these manuscripts, it also implies "making external to one's self." The noun *Entäusserung* is also explicitly defined as alienation (of property). The second German word, as rendered in English as "to alienate," connotes primarily two people becoming estranged from each other. Thus, the term "alienation" refers to a complex process with several aspects. As will be seen in a later discussion of *Capital*, Marx described the process and its consequences in great detail. Here it may be summarized in general terms.

The process begins with the separation of men from their means of production and subsistence (as was the case in England when the yeomen were driven from their land following passage of various Enclosure Acts). Men are alienated from their property and therefore compelled, if they are to avoid starving and becoming vagabonds, to sell their labour power to the capitalist entrepreneurs awaiting them. The two parties, capitalist as well as labourer, thus enter into an essentially instrumental relationship with each other. Forming that relationship is and remains an act of expediency, and the two parties remain estranged from each other because the relationship is based on conflicting interests and fundamentally different conditions of life.

Immediately upon entering the relationship, the worker begins to consume his energies in the production of things; his labour power becomes objectified in commodities over which he has no control. In that sense, the more he produces, the poorer he becomes.

> All these consequences are contained in the definition that the worker
> is related to the *product of his labor* as an *alien* object. For on this premise
> it is clear that the more the worker spends himself, the more powerful
> the alien objective world becomes which he creates over against himself,
> the poorer he himself—his inner world—becomes, the less belongs to
> him as his own.… The worker puts his life into the object; but now his
> life no longer belongs to him but to the object. Hence, the greater this
> activity, the greater is the worker's lack of objects. Whatever the product
> of his labor is, he is not. Therefore the greater the product, the less is
> he himself. The *alienation* of the worker from his product means not
> only that his labor becomes an object, an *external existence*, but that it
> exists *outside him*, independently, as something alien to him, and that
> it becomes a power on its own confronting him; it means that the life
> which he has conferred on the object confronts him as something hostile
> and alien. (p. 70)

The worker has no control over the process of production or its results; his
labour is an alienating activity, not only because he loses the product in
which he has reified a part of himself, but because the whole productive
process is external to him and his human needs. In

> his work, therefore, he does not affirm himself but denies himself, does
> not feel content but unhappy, does not develop freely his physical and
> mental energy but mortifies his body and ruins his mind. The worker
> therefore only feels himself outside his work, and in his work feels outside
> himself. He is at home when he is not working, and when he is working
> he is not at home. His labor is therefore not voluntary, but coerced; it
> is *forced labor*. It is therefore not the satisfaction of a need; it is merely a
> *means* to satisfy needs external to it. Its alien character emerges clearly
> in the fact that as soon as no physical or other compulsion exists, labor
> is shunned like the plague. (p. 72)

Consequently, he experiences the process of production as an oppressive
activity, as a loss of freedom. He

> no longer feels himself, to be freely active in any but his animal func-
> tions—eating, drinking, procreating.… And in his human functions

he no longer feels himself to be anything but an animal.… Certainly eating, drinking, procreating, etc., are also genuinely human functions. But in the abstraction which separates them from the sphere of all other human activity and turns them into sole and ultimate ends, they are animal. (p. 73)

Man, as worker, has become something less than human, because he is separated from his potential human qualities. The animal, Marx says, is immediately identical with its life activity; man, on the other hand, has the ability to make his life activity the object of his will and consciousness. That is what makes it possible for man to attain ever greater degrees of freedom. The animal produces only when dominated by his immediate physical needs; man, however, can produce "even when he is free from physical need and only truly produces in freedom therefrom" (p. 75). This is reversed under conditions of alienated labour where man's whole conscious being and life activity, "his essential being [becomes] a mere means to his existence."

Thus we have an initial alienation from his means of production that forces an individual (the worker) to form an estranged relationship with another individual (the employer). The activity itself, which he now performs for the means of existence, is an alienating activity, for the product remains alien to the worker and the process of production itself remains external to his consciousness and to his human needs and desires. Man becomes increasingly alienated from himself, a fact that expresses itself in his estrangement from others. One can then see why Marx remained unimpressed with the "forcing-up of wages" and other such ameliorative measures that would not alter the basic relationships underlying the conditions of alienation and "would therefore be nothing but *better payment for the slave*, and would not conquer either for the worker or for labor their human status and dignity" (p. 81).

It is not the worker alone, however, but the nonworker as well (albeit in a different form and in differing degrees) who is subject to the condition of alienation. Everything "which appears in the worker as an *activity of alienation, of estrangement,* appears in the nonworker as a *state of alienation, of estrangement*" (p. 83). The capitalist who regards as luxury everything the worker desires above his barest physical needs is himself subject, though to a lesser extent than the worker, to denial and want. For political economy, denial and want, or thrift and saving, were major virtues for both the capitalist and the worker:

> This science of marvelous industry is simultaneously the science of *asceticism*, and its true ideal is the *ascetic* but *extortionate* miser and the ascetic but *productive* slave.... The political economy—despite its worldly and wanton appearance—is a true moral science, the most moral of all the sciences. Self-denial, the denial of life and of all human needs, is its cardinal doctrine. The less you eat, drink, and read books; the less you go to the theatre, the dance hall, the public house; the less you think, love, theorize, sing, paint, fence, etc., the more you *save*—the *greater* becomes your treasure which neither moths nor dust will devour—your *capital*. The less you *are*, the more you *have*; the less you express your own life, the greater is your *alienated* life—the greater is the store of your estranged being. (p. 119)

This general condition, then, a consequence of specific social relationships and processes, was one that had to be abolished if men were to elevate themselves to a truly *human* status. For Marx, that was possible only "*in a practical way, by virtue of the practical energy of men*" (p. 109). If men were to develop their essential human powers, if they were to perfect themselves, they had first of all to abolish the conditions of their present malaise. That was to be a process, a movement. Therefore, the establishment of what Marx called "communism" was not an end but a means to man's greater freedom and hence to man's greater humanity. "Communism," wrote Marx in another early work, *German Ideology*, "is for us not a stable state which is to be established, an *ideal* to which reality will have to adjust itself. We call communism the *real* movement which abolishes the present state of things. The conditions of this movement result from the premises now in existence."[4] Communism is no static utopia toward which men should strive; it is a critical and revolutionary movement. "Communism ... is the *actual* phase necessary for the next stage of historical development in the process of human emancipation and recovery" (p. 114). As we shall see, Marx's conception of "communism" presupposed and entailed the enhancement of human rights and civil liberties.

It is clear, then, that Marx had a conception of what the human individual could become and that this was his measure of the existing social system.

Man's creative powers, his capacity for self-perfection and self-realization, are practically unlimited—given the abolition of those relationships and conditions which until now have so drastically impeded his development. Man is a creature of the very social conditions he himself has created, but *he need not remain a prisoner of those conditions*. To understand how, in Marx's view, men could make their history more consciously than ever before, we must examine another aspect of the Enlightenment legacy—negative-critical thinking—the dialectical form of which Marx learned directly from Hegel but fundamentally transformed.

NOTES

1. Karl Marx, *Economic and Philosophic Manuscripts of 1844* (Moscow: Foreign Languages Publishing House, 1961), p. 30. (Hereafter all page references to this work will be indicated in parentheses immediately following the quoted passage.)
2. Karl Marx, *Early Writings*, trans. and ed. T. B. Bottomore (London: C. A. Watts, 1963), pp. 43–44.
3. Ibid.
4. Karl Marx and Frederick Engels, *The German Ideology* (New York: International Publishers, 1960), p. 26.

CHAPTER 6

Marx's Relation to Hegel and Feuerbach

For Hegel, it will be recalled, reason embraced the total universe; all of its realms, the inorganic as well as the organic, nature as well as society, were governed by the Idea and its dialectical logic. Reason was an immanent force that expressed itself in the unfolding of reality. In the natural realm, development and change—things becoming actually what they always were potentially—took place in "a direct, unopposed, unhindered manner."[1] It was both a peaceful process and one of blind necessity. Not so in the human realm, where history had shown that development was a conflictive process dependent on human consciousness and will. The rational structure of being could be comprehended by the human mind and that was a necessary condition of freedom: the actualization of the potentialities inherent in reality. "Truth" was not merely a function of formal propositions; the criterion of truth was reality in process. Herbert Marcuse has explained Hegel's view rather well: "Something is true if it is what it can be, fulfilling all its objective possibilities."[2]

For Hegel, the form in which a thing immediately appears is not yet its true form. What one sees at first is a negative condition, not the real potentialities of a thing. Something becomes true "only in the process of overcoming this negativity, so that the birth of the truth requires the death of the given state of being.... All forms are seized by the dissolving movement of reason which cancels and alters them until they are adequate to their notion."[3] In those terms, there is a revolutionary side to Hegel's philosophy. The given facts as they appear can never be more than a temporary and partial truth, because they represent only one negative phase in the unfolding of truth which reveals itself precisely by the destruction and supersession of that phase.

This dialectical conception of reality which can be traced to Aristotle and even to certain pre-Socratic philosophers profoundly influenced Marx's thinking about social phenomena.[4] The realm of the "is" must always be challenged to reveal the possibilities within it. The existing factual order is a transient negativity that can be transcended. One cannot even comprehend the existing order, let alone free its potentialities, unless it is critically opposed and ultimately transcended. The data are not "positives," nor is the existing factual order inviolable. On the contrary, since that order imposes a subhuman condition of existence upon men, since they are therefore less than they can be, men must strive to change that order.

This approach is directly opposed to that of positivism, which treats facts *in their immediately given form* as truth. By their rejection of universal concepts and their reduction of truth to the immediately observable and verifiable, the positivists exclude "from the domain of knowledge everything that may not yet be a fact."[5] Marx, like Hegel—at least up to a given point in the latter's system—refused to limit truth to a particular "given"; he firmly believed "that the potentialities of men and things are not exhausted in the given forms and relations in which they may actually appear...."[6]

Of course, all this should not be taken to mean that Marx had no use or regard for "the facts"; that would be patently false and absurd. The point is, rather, that he was always conscious of the transient character of any given facts, which are but negative moments in a ceaseless historical process. The existing factual order of capitalism, for instance, had to be studied carefully, if only to learn how to negate it. The possibility of a revolution rested on certain objective economic and political conditions, which could be grasped through an analysis of the structure and tendencies of capitalism. Only with factual knowledge could Marx develop (as was his intention) a theory to guide the revolutionary action of the working class. Moreover, once he arrived at an empirical generalization or theoretical proposition that he regarded as true, he always pointed to the historically specific conditions to which it applied. The proposition, for example, that the "relations of production" tend to determine the character of men, including their consciousness, is regarded by Marx as a sociohistorical fact; but that fact is precisely what he regards as man's alienated condition. At the same time, therefore, that he describes that fact, he exposes the materialistic nature of the prevailing order in which relations of production are fundamental in forming and *deforming* human relations and in divesting man of his human character. Thus,

Marx's proposition is a *critical* one, implying that the prevailing relation between consciousness and social existence is a false one that must be overcome before the true relation can come to light. The truth of the materialistic thesis is thus to be fulfilled in its negation.

Marx emphasizes time and again that his materialistic starting point is forced upon him by the materialistic quality of the society he analyzes.[7]

Misunderstanding of that point has led to the worst distortions of Marx's theory, in which the very opposite of what he believed is attributed to him—namely, that his ideal was a materialistic society. Actually, his ideal was to invert the prevalent relationship between social being and social consciousness. Precisely, what Marx meant by leaving the domain of "necessity" and entering the domain of "freedom" was that men would now begin *consciously* to determine their future. That is the view Marx held not only in his early philosophical writings but in his maturity as well. In *Capital*, he wrote: "The life-process of society, which is based on the process of material production, does not strip off its mystical view until it is treated as production by freely associated men, and is consciously regulated by them in accordance with a settled plan."[8]

In those terms, as was pointed out earlier, Marx viewed socialism and/or communism not as ends in themselves. The abolition of private property and the socialization of the means of production are the first steps in the abolition of alienated labour. That this will lead to "an association, in which the free development of each is the condition for the free development of all" is *not* at all inevitable. Everything will depend on what men do with the socialized resources. If men do not associate freely and utilize those resources to fulfill their human needs and to further their human development, then the socialization of the means of production has merely substituted one form of subjugation for another. Marx foresaw that danger and warned against reifying "society" and setting it up against the individual. "What is to be avoided above all is the establishing of 'Society' as an abstraction *vis-à-vis* the individual. The individual is *the social being*. His life … is therefore an expression and confirmation of *social life*."[9]

The needs and freedom of the individual thus remain paramount in Marx's ideal; he therefore condemns any society that imposes a division of labour without considering the need for well-being and for maximum self-realization of each and every individual. This is his main criticism of class society: It is a situation in which an individual's entire fate tends to be determined by his class position and the function assigned to him in the system of production. The difference between this condition and the one he envisioned in the future, Marx made clear in a famous passage:

> The division of labor offers us the first example of how, as long as man remains in natural society [i.e., governed by laws which are inexorable, like natural laws over which men have no control], that is as long as a cleavage exists between the particular and the common interest, as long therefore as activity is not voluntarily, but naturally, divided, man's own deed becomes an alien power opposed to him, which enslaves him instead of being controlled by him. For as soon as labor is distributed, each man has a particular, exclusive sphere of activity, which is forced upon him and from which he cannot escape. He is a hunter, a fisherman, a shepherd, or a critical critic, and must remain so if he does not want to lose his means of livelihood; while in communist society, where nobody has one exclusive sphere of activity, but each man can become accomplished in any branch he wishes, society regulates the general production and thus makes it possible for me to do one thing to-day and another to-morrow, to hunt in the morning, fish in the afternoon, rear cattle in the evening, criticize after dinner, just as I have a mind, without ever becoming hunter, fisherman, shepherd or critic.[10]

From Hegel, then, Marx took the emphasis on negative-critical thinking, which he integrated into his intellectual consciousness.[11] With Marx, however, dialectical thinking is not only critical and revolutionary but empirical and sociological as well. Conflict, for example, is explained not abstractly but in terms of concrete and specific social relationships. One class owns the means of production whereas the other does not; that is the basis of the various forms of conflict between them. Marx views the entire capitalist system as resting on conflicting principles and tendencies: "Contradictions" exist between the social character of production and the institution of private property, or between the growth of the "productive forces" and the existing "relations of production"; between production for use and production for profit; between production and consumption, and still others. For Marx, those conflicting principles are rooted in definite social relationships, and his dialectical reasoning is therefore quite the opposite of Hegel's closed ontological system. Marx's thought is in all respects a different order of truth from Hegel's, and not to be interpreted in terms of the latter's philosophical concepts. That can only be appreciated by a further examination of Marx's work.

Marx worked out his own theory of the relationship between social existence and social consciousness—the so-called materialist conception of history—in direct opposition to Hegel's idealistic conception of that relationship. Throughout his life, Marx continued to honour his intellectual debt to that "mighty thinker" by coquetting with the Hegelian mode of expression. Nevertheless, he believed that dialectical thinking had suffered from mystification in Hegel's hands. "With him it is standing on its head. It must be turned right side up again, if you would discover the rational kernel within the mystical shell."[12] What was that rational kernel? "In its rational form," Marx wrote,

> It [the dialectic] is a scandal and abomination to bourgeoisdom and its doctrinaire professors, because it includes in its comprehension and affirmative recognition of the existing state of things, at the same time also, the recognition of the negation of that state, of its inevitable breaking up; because it regards every historically developed social form as in fluid movement, and therefore takes into account its transient nature not less than its momentary existence; because it lets nothing impose upon it, and is in its essence critical and revolutionary.[13]

In Hegel, moreover, the "existing state of things" appeared as an expression of the Idea or Spirit; he had held, apparently, to an inverted conception of the relationship between existence and consciousness. That prompted Marx to state once more in his maturity what he had already repeatedly insisted upon in his youth:

> My dialectical method is not only different from the Hegelian, but its direct opposite. To Hegel, the life-process of the human brain, i.e., the process of thinking, which, under the name of "the Idea," he even transforms into an independent subject, is the demiurgos of the real world, and the real world is only the external, phenomenal form of "the Idea." With me, on the contrary, the ideal is nothing else than the material world reflected by the human mind, and translated into forms of thought.[14]

Marx thus dissociated himself from the metaphysical premises of Hegel's philosophy, in which thinking was separated from the life-process. At the same time, however, Marx rejected the prevailing form of materialism. He vehemently opposed the mechanistic and reductionist standpoint according to which man's mental activity was nothing more than matter in motion. Chemical bodily processes, according to that doctrine, were sufficient to explain men's ideas and emotions. Materialists of that kind contended that "Ideas stand in the same relation to the brain as bile does to the liver or urine to the kidneys."[15]

The *locus classicus* of Marx's critique of mechanistic materialism is his famous "Theses on Feuerbach."[16] There Marx rejects any doctrine that ignores the active, creative, and determining side of man. In his first thesis, Marx acknowledges that the active side was in fact recognized by idealism—that is, by such great idealistic philosophers as Kant and Hegel. In the same thesis, Marx repudiates all previous materialistic philosophies, including Feuerbach's, for treating humans as if they were no more than passive, determined objects. What emerges from Marx's critique is his own conception of humanity as actively constituting itself. The external world is a humanly created world that is moulded and changed by means of man's theoretical-practical activity. Man creates the world in the sense that he produces his tools and external objects with the materials of nature, thus modifying nature, his means of acting upon it, and his relations with his fellow man.

Thus Marx developed his own distinctive view in opposition to idealism and materialism alike. With the exception of Feuerbach, whose notable achievement Marx believed was to make the social relation of man to man the basic principle of his theory, none of the Young Hegelians had advanced much beyond Hegel conceptually. But Feuerbach had committed the basic error of the mechanistic materialists: He had overlooked the creative, determining side of practical human activity. Marx's theory and method (the so-called "materialist conception of history," which he also described as "dialectical" because it took into account both the active and the passive sides) cannot therefore be adequately grasped as materialism in the traditional sense. Marx's view, as he himself characterized it, was to be distinguished from both idealism *and* materialism. Marx sought to overcome the one-sidedness of both philosophical traditions and to preserve their elements of truth. That must always be borne in mind when we hear Marx and Engels speak of their "materialist conception"; for gross misunderstandings of Marx's theory persist to this very day.

NOTES

1. Herbert Marcuse, *Reason and Revolution*, 2nd ed. (Boston: Beacon Press, 1954), p. 25.

2. Ibid., p. 25.

3. Ibid., p. 26.

4. In this connection, Hannah Arendt has remarked that "the influence of Aristotle on the style of Marx's thought seems to me almost as characteristic and decisive as the influence of Hegel's philosophy," *The Human Condition* (Garden City, N.Y.: Anchor Books, 1959), p. 365.

5. Marcuse, *Reason and Revolution*, p. 113.

6. Ibid., p. 113.

7. Ibid., pp. 273–74.

8. Karl Marx, *Capital* (Moscow: Foreign Languages Publishing House, 1954), Vol. I, p. 80.

9. Karl Marx, *Economic and Philosophic Manuscripts of 1844* (Moscow: Foreign Languages Publishing House, 1961), p. 105.

10. Karl Marx and Frederick Engels, *German Ideology* (New York: International Publishers, 1960), p. 22.

11. However, unlike his friend and colleague, Frederick Engels, Marx made no attempt to codify dialectical reasoning into a rigid system equally applicable to nature and society. A critique of Engel's view of the dialectic and his vacillation between Hegelianism and Positivism may be found in George Lichtheim's *Marxism: An Historical and Critical Study* (New York: Frederick A. Praeger, 1962), and in Sidney Hook's *Reason, Social Myths and Democracy* (New York: Harper & Row, 1940).

12. Marx, *Capital*, p. 20.

13. Ibid., p. 20.

14. Ibid., p. 19.

15. Franz Mehring, *Karl Marx* (Ann Arbor: University of Michigan Press, 1962), p. 280.

16. See T. B. Bottomore and M. Rubel, eds., *Karl Marx: Selected Writings in Sociology and Social Philosophy* (London: C. A. Watts, 1961), pp. 67–69.

CHAPTER 7

Marx's Historical Sociology

Marx died in 1883. Soon after, "Marxism" came to stand for a theory in which economic and other "material" factors explained the structure of society and the course of history. That was the dominant view among Marxists and critics of Marxism alike. Marx and Engels, it was widely believed, had proposed that callous self-interest governs individuals, classes, and nations, driving the world forward. The history of people throughout the centuries is to be explained by a changing, complex interplay of strictly material causes. Economics is everything! Marxism was thus reduced to a one-factor theory.

At the same time, Marx's theory was transformed by his followers in another respect. Marx's focus on the connections between economic development and social-class formation was reduced to a form of technological determinism. Economic and historical changes were thus made to depend directly on technical changes in the instruments of work. Changes in some important element of production—the discovery of a new raw material or fuel—was said to determine the movement of history.

In time, both economic and technological determinism came to be regarded as one-sided and misleading. Prominent Marxists, often under the influence of outstanding non-Marxist thinkers, assailed these forms of "vulgar Marxism" and exposed them as basic distortions of the founder's ideas. The efforts of these critics were largely successful, for they convincingly reconstituted the original complexity of Marx's conception of history. Under their influence, Marxism came to be regarded as an "open," nondogmatic theoretical approach. Adherents of this view stressed the relative autonomy of the noneconomic spheres of society and underscored the role of human consciousness and will in the making of history.

In recent years, however, the "open" view has itself come under attack. There has been a reversion to the older, deterministic versions of Marx's ideas. Indeed, several recent studies of Marx's social thought have attributed to him a narrow, technological and "productive force" determinism.

Such reversions to a mechanistic Marxism suggest that it is necessary to take still another look at the original texts and to address the key questions systematically.

MARX'S FAMOUS "PREFACE"

In 1859, Marx wrote a preface to *A Contribution to the Critique of Political Economy*. The preface has long been regarded as Marx's most succinct formulation of his theory, and recent interpreters of Marx have treated the preface as the *locus classicus* of Marx's conception of history. The text therefore deserves to be quoted in its entirety:

> I was led by my studies to the conclusion that legal relations as well as forms of State could neither be understood by themselves, nor explained by the so-called general progress of the human mind, but that they are rooted in the material conditions of life, which are summed up by Hegel after the fashion of the English and French writers of the eighteenth century under the name *civil society*, and that the anatomy of civil society is to be sought in political economy. The study of the latter which I had begun in Paris, I continued in Brussels where I had emigrated on account of an expulsion order issued by M. Guizot. The general conclusion at which I arrived, and which, once reached, continued to serve as the guiding thread in my studies, may be formulated briefly as follows: In the social production which men carry on they enter into definite relations that are indispensable and independent of their will; these relations of production correspond to a definite stage of development of their material powers of production. The totality of these relations of production constitutes the economic structure of society—the real foundation, on which legal and political superstructures arise and to which definite forms of social consciousness correspond. The mode of production of material life determines the general character of the social, political and spiritual processes of life. It is not the consciousness of men that determines their being, but, on

the contrary, their social being determines their consciousness. At a certain stage of their development, the material forces of production in society come in conflict with the existing relations of production, or—what is but a legal expression for the same thing—with the property relations within which they had been at work before. From forms of development of the forces of production these relations turn into their fetters. Then occurs a period of social revolution. With the change of the economic foundation the entire immense superstructure is more or less rapidly transformed. In considering such transformations the distinction should always be made between the material transformation of the economic conditions of production which can be determined with the precision of natural science, and the legal, political, religious, aesthetic or philosophical—in short ideological, forms in which men become conscious of this conflict and fight it out. Just as our opinion of an individual is not based on what he thinks of himself, so can we not judge of such a period of transformation by its own consciousness; on the contrary, this consciousness must rather be explained from the contradictions of material life, from the existing conflict between the social forces of production and the relations of production. No social order ever disappears before all the productive forces for which there is room in it have been developed; and new, higher relations of production never appear before the material conditions of their existence have matured in the womb of the old society. Therefore, mankind always sets itself only such problems as it can solve; since, on closer examination, it will always be found that the problem itself arises only when the material conditions necessary for its solution already exist or are at least in the process of formation. In broad outline we can designate the Asiatic, the ancient, the feudal, and the modern bourgeois modes of production as progressive epochs in the economic formation of society. The bourgeois relations of production are the last antagonistic form of the social process of production; not in the sense of individual antagonisms, but of conflict arising from conditions surrounding the life of individuals in society. At the same time the productive forces developing in the womb of bourgeois society create the material conditions for the solution of that antagonism. With this social formation, therefore, the pre-history of human society comes to an end.[1]

As the reader will note, Marx here speaks of an economic "foundation" and of legal and political "superstructures." He goes on to say that the "mode of production" "determines the general character of the social, political and spiritual process of life" and in a most unequivocal way he asserts that it is social existence that determines social consciousness. It also appears that Marx assigns causal priority to the "forces of production" in bringing about social change. Little wonder, then, that both his followers and critics have continued to labour under the misapprehension that Marx has advocated a form of economic determinism in which the "foundation" is the cause, and the "superstructure" the effect.

Frederick Engels, Marx's colleague and friend who coauthored many of their writings, also contributed to the misapprehension of their views. When Engels discovered after Marx's death that their so-called "materialist conception of history" was widely misunderstood, he undertook to clarify their position in several letters that are by now quite well known among Marx scholars. To J. Block, Engels wrote,

> The economic situation is the basis, but the various elements of the superstructure … also exercise their influence upon the course of historical struggles and in many cases preponderate in determining their *form*. There is an interaction of all these elements [of the superstructure] in which, amid all the endless host of accidents (that is, of things and events, whose inner connection is so remote or so impossible of proof that we can regard it as nonexistent, as negligible) the economic movement finally asserts itself as necessary.[2]

And to H. Starkenburg, Engels wrote in a similar vein,

> Political, juridical, philosophical, religious, literary, artistic, etc., development is based on economic development. But all these react upon one another and also upon the economic basis. It is not that the economic condition is the cause and alone active, while everything else only has a passive effect. There is, rather, interaction on the basis of economic necessity, which *ultimately* always asserts itself.[3]

Here we see that while Engels allows for some interaction between "base" and "superstructure," he insists in both letters that economic conditions ultimately assert themselves. The effect of these letters was to reaffirm the causal priority of economic conditions.

In the light of Engels's letters (which are representative of his many other pronouncements on the subject) and Marx's own formulation in the "Preface," we are justified in saying that Marx and Engels must share responsibility for the widespread and persistent misunderstanding of their views. That is not all. Engels and Marx must also share responsibility for the impression that they were social evolutionists and that the only difference between them and other nineteenth-century evolutionists was that Marx and Engels designated the "mode of production" as the motor of evolutionary change. In the "Preface," Marx states that the "Asiatic, ancient [slave], feudal, and modern bourgeois modes of production can be designated as progressive epochs in the economic foundation of society." Hence we have the additional question of whether Marx and Engels were in fact evolutionists.

Of course, one cannot simply dismiss either the "Preface" or Engels's letters; neither must we take the centrality of the "Preface" for granted, as a host of commentators have done. The only reliable way of assessing the importance of the "Preface" and thus ferreting out its true meaning, is to place it in the context of Marx's total scholarly output. Only by this method will we learn why Marx expressed himself as he did in the "Preface"; only by such a method will we learn whether or not Marx proposed some sort of suprahistorical theory in which economic conditions and "productive forces" constitute everywhere and always the prime movers of history. Our procedure therefore will be to examine the texts in which Marx and Engels discussed the major modes of production, or socioeconomic epochs, in history. We will then ask what those texts imply for an adequate interpretation of the "Preface."

TRIBAL OWNERSHIP

In *The German Ideology*, one of their earliest coauthored works, Marx and Engels introduced the concept "mode of production." In that work, as in the "Preface," the concept "mode of production" embraces both "productive forces" and "relations of production." A society's "productive forces" may be analyzed into several components:

1. the social cooperation of the producers themselves, as it is conditioned by,
2. the existing instruments of production,
3. the available technical knowhow and, finally,
4. the society's natural habitat.

"Relations of production," on the other hand, refers to property relations or forms of ownership. If, therefore, *productive forces* speaks to the question of how a society produces its means of livelihood and goods, *relations of production* addresses the question of who owns and/or controls a society's productive resources.

Now, from the "Preface" one may gain the impression that Marx sought the key to social change solely in the internal dynamic of the productive forces pressing upon the existing relations of production. But Marx's other writings make it quite clear that that is not at all what he had intended. In *The German Ideology*, for example, Marx writes that the entire internal structure of a society "depends on the stage of development reached by its production and its internal and *external* intercourse."[4] Moreover, Marx designates the first form of ownership as "tribal," a form coinciding with an elementary division of labour. "The social structure," he continues,

> is therefore limited to an extension of the family; patriarchal family chieftains; below them the members of the tribe; finally slaves. The slavery latent in the family only develops gradually with the increase of population, the growth of wants, *and with the extension of external relations of war or of trade.*[5]

The italicized passage makes the point we are after. It leaves no doubt that for Marx and Engels a significant social change, such as the development of slavery, could not be explained solely as a result of the growth of "productive forces"— or of any other solely internal factor.

Marx did not somehow change his mind about this matter between the time of writing *The German Ideology* (1846) and the "Preface" (1859). Throughout the *Grundrisse* (1857–58), a large draft of his chief work, *Das Kapital (Capital)*, Marx pays due regard to external relations. His discussion of nomadic and pastoral peoples, whether in the Asiatic steppes or among the Indian tribes of America, is a case in point. "The only barrier," writes Marx, which the community can encounter in relating to the natural conditions of production—the earth—as to its own property (if we jump ahead to the settled peoples) is *another community*, which already claims it as its own inorganic body. *Warfare* is therefore one of the earliest occupations of each of these naturally arisen communities, both for the defence of their property and for obtaining new property.[6]

And Marx continues,

If human beings themselves are conquered along with the land and soil as its organic accessories, then they are equally conquered as one of the conditions of production, *and in this way arises slavery and serfdom*, which soon corrupts and modifies the original forms of all communities, and then itself becomes their basis.[7]

Of course, Marx does not mean to suggest that war and pillaging are sufficient explanations of slavery. In fact, he vehemently rejects a received opinion to that effect and reminds his reader that slavery presupposes economic conditions of a certain kind. For "pillage to be possible," he writes,

there must be something to be pillaged, hence production. And the mode of pillage is itself in turn determined by the mode of production.... To steal a slave is to steal the instrument of production directly. But then the production of the country for which the slave is stolen must be structured to allow of slave labour, or (as in the southern part of America, etc.), a mode of production corresponding to the slave must be created.[8]

So the "mode of production" is essential in an analysis of how and why slavery has appeared in a given society, or why other significant changes have occurred within it. But even the fullest examination of the "mode of production" will fail to provide the whole answer. When, for instance, a pastoral people finally settles down, "the extent to which this original community is modified will depend on various external, climatic, geographic, physical, etc., conditions as well as their particular natural disposition—their clan character."[9] This is surely as far from one-factor determinism as one can get.

We have only scratched the surface. For there exists a mountain of evidence with which to demonstrate that in their actual analyses of societies and institutions Marx and Engels never confined themselves to economic conditions. In his well-known essay called "the Mark," Engels provided a historical sketch of the agrarian conditions of the ancient Germanic peoples. Basing himself on the writings of Caesar and Tacitus, Engels describes the earliest known forms of communal landed property among the German tribes. A large portion of these migratory peoples cultivated their fields in common when they temporarily settled down. Nevertheless, hereditary, private property existed among them from earliest times. How does Engels explain that fact? "The first piece of ground," he writes,

> that passed into the private property of individuals was that on which the house stood. The inviolability of the dwelling, that basis of all personal freedom, was transferred from the caravan of the nomadic train to the log house of the stationary peasant, and gradually was transformed into a complete right of property in the homestead.[10]

The free German's homestead had from earliest times been excluded from the common property of the mark. Inaccessible to officials, the homestead was a refuge for fugitives. The inviolability of the dwelling was firmly rooted in German tribal, customary law. The sacredness of the dwelling, Engels concludes,

> *was not the effect but the cause of its transformation into private property.*[11]

So much for the allegation that Marx and Engels always considered ideas as derivative from economic or other "material" conditions.

Moreover, kingship soon arose among the Germans, a tendency favoured by the existence of *retinues*. In earliest times, leaders among the Germanic tribes were elected for their military prowess. At the same time, however, leading men organized retinues, that is, private associations of warriors recruited on the basis of their military skills. Recruited from diverse clans and tribes, young men joined a retinue eager for the booty they would gain in raids upon neighbouring groups. The spoils—primarily cattle, slaves, and jewelry—remained the private property of the retinue members, and never became communal clan property. Differences of wealth thus increased inside the clans, severely weakening the democratic-communal character of Germanic society as it existed at the time. Hence the retinues, Engels observes, were

> the beginnings of the decay of the old freedom of the people and showed themselves to be such during and after the migrations. For in the first place they favored the rise of monarchic power. In the second place, as Tacitus already notes, they could only be kept together by continual wars and plundering expeditions. Plunder became an end in itself. If the leader of the retinue found nothing to do in the neighborhood, he set out with his men to other peoples where there was war and the prospect of booty.... When the Roman empire had been conquered, these retinues of the kings formed the second main stock, after the unfree and the Roman courtiers, from which the later nobility was drawn.[12]

For Engels private property among the Germanic peoples developed out of several conditions. There was first the old Germanic tradition of treating the family dwelling as sacred and inviolable. This custom, originating in the Germanic migratory culture, led to private homesteads once they settled down. Second was the Roman influence. In their conquests of Roman territory, where the soil had been private property for centuries, the Germans "borrowed" this institution. Finally, there were the retinues, which had become permanent, and of mixed clan composition. When the retinues went to war, it was increasingly the case that the men fought not side by side with their own kinsmen, but with their fellow retinue warriors. Retinues followed and obeyed their own leaders rather than the duly elected military chieftains of the people, which led to very significant social changes.

Among the early Germans, as among many early agricultural societies, tillage was typically the work of the women, while men hunted and looked after the domesticated animals, such as cattle. But with the introduction of the horse-drawn plough, tillage and other forms of heavy work in the fields was transferred to men. The growth of the retinues, however, caused a reversion to the old practice. The young men engaged in wars and forays while the women, old men, and children tended to the fields and to the running of the homes. The young men had an increasingly tenuous connection with production, and *war* became a major method of appropriation. By Tacitus' time, retinue members had acquired substantial herds of cattle and received the produce of the fields worked by their slaves. Growing dependence on booty as a source of wealth gave rise among the retinues to contempt for agricultural labour, which was left more and more to women, children, and slaves. Thus what the retinues had become in the 150-year period between Caesar and Tacitus served to undermine the older communal institutions in several ways:

1. Retinue leaders became largely independent of the discipline of their kinsmen and even of the tribal assembly of warriors.
2. Retinue leaders became monarchs and nobles whose accumulated wealth and power raised them above their kinsmen.
3. Retinues became "international," that is, they cut across the boundaries of their own various tribes and peoples.
4. Retinue leaders and members alike bequeathed their property to their own children rather than to their entire kindred, thus undermining the clan and elevating the family at the clan's expense.

We see that Engels's analysis of early Germanic society was quite complex. The developments leading to the emergence of private property as an institution, to the crystallization of socioeconomic classes and to the rise of the monarchical state, were partly economic and partly noneconomic. An understanding of these changes required a study of the history of the Germanic peoples from the time of Caesar's *Memoirs of the Gallic Wars* (51 B.C.) to the time of Tacitus' *Germania* (98 A.D.). The structural changes that Germanic society had undergone in that 150-year period, Engels clearly understood, could never be adequately grasped by any theoretical formula. No economic or "productive force" determinism could ever explain why the highly communal Germanic people were transformed into a class society.

Indeed, what is striking about Engels's analysis is the prominent role he assigns not to "productive forces," but to "force" in general. The decline of the "mark," that is, German communal institutions and the prevalence of the retinues, was accompanied by the formation of feudalism. The constant wars of the early Middle Ages, wrote Engels, whose regular consequences were confiscations of land, ruined a great number of peasants, so that even during the Merovingian dynasty, there were very many free men owning no land. The incessant wars of Charlemagne broke down the mainstay of the free peasantry.… [The] eternal wars between kings, and feuds between nobles, compelled one free peasant after another to seek the protection of some lord …; by fraud, by promises, threats, violence, they forced more and more peasants and peasants' land under their yoke.… [The] peasants' land was added to the lord's manor, and was, at best, only given back for the use of the peasant in return for tribute and service. Thus this peasant, from a free owner of the land, was turned into a tribute-paying, service-rendering appanage of it, into a serf.[13]

For Marx and Engels, it is clear, feudal serfdom was an outgrowth of war and military conquest which disrupted the old tribal pattern by turning retinue leaders and other military chieftains into sovereigns and lords.

PRODUCTIVE FORCES: DID MARX IN FACT ASSIGN THEM CAUSAL PRIORITY?

Earlier we observed that some commentators ascribe to Marx a form of "productive force" or technological determinism. So before we examine other modes of production, we should pause to ask this question: Are "productive forces," for Marx, some kind of inexorable, prime mover of history?

It is true that not only in the "Preface" but elsewhere as well, Marx occasionally expressed himself in a manner that lends support to a technological interpretation of his theory. There is, for instance, that famous passage in *The Poverty of Philosophy* (1847), where Marx remarks

The hand-mill gives you a society with the feudal lord; the steam-mill, a society with the industrial capitalist.[14]

Many commentators have taken this aphorism literally. They have ignored the more careful formulation Marx introduced some twenty pages later in the same book:

> Labour is organized, is divided differently according to the instruments it disposes over. The hand-mill presupposes a different division of labour from the steam-mill.[15]

Here we see clearly the meaning Marx had intended; as the instruments of production vary, so does the *division of labour*—but not necessarily the nature of the society as a whole, or even its class structure.

Similarly, in *Capital*, Vol. I, Marx wrote:

> Relics of bygone instruments of labour possess the same importance for the investigation of extinct economical forms of society, as do fossil bones for the determination of extinct species of animals. It is not the articles made, but how they are made, and by what instruments, that enables us to distinguish different economical epochs. Instruments of labour not only supply a standard of degree of development to which human labour has attained, but they are also indicators of the social conditions under which that labour is carried on.[16]

Thus Marx proposes a kind of "archeology" based on changing forms of instruments of labour. But, as we shall see, Marx understood, as does every good archeologist, that from tools alone only limited inferences can be made about social forms.

"Productive forces" are fundamental for Marx in this sense: The level of their development is the necessary but not sufficient condition for the emergence of certain social formations. If a labourer needs all of his time to produce the necessary means of subsistence for himself and his dependents,

> he has no time left to work gratis for others. Without a certain degree of productiveness of his labour, he has no such superfluous time at this disposal; without such superfluous time, no surplus labour, and therefore no capitalists, no slave-owners, no feudal lords, in a word, no class of large proprietors.[17]

Production, writes Marx, the rudimentary process of producing use-values,

> is the necessary condition for effective exchange of matter between man and Nature; it is the everlasting Nature-imposed condition of human

existence, and therefore is independent of every social phase of that existence, or rather, is common to every such phase.[18]

But in the very same paragraph Marx adds:

as the taste of porridge does not tell you who grew the oats, *no more does this simple process [i.e., production] tell you of itself what are the social conditions under which it is taking place, whether under the slave-owner's brutal lash, or the anxious eye of the capitalist.…*

The last passage speaks loudly, for it demonstrates that though the hand-mill presupposes a division of labour different from the steam-mill, neither type of mill, in and of itself, tells us anything about the "property relations" under which it is being employed.

For a proper understanding of the concept "productive forces," we must remember that Marx makes a fundamental distinction between capitalist and precapitalist modes of production. Modern capitalist industry, Marx writes,

never looks upon and treats the existing form of a process as final. The technical basis of that industry is therefore revolutionary, while all earlier modes of production were *conservative*.[19]

This is the same point Marx made in the *Communist Manifesto*, where he stated that whereas the bourgeoisie could not exist without revolutionizing the instruments of production:

Conservation, in an unaltered form, of the old modes of production was, on the contrary, the first condition of existence of all earlier industrial classes.[20]

An example of such earlier classes would be the guilds of the Middle Ages where traditional ways of producing were highly valued and preserved.

The conclusion is beyond doubt. If, for Marx, precapitalist modes of production were *conservative*, he never could have intended his formulation in the "Preface" to mean that "productive forces" are a constantly and invincibly expanding force in history—the major cause of the historical changes that societies have undergone. And, of course, more direct evidence is plentiful that Marx and Engels never proposed such an untenable notion.

In *The German Ideology*, in their discussion of the conditions of emerging feudalism, Marx and Engels wrote:

> The last centuries of the declining Roman Empire and its conquest by the barbarians *destroyed a number of productive forces;* agriculture had declined, industry had decayed for want of a market, trade had died out or been violently suspended, the rural and urban population had decreased. From these conditions and the mode of organization of the conquest determined by them, feudal property developed under the influence of the Germanic military constitution.[21]

And in a later context they wrote:

> *It depends purely on the extension of commerce whether the productive forces achieved in a locality, especially inventions, are lost for later development or not.* As long as there exists no commerce transcending the immediate neighborhood, every invention must be made separately in each locality, and mere chances such as irruptions of barbaric peoples, even ordinary wars, are sufficient to cause a country with advanced productive forces and needs to have to start right over again from the beginning. In primitive history every invention had to be made daily anew and in each locality independently. That highly productive forces are little safe from complete destruction, given even a very extensive commerce, is proved by the Phoenicians, whose inventions were for the most part lost for a long time to come through the ousting of this nation from commerce, its conquest by Alexander and its consequent decline.... *Only when commerce has become world-commerce and has as its basis big industry*, when all nations are drawn into the competitive struggle, is the permanence of the acquired productive forces assured.[22]

A similar point is made by Engels while describing the conditions of the declining Roman Empire:

> the level of production had neither risen nor fallen significantly during the following four centuries and had therefore with equal necessity again produced the same distribution of property and the same classes in the population.[23]

In light of such evidence we can see that there are no good grounds for believing that Marx viewed productive forces as a universal, ever-expanding lever of social change. Only in the epoch of modern capitalist industry and world commerce was there a consolidated growth of productive forces. Furthermore, there is a good deal more evidence with which to support this interpretation.

THE FEUDAL MODE OF PRODUCTION

Whether it was a matter of explaining the rise of the ancient slave systems of Greece and Rome or the feudal order of medieval Europe, Marx and Engels considered a variety of factors. Nowhere did they attempt to explain historical change by means of economic or technological factors alone.

In the history of European society, the chattel slavery of antiquity eventually gave way to a different type of organization called "feudalism." With the decline of the Roman Empire, the seminomadic cultivators were tied down to the soil. Although ultimately that may have increased the productivity of the temperate forest zone, Marx nowhere attempts to explain the establishment of feudalism as a result of the growing "productive forces." On the contrary, he sees the origins of feudalism in several closely connected circumstances—the disintegration of the Roman Empire into a multiplicity of military chieftainships, a process accompanied by the barbarian invasions and the decline of the towns. Originally the mode of production in many of the empire's provinces was based on common possession or access to the soil. "Part of the land," Marx notes,

> was cultivated in severalty as freehold by the members of the community, another part—*ager publicus*—was cultivated by them in common. The products of this common labour served partly as a public store for providing costs of war, religion, and other common expenses. In the course of time military and clerical dignitaries usurped, along with the common land, the labour spent upon it. The labour of the free peasants on their common land was transformed into corvée for the thieves of the common land.[24]

Corvée gave rise to the servile relationship called serfdom. The corvée rarely arose from serfdom. On the contrary, "serfdom much more frequently ... took origin from the corvée."[25]

Throughout their scattered remarks on the formation of feudalism, Marx and Engels stress the role of force and violence. Not only that, they also criticize others for neglecting the role of force and for interpreting the transition from slavery to serfdom as unambiguous evolutionary progress. In 1882, Engels published his essay, "The Mark," basing his analysis largely on the work of the eminent German historian Georg Ludwig Maurer (1790–1872). Although Engels much admired Maurer and acknowledged his debt to him, he nevertheless criticized him in a letter to Marx. Maurer's errors, Engels argued, were a consequence of the

> insufficient importance which he attaches to *force* and the part it plays [and] from his enlightened prejudice that since the dark Middle Ages a steady progress to a better state of things must simply have taken place; *this prevents him [Maurer] from seeing not only the antagonistic character of real progress, but also the individual retrogressions.*[26]

Unlike Maurer, then, Engels gave due attention to *force*, and to antagonisms and retrogressions. If the conditions of the peasants improved in the middle of the thirteenth century, it was thanks to the consequences of the Crusades. "Many of the lords," write Engels,

> when they set out to the East, explicitly set their peasant serfs free. Others were killed and never returned. Hundreds of noble families vanished, whose peasant serfs frequently gained their freedom.[27]

Yet the rise of towns in the fourteenth and fifteenth centuries had the opposite effect on the peasants. The luxurious life of the town patricians aroused the envy of the coarsely fed and clothed country lords in their roughly furnished dwellings. Engels continued:

> Lying in wait for traveling merchants became more and more dangerous and unprofitable. But to buy them [the goods the merchants had to sell], money was requisite. And that the peasants alone could furnish. Hence, renewed oppression of the peasants, higher tributes, and more corvée; hence renewed and always increasing eagerness to force the free peasants to become bondmen, the bondmen to become serfs, and to turn the common mark land into land belonging to the lord.[28]

In that way the flourishing towns gave the manorial lords an interest in the expanding market economy and prompted them to intensify the exploitation of their peasants—that is, to squeeze larger surpluses out of them.

Despite widespread usurpation of the peasant's common lands in the earlier feudal period, there remained for common use uncultivated soil as well as forest and pasture land in many parts of Germany. When the lords moved to usurp those common lands, they provoked the great peasant uprisings of the early sixteenth century.[29] With the defeat of the peasants by the princes and lords, a renewed serfdom became prevalent. "In those places where the fighting raged," writes Engels,

> all remaining rights of the peasants were now shamelessly trodden under foot, their common land turned into the property of the lord, and themselves into serfs.[30]

Then came the devastations of the Thirty Years' War breaking the peasants' last power of resistance; unlimited corvée was introduced anew and serfdom became general until it was shattered from without by the French Revolution.

For Marx and Engels, the establishment and development of feudal serfdom are complex processes to which war and other historical events contributed. And the emergence of the market economy, instead of alleviating the peasant's burden, accomplished the exact opposite. In any event, it is indisputable that for these thinkers there certainly was no straight line of progress from the ancient society to that of feudal serfdom.

Historically, feudalism has been associated with simple instruments of production, with production for the immediate needs of the household or village community, and with a politically decentralized system. The lord of each manor rendered the juridical function for the dependent population. In the earliest period, production for the market was either nonexistent or minimal. Hence the feudal mode of production as a pure type, was not an exchange economy. That is to say that what was produced on the manor had not yet become a "commodity." For Marx, the term "commodity" refers to an article produced for exchange, for the market. Only when the peasant family began to produce more than enough for its own wants and for the dues payments to the lord, did exchange begin. The surplus products were offered for sale. These products became commodities, thus providing the manorial lords with money income. It is true that in the towns the artisans produced for the market from the very beginning. As Engels observed, however, even the artisans:

> supplied the greatest part of their own individual wants. They had gardens and plots of land. They turned their cattle out into the communal forest, which also yielded them timber and firing. The women spun flax, wool, and so forth. Production for the purpose of exchange, production of commodities, was only in its infancy. Hence exchange was restricted, the market narrow, *the methods of production stable....*[31]

Under feudalism the methods of production were stable. In time, however, the "natural economy," producing for self-subsistent village communities, gave way to an exchange economy. In Marx's vocabulary, products that earlier had only "use-value," now acquired "exchange-value" as well.

Commodity production became a growing tendency. It was only with respect to this epoch and the emergence of capitalism that one could justifiably speak of growing "productive forces" coming into conflict with the existing "relations of production." For it was capitalism, as we have seen, that Marx regarded as the first revolutionary mode of production in history. But before we turn our attention to that revolutionary mode, we must explore another conservative mode of production.

THE ASIATIC MODE OF PRODUCTION: ITS SIGNIFICANCE FOR MARX'S THEORY

In developing his conception of the Asiatic mode of production, Marx relied heavily on English classical economics. Adam Smith had already noted that similarities among several governments in Asia appeared to be related to the complex irrigation and water-regulation projects of those societies, and he commented upon the extraordinary power of the rulers in ancient Egypt, China, and India.[32] James Mill viewed the "Asiatic model of government" as a distinct institutional type not to be confused with European feudalism.[33] Richard Jones provided a general portrait of Asiatic society,[34] and John Stuart Mill placed that society in a comparative framework.[35]

Other thinkers had noted the peculiarities of Asiatic society and government, even earlier than the English economists. Montesquieu, for example, in his classification of societies, included a type he called Asiatic "despotism." That was a type in which all groups in society were so weak that organized resistance to the despot was impossible. Everyone was equal in his condition of servitude to the ruler. Machiavelli contrasted two different types of government exemplified by the Turkish Empire and the kingdom of France. Though he made no explicit use of the term despotism, his discussion shows that he understood the basic *political* differences between oriental despotism and feudalism.[36]

It was in 1853 that Marx and Engels began, for the first time, to give more sustained attention to Asia. Their interest was prompted by British colonial behaviour in China and India. From that time on, Marx employed not only the concept "Asiatic mode," but in addition, the terms "Oriental despotism," "Asiatic society," and other such designations. The Marx-Engels conception of the Asiatic mode must be constructed from their correspondence, from several articles that Marx wrote for the *New York Daily Tribune*, and from numerous remarks scattered throughout the writings of both men.

In a letter to Engels, dated Jun 2, 1853, Marx relates how informative and insightful he found François Bernier's *Travels Containing a Description of the Dominions of the Great Moguls*. Quoting several passages from Bernier's work, which he describes as "brilliant," Marx notes the distinctive condition of Eastern society, "namely, that the *king is the one and only proprietor of all the land* in the kingdom." Marx then goes on to say that "Bernier rightly considered the basis of all phenomena in the East—he refers to Turkey, Persia, Hindustan—to be the *absence of private property in land*. This is the real key, even to the Oriental heaven."[37]

In his reply (June 6, 1853), Engels agreed that the "absence of property in land is indeed the key to the whole of the East," but he then went on to ask how it came about that the Orientals never arrived "at landed property, even in its feudal form?" Here is Engels's explanation:

> I think it is mainly due to the climate, taken in connection with the nature of the soil, especially with the great stretches of desert which extend from the Sahara straight across Arabia, Persia, India, and Tatary up to the highest Asiatic plateau. *Artificial irrigation is here the first condition of agriculture* and this is a matter either for the communes, the provinces or the central government.... The artificial fertilization of the land, which immediately ceased when the irrigation system fell into decay,

explains the otherwise curious fact that whole stretches which were once brilliantly cultivated are now waste and bare (Palmyra, Petra, the ruins in the Yemen, districts in Egypt, Persia and Hindustan); it explains the fact that one single devastating war could depopulate a country for centuries and strip it of its whole civilization.[38]

Marx took the analysis further in his response to Engels on June 14, 1853. In that letter Marx stressed the *stationary* character, economically speaking, of that part of Asia, and suggested that it is to be explained by two related facts:

1. that the public water and other works were under the control of the central government; and
2. that the entire empire "was divided into *villages*, each of which possessed a completely separate organization and formed a little world in itself."[39]

Every village was a *self-sufficient* community, almost identical to every other. At the head of each village stood a representative of the central government. He was a kind of superintendent of affairs who settled the disputes of inhabitants, supervised the police, and collected the village taxes. The economic organization of the village typically included a record keeper, a watchman of the village crops, an official who ensured that irrigation water was justly distributed to the several fields, and an astrologer who determined the planting and harvest times. In addition, every village had its own craftsmen and artisans: a smith, carpenter, potter, washerman, barber, and a silversmith, who often also served as poet and schoolmaster. Finally, there was the Brahmin for worship.

Marx quoted a parliamentary report describing this village structure in which:

the inhabitants of the country have lived from time immemorial.... The inhabitants give themselves no trouble about the breaking up and division of kingdoms; while the village remains entire, they care not to what power it is transferred, or to what sovereign it devolves; its internal economy remains unchanged.

And Marx comments,

> I do not think anyone could imagine a more solid foundation for stagnant Asiatic despotism.[40]

For Marx and Engels, Oriental despotism was a system in which all power was centralized in the hands of the emperor, the political sovereign *and* the absolute landlord. The absolute power of the emperor rested on the fact that the myriad villages were like so many disunited atoms incapable of offering resistance to the central government. Villages had no real property in land and depended totally on the central government and its officials for the proper and adequate irrigation of the soil.

All governments associated with the Asiatic mode of production performed the economic function of providing public works, mainly irrigation and drainage or, in a word, the artificial fertilization of the soil. Those are the distinctive circumstances that account for the fact, writes Marx, that

> However changing the political aspect of India's past must appear, its social condition has remained unaltered since its remotest antiquity, until the first decennium of the nineteenth century.[41]

It was only under British colonial rule that the Asiatic mode was undermined. For the British, unlike previous rulers, had entirely neglected the public water works of India, thus causing a fateful deterioration of agriculture.

For Marx, the Asiatic form thus hung on so tenaciously for so long a time owing to its "presupposition that the individual does not become independent *vis-à-vis* the commune; that there is a self-sustaining circle of production, unity of agriculture and manufactures."[42] Engels, in his book *Anti-Dühring*, made similar points. The self-sufficiency of the Asian village communities was such that for

> thousands of years Oriental despotism and the changing rule of conquering nomad peoples were unable to injure the old communities....[43] However great the number of despotisms [Engels continues in another context] which arose and fell in Persia and India, each was fully aware that above all it was the entrepreneur responsible for the collective maintenance of irrigation throughout the river valleys, without which

no agriculture was possible there. It was reserved for the enlightened English to lose sight of this in India; they let the irrigation canals and sluices fall into decay, and now at last are discovering, through the regularly recurring famines, that they have neglected the one activity which might have made their rule in India at least as legitimate as that of their predecessors.[44]

The Asiatic mode of production thus formed the basis for thousands of years of "the cruelest form of state, Oriental despotism, from India to Russia."[45]

It is important to emphasize that for Marx and Engels there was a sharp contrast between the Asiatic and feudal modes of production. The dominance of the Oriental despot precluded genuine, private ownership of land, the precondition of feudalism. If anything distinguished the Orient, it was the absolute supremacy of the State, so that even the advantaged and privileged elements were never genuine land *lords*. No real feudalism had existed in India and China, the two Asian countries that received the most attention from Marx and Engels.

THEORETICAL IMPLICATIONS

It follows from everything that has been said so far that Marx's conception of the Asiatic mode of production has definite implications for an understanding of his theory and method. If the Asiatic mode was above all a *stationary* one from time immemorial until the nineteenth century, that can only mean that the "productive forces" were stable and unchanging. That fact alone is sufficient to refute the erroneous but widespread view that Marx, in the "Preface," had set forth a theory that growing "productive forces" are the *universal* source of social change.

It also follows from Marx's conception of the Asiatic mode that he never proposed a theory of *unilinear* development. Even if one insists that Marx did in fact propose a theory of social evolution or development—a view that we shall later challenge—the Asiatic mode allows for only one inference: Marx and Engels discerned at least *two* lines of development, the Western and the Eastern.

Our rejection of the universal, unilinear interpretation of Marx's conception of history may appear to be irreconcilable with one statement in particular that he made in the "Preface." There, we will recall, Marx wrote,

"In broad outline we can designate the Asiatic, the ancient, the feudal, and the modern bourgeois modes of production as progressive epochs in the economic formation of society." This statement has traditionally reinforced the impression that Marx perceived only one line of development. To attain a full understanding of why such an impression is quite mistaken, we must first consider Marx's view of capitalism, its origin, and its development.

THE CAPITALIST MODE OF PRODUCTION

One cannot, of course, date the beginnings of a historical process with precision. Marx relied on the historians of the time who largely agreed that it was from the thirteenth and fourteenth centuries on that the "natural economy" of Europe, producing for self-subsistent manorial villages, was increasingly replaced by an exchange economy. In Marx's vocabulary, products that earlier had only "use-value" now acquired "exchange-value" as well. Commodity production, or production for the market, became a growing tendency. Yet this was not capitalism, as yet, but rather a preparatory stage for it.

For Marx, money and commodities were transformed into *capital* under specific historical circumstances. Capitalism requires that "two very different kinds of commodity-possessors must come face to face and in contact; on the one hand, the owners of money, means of production, means of subsistence, who are eager to increase the sum of values they possess, by buying other people's labor power; on the other hand, free laborers, the sellers of their own labor-power and therefore the sellers of labor." [46] The labourers are free in two senses, the first literal and the second ironic. The typical labourers of capitalism are neither a part of the means of production, as are slaves and bondsmen; nor do they possess means of production of their own, as do peasant proprietors. Labourers under capitalism have been "freed" or *separated* from their means of production, and are now entirely dependent for their survival on the sale of their labour. In the absence of "free labour" in the double meaning of the term, capitalism never could have arisen.

The origins of the capitalist mode of production may therefore be traced to the process that separates the producer from his means of production and means of subsistence, while placing those means under exclusive control of the capitalist. Capitalism thus required the proletarianization of the agricultural population. A "proletarian" possesses nothing but the labour of his hands. How, then, did such a socioeconomic class emerge for the first time?

By the end of the fourteenth century, serfdom was almost nonexistent in England. The vast majority of the population consisted of free peasant proprietors. They worked with their own instruments of production and provided for their own subsistence. These peasant proprietors also enjoyed the usufruct of the common lands that provided them with timber and firewood, and provided their cattle with pasture. A century later, however, that state of affairs had begun to change. The power of the feudal lords had been so greatly reduced by the monarchy that it was not difficult for the Crown to break up the feudal retainers and to confiscate their estates. As a result, a mass of peasants and yeomen were driven from the soil. At the same time, the more powerful feudal lords created an even larger proletariat by the forcible eviction of their peasants and by the usurpation of the common lands.

The forceful evictions were economically motivated. The continental wool manufacturers were prospering, which led, in turn, to a marked rise in the price of English wool. Marx describes the new nobility as a child of its time, for whom "money was the power of all powers. Transformation of arable land into sheepwalks, was, therefore, its cry."[47] Humans were displaced by sheep. Describing the tragic spectacle in his book *Utopia*, Thomas More wrote: "Your shepe that were wont to be so meek and tame, and so small eaters, now, as I hear saye, be become so great devourers and so wylde that they eate up, and swallow downe, the very men themselves."[48] The evicted became vagabonds helplessly roaming the countryside; their descendants eventually became wage-labourers.

Thus what was formerly the peasant's means of production now became *capital* in the hands of the new commercial lords and big farmers, and what was formerly produced by the peasants for their own use and consumption, now became means of subsistence that the new proletarians could acquire only by selling their labour for wages. Labour had become a commodity subject to market forces. The expropriation of self-supporting peasants necessarily led to the destruction of their distinctive rural domestic industry. As a consequence, Marx writes,

> The spindles and looms, formerly scattered over the face of the country, are now crowded together in a few great labor-barracks, together with the

> laborers and the raw material. And spindles, looms, raw materials, are
> now transformed from means of independent existence for the spinners
> and weavers, into means for commanding them.[49]

Manufacture was thus separated from agriculture, and in time the new class of proletarians created an internal market for the emerging capitalist mode of production.

The first phase of capitalism was "manufacture" quite literally, that is, hand production. Capitalist production at this stage is distinguished from handicraft production in the guilds only by the greater number of workers simultaneously employed by one and the same capitalist. Capitalist manufacture thus arose out of handicraft, in some cases uniting the formerly distinct crafts and in others uniting the members of the same craft. In this increasingly complex division of labour, each worker is forced to engage in one simple operation. He is therefore alienated from the creative prerogatives he enjoyed as a craftsman. His entire body now becomes an "automatic, specialized implement of that operation."[50] What the worker loses in creativity, the organization gains in efficiency. The worker now takes less time in performing a specific operation than the craftsman who performed the entire series of operations in succession. The division of labour among many workers, each with its specialized operation, is the basis of capitalist manufacture, a new organization of labour under which *the socially productive power of labour is greatly enhanced.* Manufacture produces the detail labour "by reproducing, and systematically driving to an extreme within the workshop, the … differentiation of trades which it found ready to hand in society at large."[51]

The concentration of the various skills and trades in one workshop, entailed changes in the tools employed. Unlike the craftsman who used a few tools for many operations, the worker employed one tool in a specialized operation. Radical changes were taking place in the world of work. The transformation of the worker into a detail labourer, Marx believed, had far-reaching consequences. The new industrial division of labour effectively alienated the worker from his creative powers, thus diminishing him as a human being. The higher productivity of the new organization of labour was made possible by classifying and grouping workers according to their specific functions. What was taken away from the individual worker in artistic skill, creativity, and reflective powers was imparted to the organization.

The organization as a whole was enriched by alienating the worker from his individual human gifts.

With machine production, a later stage of capitalist development, the individual worker pays an even bigger price for his increased productivity. If manufacture was somewhat adapted to the skills of the worker, the machine system compelled the worker to adapt to it. Production is analyzed into a sequence of phases, each of which is solved by means of machinery. The capitalist now strives for a productive process that is continuous and uninterrupted in its various phases; shifts from one phase to another are made not by hand, but by machinery. "The life-long specialty," wrote Marx, "of handling one and the same tool, now becomes the life-long specialty of serving one and the same machine."[52] In manufacture the worker used the tool; in the factory the machine uses the worker. Under such circumstances the intellectual and creative powers of the worker become superfluous.

Machine production greatly accelerated the concentration of capital and led to the prominence of the factory system. Older forms of production were increasingly displaced by the modern capitalist form and by the power of capital. Hence, the expansion of productive forces under capitalism was accompanied by growing alienation. For it was only by forfeiting his creative human faculties that the worker contributed to the growth of the productive organization. He had lost all control over the productive process. Marx's revolutionary reply to that condition is well known: while labour itself could never be abolished—it being the process by which human beings produce and reproduce their very life—*alienated* labour, exploitation, and oppression could be eliminated from human experience. Those who suffered most directly from those conditions would sooner or later find them intolerable and wrest all power from their oppressors. With that as a beginning and with the gradual abolition of classes and class conflicts, humanity might some day create a society in which "the free development of each is the condition for the free development of all." [53]

Marx's conception of the genesis and development of capitalism is therefore essential for a clarification of his theory: *Only in the capitalist epoch and in the transition to it, do "productive forces" become a dynamic element. Precapitalist modes of production in the West were "conservative," and the Asiatic mode of production was "stationary."*

Therefore when Marx, in the "Preface," speaks of the Asiatic, ancient, feudal, and modern bourgeois modes of production as "progressive epochs," all he means to convey by that phrase is that those have been the major epochs in the history of human civilization. "Progressive," in the context of the "Preface," simply refers to the chronological sequence of epochs beginning with the Asiatic mode of production in ancient Mesopotamia and Egypt, and culminating in the capitalism of nineteenth-century Europe. Marx was *not*, as we shall see from additional evidence, proposing that the Asiatic mode evolved stage by stage into capitalism; nor was he proposing that the "progressive epochs" were necessary stages through which every society was fated to pass.

So we are now ready to confront the central question: Did Marx subscribe to social evolutionism or to any other *suprahistorical* theory?[54]

WAS MARX A SOCIAL EVOLUTIONIST?

To answer this question, we need first to have a look at some of the typical nineteenth-century theories of social evolution. The nineteenth century was the heyday of social evolutionism. Edward Burnett Tylor, Lewis Henry Morgan, Auguste Comte, Herbert Spencer, and numerous others all subscribed to a doctrine according to which the human race has progressed from lower to higher stages. Doubtless we owe an immense intellectual debt to those extraordinary thinkers, for we have acquired from them a large body of substantive knowledge about a wide range of human societies and cultures. The question remains, however, whether their conception of social evolution was scientifically sound.

Most nineteenth-century evolutionary schemes had in common certain stated and unstated premises that may be summed up in the following statement: Change is natural, directional, immanent, continuous, and derived from uniform causes.[55] These premises were shared by such otherwise diverse thinkers as Hegel, Saint-Simon (and his pupil Comte), Tocqueville, Spencer, Morgan, and Durkheim. For Hegel, the developmental idea expressed itself in his view of the spirit of freedom, which grew from its modest beginnings in the ancient Orient until it attained its highest form in the Prussia of his day. In Saint-Simon and Comte, the idea is evident in their law of three stages: Knowledge evolves from the religious through the metaphysical to the positive (or scientific) stage. In Tocqueville, we find societies increasingly embodying the spirit of equality, thus proceeding from aristocracy to democracy. For Spencer, the direction of evolution was from the relatively homogeneous "military" society to the complex "industrial" one. Morgan perceived three main stages of societal development: "savagery," "barbarism," and "civilization." And Durkheim, finally, placed the subject of social solidarity into an evolutionary framework, arguing that society normally progresses from a mechanical to an organic stage of solidarity. Many more thinkers could be mentioned to illustrate the prevalence in the nineteenth century of evolutionary schemes. As Robert A. Nisbet has stressed in his illuminating monograph *Social Change and History,* all such schemes are drawn "from the metaphor of growth, from the analogy of change in society to change in the growth-processes of the individual organism."[56]

How did the idea of growth, development, and evolution become so pervasive in the nineteenth century? Historians have sought the answer to that question in the Romantic-Conservative Reaction to the French Revolution, which we already have explored in previous chapters of this book. Conservatives throughout Europe deplored the consequences of that great social upheaval. They looked upon it as a disaster resulting from the folly of the revolutionaries who, intoxicated with Enlightenment ideas, attempted to reorder society according to mechanistically rational principles. In opposition to the eighteenth-century exaltation of the individual, conservatives elevated the *group,* the *community,* and the *nation* to paramountcy. Eighteenth-century thought had been dominated by mechanistic metaphors: The Newtonian universe was "spring and wire," and even the human being was likened to a machine. Nineteenth-century thought, in contrast, adopted organic metaphors. This is exemplified in the political philosophy of Edmund Burke who insisted that society was a living organism.

Burke was only one among numerous other nineteenth-century thinkers whose categories of analysis had become thoroughly dominated by evolutionary metaphors or by what J. B. Bury called "the idea of progress." Bury identified that idea as a distinctively modern product which emerged in its earliest forms in the seventeenth century and reached its fullest expression in the nineteenth.[57] The idea of progress stands in sharp contrast to the idea of cycles in Greco-Roman antiquity.

With knowledge of the historical grounds of the evolutionary idea, we are better prepared to address this question: Are nineteenth-century evolutionary theories to be regarded as objective and scientific accounts of social change? If, following Robert A. Nisbet, we define social change "as a succession of differences in time in a persisting (social) entity," then we have to answer that question in the negative. For the theories with which we are concerned have failed to demonstrate a series of developmental steps in the transformation of a single social entity. Typically, evolutionists selected their evidence for stages from diverse societies and from various historical periods. The great anthropologist Lewis Henry Morgan, for example, illustrated "savagery" with one society, "barbarism" with a second, and "civilization" with a third. Selecting their data from divergent cultural areas and historical periods, the evolutionists then arranged them in a series resembling the actual historical series in the West. Thus this school of thought has given us, Nisbet has convincingly noted, not a theory of the actual course of development of a single social entity, but rather a

> series of "stills" as in a movie film. It is the eye—or rather in this instance, the disposition to believe—that creates the illusion of actual development, growth, or change.
>
> It is all much like a museum exhibit. (It might be observed in passing that the principles of museum arrangement of cultural artifacts have not been without considerable influence on the principles of cultural evolution.) The last one I saw was an exhibit of "the development of warfare." At the beginning were shown examples of primitive war-making—spears, bows and arrows, and the like. At the far end of the exhibit were examples (constructed miniatures) of the latest and most awful forms of warfare. In between, constructed in fullest accord with the principles of logical continuity, was the whole spectrum or range of weapons that have been found or written about anywhere on the earth's surface at whatever time. All of this, observers were assured, represented the development of warfare. But the development of warfare where? Not, certainly, in the United States, or in Tasmania, or in China, or in Tierra del Fuego, or in any other concrete, geographically identifiable, historically delimited, area. What "develops" is in fact no substantive, empirical entity but a hypostatized, constructed entity that is called "the art of war."[58]

That is a telling criticism. The social evolutionists, far from having proved the validity of their theories, have merely given expression to the dominant intellectual and cultural ideas of their time. The entire evolutionary theory and method rested on the prior acceptance of the idea of progressive development. Thus evolutionary theory has suffered from an inherent circularity that it has never overcome. Robert Nisbet and other scholars have included Marx among the evolutionists. As we shall see, however, the view that Marx belongs in that category is quite erroneous.

It would not be surprising at all if Marx and Engels, for all their originality, had been influenced by the evolutionary ideas of their time. Indeed, scholars who classify Marx and Engels with the evolutionists support their claim by pointing to apparent signs of evolutionary thinking throughout their writings. Here are some of those apparent signs: In their early coauthored book, *The German Ideology*, Marx and Engels described several stages of ownership forms—tribal, ancient, feudal, and capitalist. In the "Preface," to which we have referred throughout this study, Marx again speaks of "progressive epochs." That Marx and Engels had viewed society as developing in stages is further suggested by their enthusiastic reception of Lewis Henry Morgan's *Ancient Society*, and by Engels' heavy reliance on that work in his *Origin of the Family, Private Property, and the State*. In addition, the argument continues, Marx and Engels frequently employed progressivist-evolutionary language and apparently saw some parallels between organic and social evolution. In his funeral oration over Marx's grave in 1883, Engels stated "just as Darwin discovered the law of evolution in organic nature, so Marx discovered the law of evolution in human history."[59] In 1888, in his preface to the English edition of the *Communist Manifesto*, Engels prophesied that Marx's ideas are "destined to do for history what Darwin's theory has done for biology." Analogies between historical processes and evolutionary biology may be found in *Capital*. In Marx's own preface to the second edition of *Capital* in 1873, he states that capitalism is "a passing historical phase" and quotes from a Russian review of the first edition. The review praises Marx's work for demonstrating that the unfolding processes of economic life are analogous with biological evolution; and for "disclosing the special laws that regulate the origins, existence, development, and death of a given social organism and its replacement by another and higher one." And Marx approvingly comments that the reviewer has accurately portrayed his "dialectical method."[60] Marx's study of England as the most advanced capitalism of his time has also suggested that for him the "less developed" societies were ultimately destined to mirror the conditions of the "more developed."

In light of such utterances it is clear that Marx and Engels must bear some responsibility for the widespread and persistent misapprehension of their theory. As we have seen, however, a careful and open-minded examination of their writings demonstrates that it would be a gross error to take their evolutionary metaphors as anything more than rhetoric. For this much is incontrovertible as a result of our study thus far: For Marx and Engels there was no unambiguous, unilinear progress from lower to higher stages. Even in terms of technology and "productive forces," there was no such pattern of onward and upward. Instead, there were ups and downs and zigzags in the precapitalist epochs, which were predominantly *conservative* modes of production.

Furthermore, the Asiatic mode of production decisively foils any attempt to foist a unilinear evolutionism upon Marx and Engels. For, as we have seen,

1. their conception of the Asiatic mode implies not one but at least two major lines of development, a Western and an Eastern; and,
2. the Asiatic mode was stationary, which is to say that it had undergone no socioeconomic development at all.

And in point of fact, we have rather direct evidence that Marx never intended to set forth a universal-unilinear conception of history. In a letter to N. K. Mikhailovsky, a Russian author of an article discussing *Capital*, Marx emphasizes that the chapter on Primitive Accumulation of Capital (in which Marx describes the separation of the peasant producers from their means of production) "does not pretend to do more than trace the path by which, *in Western Europe*, the capitalist order of economy emerged from the womb of the feudal order of economy." Marx then goes on vehemently to reject Mikhailovsky's attempt to transform Marx's sketch of the origins of capitalism in *Western Europe* into a universal theory "of the general path every people is fated to tread, whatever the historical circumstances in which it finds itself." And Marx concludes the letter by dissociating himself from all attempts to turn his economic emphasis, which he applied to specific historical circumstances, into a universal generalization.[61]

Marx made the same point in a letter to Vera Zasulitch, another Russian who had queried him about his theory. She had asked him what implications his theory had for the vitality of the *Mir*, the Russian rural community and, in particular, its institution of common property. In his reply Marx reminded her, as he had Mikhailovsky, that his sketch in *Capital* of the genesis of capitalism "is expressly limited to the countries of *western Europe*;" and that his analysis in *Capital* therefore had no necessary implications either "for or against the vitality of the [Russian] rural community." Moreover, he added, in Western Europe the genesis of capitalism entailed the transformation of one form of private property (the peasant's or yeomen's) into another form of private property (the capitalist's); while in Russia, capitalism would require the transformation of the Russian peasants' common property into private property.[62]

If one examines Marx's writings in the light of the foregoing qualifications, it becomes perfectly evident that he always had intended his emphasis on socioeconomic processes as a *historically specific* proposition relating to the West European origin of capitalism, and not to societies in general. Marx subscribed neither to social evolutionism nor to any other suprahistorical doctrine. That Marx had no dogmatic commitment to "economic determinism" is further evident in such writings as the "Class Struggles in France" and "The 18th Brumaire of Louis Bonaparte," where Marx's analysis is almost exclusively concerned with political struggles and political events. In fact, Marx's preface to the second edition of "The 18th Brumaire of Louis Bonaparte" where Marx's analysis is almost exclusively concerned with political struggles and political events, demonstrates that he rejected rigid determinisms of all kinds. To clarify the purpose of his essay on the *coup d'état* of Louis Napoleon, Marx compares his own treatment with that of Victor Hugo and Pierre-Joseph Proudhon. Bonaparte's *coup*, says Marx, appears in Hugo's work as a

> bolt from the blue. He sees in it only the violent act of a single individual. He does not notice that he makes this individual great instead of little[63] by ascribing to him a personal power of initiative such as would be without parallel in world history. Proudhon, for his part, seeks to present the *coup d'état* as the result of an antecedent historical development. Unnoticeably, however, his historical construction of the *coup d'état* turns into a historical *apologia* for its hero. Thus he falls into the error of our so-called *objective* historians. I, on the contrary, demonstrate how the class struggle in France created circumstances and relations that made it *possible* for a grotesque mediocrity to play a hero's part.[64]

In other words, while Hugo made the error of turning Louis Napoleon into a "great man," who presumably made history quite by himself, Proudhon committed the opposite error of interpreting the *coup* as if it had been fatal-istically predetermined. Marx, in contrast to both Hugo and Proudhon, analyzed the social and historical circumstances that made it *possible* for a mediocrity to become the dictator of France.

In sum, the ups and downs of history, the conservative character of the precapitalist modes of production, the implications of the Asiatic mode of production, Marx's all-important repudiation of suprahistorical theory and fatalistically determined historical processes—all of these facts make it quite impossible to argue that for Marx "productive forces" or economic processes more generally, determined everything else.

We may therefore safely conclude that Marx had never meant to propose a rigid determinism of any kind, that he had never intended to advance a universal theory, good for all times and all places. To be sure, his method enjoins the investigator to give due attention to the "mode of production." But nowhere does Marx assert that the mode of production is the universally decisive factor in determining the various forms of society. It is strictly a matter of empirical-historical investigation whether economics, politics, war, religion or ideology—or, indeed, any or all of these in combination—will be decisive for change or nonchange in any particular case.

In Marx's historical-sociological method, there is no universal "prime mover" of history; there are no "iron laws," no universally necessary stages. *The major scientific aim of Marx's method was to guide the exploration of the manifold and historically changing connections between the economy and all other facets of society.* It is such a reading of Marx that will enable contemporary social scientists to recover the fruitful elements, both methodological and substantive, of Marx's historical sociology.

NOTES

1.   Karl Marx, *A Contribution to the Critique of Political Economy* (Chicago: Charles H. Kerr, 1904), pp. 11–12.

2.   Karl Marx and Frederick Engels, *Selected Works*, 2 vols. (Moscow: Foreign Languages Publishing House, 1951), Vol. II, p. 443. These volumes are hereafter cited as *MESW*.

3.   *MESW*, Vol. II, p. 457.

4.   Karl Marx and Frederick Engels, *The German Ideology*, Parts I and III (New York: International Publishers, 1947), p. 8, italics added.

5. Ibid., p. 9, italics added.

6. Karl Marx, *Grundrisse*, trans. Martin Nicolaus (Middlesex, England: Penguin Books, 1973), p. 491, italics in original.

7. Ibid., italics added.

8. Ibid., p. 98.

9. Ibid., p. 472.

10. Frederick Engels, *The Peasant War in Germany* (Moscow: Foreign Languages Publishing House, 1956), p. 165. Engels's essay "The Mark" is in the appendix.

11. Ibid., italics added.

12. Frederick Engels, *The Origin of the Family, Private Property, and the State* (New York: International Publisher, 1942), p. 131.

13. Engels, *The Peasant War in Germany,* "The Mark," p. 173.

14. Karl Marx, *The Poverty of Philosophy* (Moscow: Foreign Languages Publishing House, n.d.), p. 105.

15. Ibid., p. 127.

16. Karl Marx, *Capital,* Vol. I. (Moscow: Foreign Languages Publishing House, 1954), pp. 178–80.

17. Ibid., p. 511.

18. Ibid., pp. 183–184, italics added.

19. Ibid., p. 486, italics added.

20. *MESW*, Vol. I, p. 36.

21. Marx and Engels, *The German Ideology,* pp. 11–12.

22. Ibid., p. 141, italics added.

23. Engels, *The Origin of the Family,* p. 141.

24. Marx, *Capital*, Vol. I, p. 237.

25. Ibid.

26. Karl Marx and Frederick Engels, *Selected Correspondence* (Moscow: Foreign Languages Publishing House, 1953), p. 428, italics added.

27. Engels, "The Mark," pp. 174–75.

28. Ibid., p. 175–76.

29. See Engels, *The Peasant Wars in Germany.*

30. Engels, "The Mark," p. 176.

31. Frederick Engels, *Anti-Dühring* (Moscow: Foreign Languages Publishing House, 1954), p. 377, italics added.

32. Adam Smith, *An Inquiry into the Nature and Causes of the Wealth of Nations* (New York: Modern Library, 1937), pp. 645ff., 687ff., 789.

33. James Mill, *The History of British India*, 2nd ed., 12 vols. (London: Baldwin, Cradock, and Joy, 1820), Vol. I, p. 175ff.

34. Richard Jones, *An Essay on the Distribution of Wealth, and on the Sources of Taxation*, (London: John Murray, 1931), pp. 7ff, 109ff.

35. John Stuart Mill, *Principles of Political Economy* (London: Longmans, Green, 1909), p. 12ff.

36. Niccolo Machiavelli, *The Prince*, trans. George Bull (Middlesex, England: Penguin Books, 1979), p. 44ff.

37. Marx and Engels, *Selected Correspondence*, pp. 98–99.

38. Ibid., p. 99.

39. Ibid., p. 102.

40. Ibid., pp. 102–03.

41. See Marx's article, "The British Rule in India," in *The New York Daily Tribune*, June 25, 1853; reprinted in Henry M. Christman, ed., *The American Journalism of Marx and Engels* (New York: The New American Library, 1966), p. 97.

42. Marx, *Grundrisse*, p. 486; see also pp. 474 and 493.

43. Engels, *Anti-Dühring*, p. 224.

44. Ibid., p. 249.

45. Ibid., p. 251.

46. Marx, *Capital*, Vol. I, p. 714.

47. Ibid., pp. 718–19.

48. Ibid., p. 720.

49. Ibid., p. 746.

50. Ibid., p. 339.

51. Ibid.

52. Ibid., p. 422.

53. Marx and Engels, "Communist Manifesto," *Selected Works*, Vol. I, p. 51.

54. By "suprahistorical" I mean a theory which, like social evolutionism, attempts to account for social change by means of laws of development that are immanent, objective, and inexorable.

55. See Robert A. Nisbet, *Social Change and History* (New York: Oxford University Press, 1969), p. 166ff.

56. Ibid.

57. J. B. Bury, *The Idea of Progress: An Inquiry into Its Origin and Growth* (London: Macmillan, 1928).

58. Nisbet, *Social Change and History*, p. 197.

59. Marx and Engels, *Selected Works*, Vol. II, p. 153.

60. Marx, *Capital*, Vol. I, p. 19.

61. Marx and Engels, *Selected Correspondence*, pp. 376–79, italics added.

62. Ibid., p. 411–12, italics added.

63. Hugo called his study *Napoleon the Little*.

64. Marx and Engels, *Selected Works*, Vol. I, pp. 221–22, italics added.

CHAPTER 8

Max Weber[1] (1864–1920)

Talcott Parsons, who was among the first to introduce Weber's writings to English readers, declared in 1929 that *The Protestant Ethic and the Spirit of Capitalism* was intended by Weber as a "refutation of the Marxian thesis in a particular historical case."[2] In the late 1940s, in his translation of parts of Weber's *Economy and Society*, Parsons again declared that after an early contact with the Marxian position Weber "soon recoiled from this, becoming convinced of the indispensability of an important role of 'ideas' in the explanation of great historical processes."[3] Parsons thus implied that Marx and his followers had somehow failed to understand that ideas are important in history. Soon it became common opinion in the American social sciences that much of Weber's work had been intended as a refutation of Marxian theoretical and methodological principles.

That view still prevails. In a recent textbook on the history of social thought, the authors make the following allegations:

> Like all his works, Weber's essays on social stratification are an attempt at refuting Marxist thought.
>
> The originality of Max Weber's sociology lies in its dual rejection of both Marxism and theory that is modelled after the natural sciences.
>
> Thus, as in the *Protestant Ethic*, Weber's analysis of social stratification also showed how cultural phenomena circumscribe social action and, in so doing, refuted the Marxist emphasis on economic factors as the primary causal agents in history.[4]

Although this view of Weber's relation to Marx remains dominant, it has not gone unchallenged. In a 1945 essay on German sociology, Albert Salomon stated that Weber "became a sociologist in a long and intense debate with the ghost of Karl Marx," and that Weber's *Economy and Society* was a reexamination of the Marxian thesis.[5] At about the same time Hans Gerth and C. Wright Mills wrote "throughout his life, Max Weber was engaged in a fruitful battle with historical materialism."[6] And somewhat later George Lichtheim observed "the whole of Weber's sociology of religion fits without difficulty into the Marxian scheme."[7] Such interpretations of Weber became the starting point for the present author's 1968 essay in which he attempted to substantiate the thesis that Weber's work "must be read not as a repudiation of Marx's methodological principles but rather as a 'rounding out' and supplementing of his method."[8] In the present discussion of sociology and history in Max Weber, fuller documentation will be provided to support this thesis. In their respective conceptions of history, it will be argued, Weber and Marx are compatible and complementary; this is true in spite of the obvious political and ideological differences that exist between the two thinkers.

Before we begin to consider the evidence, however, a word must be said about an objection that has been raised against the complementarity thesis. Guenther Roth has insisted "Weber and Marx were further apart" than proponents of the complementary view have suggested. Roth, primarily interested in the question of whether Weber's work was in fact influenced by Marx, contends that Weber's concern with social classes, strata, and interests emanated from August Meitzen, the scholar under whom Weber wrote his second dissertation. Meitzen had also been interested in the historical antagonism between property and labour, and it was under his direction that Weber wrote his *Roman Agrarian History*. Roth agrees that one may discern in that work a "quasi-Marxist approach," but he maintains that "it was adopted from Meitzen, not Marx."[9] It is beyond doubt, however, that Weber knew Marx's writings quite well, and that he took them into account. That is a fact we shall demonstrate in due course and, indeed, a fact acknowledged by Roth when he writes that Weber "accepted the heuristic utility of historical materialism."[10]

Roth has highlighted certain criticisms that Weber made of the Marxism of his time. In his remarks to the first meeting of the German Sociological Association in 1910, Weber said:

I would like to protest the statement by one of the speakers that some one factor, be it technology or economy, can be the "ultimate" or "true" cause of another. If we look at the causal lines, we see them run, at one time, from technical to economic and political matters, at another from political to religious and economic ones, etc. There is no resting point. In my opinion, the view of historical materialism, frequently espoused, that the economic is in some sense the ultimate point in the chain of causes is completely finished as a scientific proposition.[11]

Weber also criticized Marxism for confusing technological with economic conditions:

To my knowledge, Marx has not defined technology. There are many things in Marx that not only appear contradictory but actually are found contrary to fact if we undertake a thorough and pedantic analysis, as indeed we must. Among other things, there is an oft-quoted passage: The hand-mill results in feudalism, the steam-mill in capitalism. That is a technological, not an economic construction, and as an assertion it is simply false, as we can clearly prove. For the age of the hand-mill, which extended up to modern times, had cultural "superstructures" of all conceivable kinds in all fields.[12]

Weber was among the first to raise such objections against Marxism. And it is true, of course, that in Marx's and Engels's copious writings one can find such ill-fated aphorisms as the one about the hand- and steam-mills. Yet a careful examination of the context shows that Marx had never intended this statement as a form of technological determinism, in which one could infer feudalism from the hand-mill. As we have seen, Marx's real meaning is that

Labour is organized, is divided differently according to the instruments it disposes over. The hand-mill presuppose a different *division of labour* from the steam-mill.[13]

So we see that it was not Marx himself, but rather some of his followers and critics who wrongly attributed to him a form of technological determinism. To be sure, one finds ambiguous statements in the writings of Marx and

Engels; one finds formulations apparently lending credence to the view that they proposed a form of economic and even "productive-force" determinism. But as we have seen, such interpretations have ignored important pieces of evidence. And it is precisely because the so-called "materialist conception of history" is *not a rigid, deterministic, suprahistorical theory, but rather a methodological approach, that we insist on the compatibility and complementarity of Marx and Weber.*

Before we begin to substantiate this thesis, one more point needs to be made. Roth's primary interest is "with the way in which certain ideas were transmitted and transformed in a particular intellectual and institutional setting."[14] We, in contrast, shall focus attention primarily on the methodological and substantive affinities between Marx and Weber. Nothing in our interpretation is intended to detract from Weber's originality and greatness; least of all is our interpretation intended to reduce Weber to a mere elaborator of Marx. Our sole objective is to extract the most fruitful analytical elements from both of these extraordinary thinkers, and thus to lay firm foundations for a historical sociology.

WEBER'S DIALOGUE WITH MARXISM

It is not at all difficult to show that Weber did in fact carry on such a dialogue. We have already cited Albert Salomon's remark that Weber became a sociologist in the course of a "debate with Marx's ghost." Dialogue is a better word for our purposes because at times, Weber criticizes either Marx himself or his followers; at other times, Weber affirms the correctness of Marx's economic emphasis and of his substantive analyses; and at still other times, Weber applies Marx's concepts, extending his analysis and rounding it out.

The title of one of Weber's chief works, *Economy and Society*, his concern with the Protestant ethic, and with the religions of East and West, all attest to his sustained interest in the questions and issues Marx had raised. Weber's lifelong intellectual preoccupation was with the origin and nature of modern capitalism and with the question of why it emerged first in the West. Ultimately, the answer to that question became a matter of grasping the distinctive nature of Western civilization and its fundamental contrasts with the civilizations of the East. In his investigations of that complex problem, Weber employed a historical-sociological method wholly compatible with Marx's. Marx's major scientific aim, as we have seen, was not to prove that economics everywhere always determined all other facets of society. His aim was rather to guide the exploration of the manifold and historically changing connections between the economy and other social institutions. That was also Weber's scientific aim. He was not concerned with refuting Marx, as is still widely believed, nor did he see himself as having bested Marx. On the contrary, he looked upon Marx's major analytical concepts as extraordinarily fruitful. Insofar as any refutation of Marxism was intended by Weber, it was of the dogmatic, vulgar, and mechanistic varieties that had become common in his day.

The "economic" for Weber as for Marx, referred to the "material struggle for existence."[15] How economics conditioned other institutions and how they, in turn, affected economic processes, was the lifelong focus of Weber's intellectual work. As an editor of the *Archiv für Sozialwissenschaft und Sozialpoltik*, an important social science journal, Weber decided "the scientific investigation of the general cultural significance of the social-economic structure of the human community and its historical forms of organization" was to be the journal's central aim. Why the journal adopted that editorial policy Weber explained this way: "The analysis of social and cultural phenomena with special reference to their economic conditioning and ramifications was a scientific principle of creative fruitfulness and, with careful application and freedom from dogmatic restrictions, will remain such for a very long time to come. The so-called "materialistic conception of history" as a *Weltanschauung* or as a formula for the causal explanation of historical reality is to be rejected most emphatically. The advancement of the economic *interpretation* of history is one of the most important aims of our journal."[16]

For Weber, then, the reaction against the dogmatic and vulgar types of Marxism had brought with it the danger of underestimating the fecundity of Marx's method conceived as a heuristic principle, not as a key for unlocking all doors.

If, for example, one carefully examines Weber's *Protestant Ethic and the Spirit of Capitalism,* it becomes quite clear that he was by no stretch of the imagination attempting to refute Marx. Throughout these studies, Weber acknowledges the fundamental importance of economic developments and insists that one must "take account of the economic conditions."[17] In the *Protestant Ethic,* however, he set himself a special task, namely, to examine the economic relevance of a specific religious ethic which, in his judgment, had not been given the consideration it deserved. Hence he is deliberately examining "only one side of the causal chain," that is, the impact of religious values on economic conduct. Again and again Weber returns to remind the reader of his limited purpose: "to clarify the part which religious forces have played in forming the developing web of our specifically worldly modern culture, in the complex interaction of innumerable different historical factors" (p. 90). Weber is fighting on two fronts. He wishes, on the one hand, to disprove the idea held by some Marxists, that the Reformation was a historically necessary consequence of economic developments. But, on the other hand, he has

> no intention whatever of maintaining such a foolish and doctrinaire thesis as that the spirit of capitalism (in the provisional sense of the term explained above) could only have arisen as the result of certain effects of the Reformation, or even that capitalism as an economic system is a creation of the Reformation. In itself, the fact that certain important forms of capitalistic business organization are known to be considerably older than the Reformation is a sufficient refutation of such a claim. On the contrary, we only wish to ascertain whether and to what extent religious forces have taken part in the qualitative formation and the quantitative expansion of that spirit over the world. (p. 91)

It was Weber's intention to assess the contribution of the Protestant ethic to the shape of the modern economic system, and to shed light on the process by which "ideas become effective forces in history." Thus Weber is proposing to "round out" Marx's method by systematically exploring the role of religion. He is not denying or belittling the importance of economic processes; nor, on the other hand, is he arguing that Protestantism caused capitalism. In the last paragraph of his study, Weber reminds his reader once again that he has been tracing influence in one direction, and that he has done only half a job since it is equally

> necessary to investigate how Protestant asceticism was in turn influenced in its development and its character by the totality of social conditions, especially economic. The modern man is in general, even with the best will, unable to give religious ideas a significance for culture and national

character which they deserve. But it is, of course, not my aim to substitute for a one-sided materialistic an equally one-sided spiritualistic
causal interpretation of culture and of history. Each is equally possible,
but each, if it does not serve as a preparation, but as the conclusion of
an investigation, accomplishes equally little in the interest of historical
truth. (p. 183)

Weber viewed capitalism as a modern phenomenon: a very complex
system of institutions, characterized by a high degree of formal, or technical,
rationality. Modern capitalism was not to be confused with the various forms
of capitalistic activity (for example, speculative, commercial, adventurous,
political) which were known in previous periods of history in the West and
East alike. The new economic system had to fight its way to supremacy by
overcoming a world of hostile traditional forces; its victory over those forces
could not be viewed as "historically necessary" or "historically inevitable."
When the capitalist economy first made its appearance in sixteenth- and
seventeenth-century Europe, it entailed a sharp break with the past. It involved
a new code of economic conduct and new social relations at odds with the
accepted conventions and laws of Church and State. How did the pioneers
of the capitalist system overcome the resistance of the old order and elbow
their way to success?

The answer to that question typically given by the Marxists was
roughly this: The successful emergence of the new system was made possible by changes in the economic world. The influx of precious metals from
America, capital accumulated in commerce, expanding markets, the growth
of population, and new technology resulting from the advance of natural
science—those were the major factors.

Weber did not deny the importance of those conditions. He nevertheless
believed that the Marxian answer was incomplete, for there were countries
in which all of the enumerated conditions were present, but which failed
to give birth to capitalist industry. France in the reign of Louis XIV, for
example, commanded immense resources by the standards of the time,
but dissipated them in luxury and war. Hence the economic explanation
is insufficient and one must look outside economics for the supplementary
factor. If the first entrepreneurs engaged in their economic pursuits with
a special vigour and dedication, that fact may be traced to the Protestant
ethic—to the new moral values that emerged with the religious changes

of the sixteenth century, the Reformation. Let us follow Weber as he puts his thesis together step by step.

Weber begins by drawing attention to certain significant cultural differences between Protestants and Catholics. In their education, Protestants were more inclined to study technical subjects; they were also more prominent as proprietors of industrial enterprises. Catholics, on the other hand, seemed to prefer more traditional humanistic studies and nonindustrial occupations such as crafts. Those differences remained evident even when one controlled for the social-class background of the two religious categories. Protestants, whether from upper or lower strata, "have shown a special tendency to develop *economic rationalism* which cannot be observed to the same extent among Catholics" (p. 40, italics added). What is the source of the more pronounced economic rationalism among Protestants?

At first glance, it might appear that they have been more worldly and hedonistic than Catholics. But closer examination shows that that has not been the case. The "English, Dutch and American Protestants," writes Weber, "were characterized by the exact opposite of the joy of living" (p. 41). Indeed, they adhered to a straight religious and moral code of self-denial. They were, in a word, *ascetic*. Ironically, it was their ascetic Protestant ethos that made them especially receptive to the rational spirit of capitalism.

To document his thesis, Weber employs the figure of Benjamin Franklin. From *Necessary Hints to Those That Would Be Rich* and *Advice to a Young Tradesman,* Weber selects some typical sayings that illustrate Franklin's commitment to industry, frugality, hard work, and punctuality. Franklin was important to Weber because, though he said, "Time is money," his attitude toward wealth was different from that of the rich man of earlier eras. Franklin's motives for making money, argues Weber, were devoid of hedonism. They were rooted in his strict Calvinist upbringing. Why should men make money, and why should "money be made out of men?" To that, Ben Franklin replies by quoting the Bible: "Seest Thou a man diligent in his business? He shall stand before kings." Franklin's business interests were thus religiously motivated and justified. For Weber, Franklin was rather typical of the early entrepreneurs who found clear sanction for their business dealings in their new Protestant teachings. Not all Protestants, however, shared the emphasis on an ascetic way of life with the resulting stimulation of capitalistic spirit and enterprise. Asceticism was to be traced to Calvin, not Luther.

With Luther, Weber observed, a new concept had emerged, which heretofore had been absent from Christian theology. That concept, expressed in the German word *Beruf* and even more clearly in the English word *calling*, referred to the morally dutiful fulfillment of a task assigned by God. The concept with that connotation, first appearing in Protestant translations of the Bible and thereafter assuming special importance among Protestants, imparted for the first time in the West a religious significance to men's daily, worldly activities.

And yet, Luther's general doctrine, far from being favourable to the ethos of capitalism, was positively hostile to it. His attitude toward capitalistic activity was quite traditional and in some respects less accommodating than that of the medieval Scholastics. Moreover, after the peasant uprising, when Luther had firmly aligned himself with the princes, he became a defender of the status quo. Hence, although Luther had introduced the idea of the "calling," that idea assumed a traditionalistic meaning and failed to provide a congenial environment for capitalistic activity. It is not in Luther's teachings, therefore, but in Calvinism that one must seek the ethical elements that fostered the capitalistic spirit. (Of course, the fostering of that spirit was an unforeseen and even unwished-for result of Calvin's labours.)

How, then, did Calvin's doctrine of predestination lead to worldly activity such as business? Actually, Weber explains, it was not the teachings of Calvin himself but rather of his followers that yielded that result. Calvin, though certain of his own election, rejected the principle that one could learn whether one was chosen or damned as an attempt to force God's secrets. But that doctrine proved to be too heavy a psychological burden for ordinary people who needed to know their fate and who required a "sign." Thus Calvin's followers increasingly gave way to the expressed need for "infallible criteria by which membership in the *electi* could be known." (p. 110). The original doctrine was therefore modified, and now stressed the

> absolute duty to consider oneself chosen, and to combat all doubts as temptations of the devil, since lack of self-confidence is the result of insufficient faith, hence of imperfect grace. The exhortation of the apostle to make fast one's own call is here interpreted as a duty to attain certainty of one's own election and justification in the daily struggle of life. In the place of the humble sinners to whom Luther

promises grace if they trust themselves to God in penitent faith are bred those self-confident saints whom we can rediscover in the hard Puritan merchants of the heroic age of capitalism and in isolated instances down to the present. On the other hand, in order to attain that self-confidence, intense worldly activity is recommended as the most suitable means. It and it alone disperses religious doubts and gives the certainty of grace. (pp. 111–12)

Good works, then, though useless for the attainment of salvation, became a possible *sign* of election. They served to allay fear of damnation. Hard work in the morally dutiful pursuit of a worldly calling, and absolute avoidance of anything which detracts from an ascetic way of life—that was the Protestant ethic. It was embodied, in varying degrees, in Puritanism, Pietism, Methodism, and the Anabaptist sects, and it had the "greatest significance for the development of the spirit of capitalism" (p. 151).

This brings us to the point at which Weber's method of presenting his thesis—the ideal-type—must be carefully examined if we are to understand the charges brought against him even by the most friendly of his critics. Just as earlier he had accentuated what he considered the characteristics of the new "spirit of capitalism" by employing Benjamin Franklin, as its ideal representative, so now he treated ascetic Protestantism as a unified whole by placing one of its major representatives at the centre of the discussion. For Weber, it was Richard Baxter, an English Puritan minister and writer, who "stands out above many other writers on Puritan ethics, both because of his eminently practical and realistic attitude, and, at the same time, because of the universal recognition accorded to his works" (pp. 155–56). So, if Franklin epitomized at one and the same time the new capitalistic ethos as well as the Protestant conception of the pursuit of a calling in a morally dutiful manner, so Baxter expressed through his religious writings "a practical and realistic attitude." Baxter does not quite say "Time is money," but he does say the spiritual equivalent, Weber argues. A waste of time is "in principle the deadliest of sins." Every "hour lost is lost to labor for the glory of God." Out of strictly religious motives, Baxter preaches "hard, continuous, bodily or mental labor"; but unlike St. Paul or Thomas Aquinas, who exempted some from the rule that "He who will not work shall not eat," Baxter exempts no one—not even the wealthy. Weber grants that there are certain secular, utilitarian elements in Baxter's thought, as when he expresses himself on the division of labour. The manufacturing system tends to serve "the common good, which is identical with the good of the greatest possible number"; yet even that has a characteristic Puritan element that becomes perfectly clear in his insistence on the methodical and systematic pursuit of a calling—everyday and for everyone. Baxter's doctrine detests both the "superior indulgence of the *seigneur* and the parvenu ostentation of the *nouveau riche*," but "it has the highest ethical appreciation of the sober, middle-class, self-made man" (p. 163). Puritanism, Weber writes, carried with it "the ethos of the rational organization of capital and labor," and "turned with all its force against one thing: the spontaneous enjoyment of life and all it had to offer" (p. 166). Asceticism

> looked upon the pursuit of wealth as an end in itself as highly reprehensible; but the attainment of it as a fruit of labor in a calling was a sign of God's blessing. And even more important: the religious valuation of restless, continuous, systematic work in a worldly calling, as the highest means to asceticism, and at the same time the surest and most evident proof of rebirth and genuine faith, must have been the most powerful conceivable lever for the expansion of that attitude toward life which we have here called the spirit of capitalism. (p. 172)

That becomes clear not only in Baxter's work, but also in the work of John Wesley, the founder of Methodism. The latter, Weber notes, even anticipated his own thesis, for he actually wrote that

> the full economic effect of those great religious movements, whose significance for economic development lay above all in their ascetic educative influence, generally came only after the peak of the purely religious enthusiasm was past. Then the intensity of the search for the Kingdom of God commenced gradually to pass over into sober economic virtue; the religious roots died out slowly, giving way to utilitarian worldliness. (p. 176)

Protestant asceticism thus provided a positive religious sanction for the exploitation of the worker's willingness to labour; it eased the employer's conscience and at the same time provided the worker with religious motives for treating his labour as a calling. Weber therefore concludes:

> One of the fundamental elements of the spirit of modern capitalism, and
> not only of that but of all modern culture: rational conduct on the basis
> of the idea of the calling, was born—that is what this discussion has
> sought to demonstrate—from the spirit of Christian asceticism. (p. 180)

If we keep in mind the many qualifications Weber drew around his thesis—that in these essays he is tracing causal influence in only one direction,
that he recognizes the fundamental importance of the economic conditions,
and that in a subsequent essay he hoped to trace the influence in a reverse
direction—then he is asserting on the basis of half-completed research
that there was a mutually reinforcing convergence of the Protestant ethic
and the capitalist ethos; and he is examining in this instance the degree to
which the latter was derived from the former. Once the capitalist system had
become established, however, the Protestant ethic was no longer a necessary
ingredient for the maintenance of the system. Moreover, the ethic was not
a necessary precondition for the emergence of the capitalist system per se,
but rather for its markedly energetic character during the early phases of
the system's development.

Whom did Weber select to illustrate the ethical injunctions of ascetic
Protestantism? Never its founder!—which led some of his critics to wonder whether in Weber's view Calvin was a Calvinist. If indeed it were
Weber's position—and some of his critics have thus wrongly interpreted
him—that Calvin's religious teachings were of crucial causal importance
in generating the capitalistic spirit, then it would have been methodologically impermissible to use anyone but Calvin as a representative of the new
religious doctrine. But Weber does not do that; instead, as we have seen,
he used Richard Baxter (1615–1691), John Wesley (1703–1791), Benjamin
Franklin (1706–1790), and others, all of whom lived a hundred years after
Calvin. Obviously, Weber was not employing them in order to show what
Calvinism was in the middle of the sixteenth century, but rather to show
what Calvinism became in the course of its development. Furthermore, he
was showing what it became, not in isolation from other developments, but
under the influence of economic and other developments. That is why the
thinkers Weber cites embody elements of both Protestant asceticism and the
capitalistic spirit. On the theoretical level, then, Weber is suggesting that
two relatively autonomous developments intersected at a given historical
point to contribute to the formation of the modern rational temperament:

There was a great "elective affinity" between the norms of the new religious movement and the ethos of the new economic system.

It should be clear, then, that those commentators who describe the *Protestant Ethic* as a refutation of Marxism simply have not read the essay with sufficient care. Furthermore, insofar as such commentators claim that Weber's analysis stressed religious and other spiritual "factors" at the expense of economic conditions, they are quite wrong. No one had to persuade Max Weber, who was, among other things, an outstanding economic historian, of the importance of economics. The fact of the matter is that economic conditions remained central to his analyses of both capitalist and precapitalist formations. This statement is best documented by reviewing what Weber had to say about the several epochs that Marx called "modes of production."

FEUDALISM: WEBER'S VIEW AND ITS AFFINITIES WITH THAT OF MARX

For Marx and Engels, as we have seen, it was the institution of *retinues* that eventually favoured the rise of kingship. Among the Germanic tribes, for instance, such permanent associations had become evident in earliest times. A retinue was formed, wrote Engels, when

> a military leader who had made himself a name gathered around him a band of young men eager for booty, whom he pledged to personal loyalty, giving the same pledge to them.[18]

As the Roman Empire disintegrated, and Germanic and other groups conquered ever greater areas, the leaders of such retinues had already become kings, while the retinues themselves, together with the Roman chiefs and courtiers, formed the later feudal nobility. Even in earlier times, the retinues had evaded the discipline of the community and had held their booty as private property. In due course the retinue became a firmly established institution—the major force that served to undermine communal property in land. The effects wrought by the powerful retinues may be illustrated with the history of the Frankish tribes that conquered Gaul. With victory, these West Germanic groups acquired possession of extensive Roman state domains. Large tracts of land were distributed to district and mark communities, while the rest, large forest areas, was designated as the commons, the land of the people as a whole. The land, however, did not remain in the people's hands for long. Engels writes:

> on his transformation from a plain military chief into a real sovereign of a country, the first thing which the king of Franks did was to transform this property of the people into crown lands, to steal it from the people and to give it, outright or in fief, to his retainers. This retinue, which originally consisted of his personal following of warriors and of other lesser military leaders, was presently increased not only by Romans … but also by [all those] who composed his court and from whom he chose his favorites. All these received their portions of the people's land, at first in the form of gifts, later of benefices, usually conferred, to begin with, for the king's life time. Thus at the expense of the people the foundation of a new nobility was laid.[19]

Like Marx and Engels, Weber also viewed feudalism as having emerged from the personal retinues of tribal chiefs. Both in antiquity and in the Middle Ages the followers of a chief soon became a royal retinue, the members of which, Weber observes,

> were often regarded as foreign or, at least, as standing outside the regular law of the land and subject only to the royal ban. In both periods steps are taken to establish a royal storehouse system and to supply the army with it … In both periods, too, the royal retinue was the institution from which a knightly aristocracy developed (other institutions played a role too), and this became so powerful and indispensable as to make kings dependent, sometimes reducing them to elective status and so dominating the state completely.[20]

But there were, of course, basic differences between the royal retinues of antiquity and those of the Middle Ages. The medieval king was not an urban ruler just as the medieval nobility never became an urban aristocracy. To explain the divergent path taken by the royal retinues and manorial institutions of medieval times, Weber repeats the argument he had made in his "The Social Causes of the Decline of Ancient Civilization." In antiquity the manors remained the economic foundation of an *urban* rentier class.

Ancient civilization was actually centred in the coastal cities and rested on their commercial economies. As one moved farther inland, one found a manorial organization similar to that of medieval times. In contrast to antiquity, a great change occurred in the Middle Ages:

> throughout the great area linked by a continuous historical tradition stretching from pharaonic to modern times there was a great shift in the centre of gravity from the coastal to the inland areas. Most of the manors were not suburban but rural institutions, and they supported an agrarian ruling class—princes, free vassals, and their knightly ministeriales.[21]

For Weber, as for Marx, the "retinue" is a pivotal concept in explaining the origins of the feudal social structure. Everywhere military chieftainship was transformed into seignorial power, which became hereditary. The leader and his followers had a privileged claim in the distribution of booty and conquered land. They imposed their authority on the people, the occupiers of small holdings, who cultivated the seignorial land as well as their own. The transition from tribal ownership to seignorial and the growing internal differentiation of society developed with the establishment of a professional warrior class that monopolized the military means of violence. Neither the weapons, equipment, training, nor horses were available to men with ordinary holdings. There thus arose, writes Weber,

> a distinction between those classes which by virtue of their possessions were in a position to render military service and to equip themselves for the same, and those who could not do this and consequently were not able to maintain the full status of free men. The development of agricultural technique worked in the same direction.... The result was that the ordinary peasant was increasingly bound to his economic functions. Further differentiation came about through the fact that the upper classes, skilled in fighting, and providing their own equipment, accumulated booty in varying degrees through their military activity, while non-military who could not do this became more and more subject to various services and taxes.[22]

The internal differentiation of tribal society was also brought about by the conquest and subjugation of other societies and by the voluntary submission of a defenseless man to the overlordship of a military leader. Because the former needed protection he recognized a lord as *patronus* (in Rome) or as a *senior*, among the Merovingian Franks.[23]

So for Weber as for Marx the development of feudal society reflected the growing wealth and power of the retinues.

Since the feudal lord was a professional warrior, not a farmer, he had nothing to do with agriculture. He received dues in kind from his dependents and, in return, guaranteed them protection. The resulting economy or "mode of production" was "conservative" in Marx's sense, and, indeed, Weber quotes Marx approvingly in this regard:

> The dues of the peasants originally served only to satisfy the requirements of the lord and were readily fixed by tradition. The peasants had no interest in making the soil yield more than was necessary for their own maintenance and for covering their obligatory payments, and the lord had as little interest in increasing the payments, as long as he did not produce for the market. The mode of life of the lord was but little different from that of the peasant. Thus "the walls of his stomach set the limits of his exploitation of the peasant," as Karl Marx observed.[24]

Lord and peasant had a common interest in maintaining the traditionally fixed dues.

The common interest in fixed dues came to an end, however, with the emergence of a market economy. Now kings, princes, and great lords all wanted to gain profit from commerce. The "natural economy" of the manor evinced a strong tendency to change in a capitalistic direction. Both the manorial lord and the peasant acquired a material interest in the emerging exchange economy, an interest that grew all the more intense as the market for agricultural products and the money economy expanded. Yet the internal changes in the manor, in the relations of lord to peasant, were insufficient to bring about the dissolution of the manor. For that to occur, other interests from without had to come into play, namely,

> the commercial interests of the newly established bourgeoisie of the towns, who promoted the weakening or dissolution of the manor because it limited their own market opportunities.[25]

Weber thus agrees with Marx that the town and the manor "were antagonistic" (Weber's words), and that feudal relations of production tended to "fetter" (Marx's term) and "set limits" (Weber's phrase) on capitalistic development. "Through the mere fact," writes Weber,

> of the compulsory services and payments of the tenants, the manorial system set limits to the purchasing power of the rural population because it prevented the peasants from devoting their entire labor power to production for the market and from developing their purchasing power. Thus the interests of the bourgeoisie of the towns were opposed to those of the landed proprietors. In addition, there was the interest on the part of the developing capitalism in the creation of a free labor market, to which obstacles were opposed by the manorial system through the attachment of the peasants to the soil. The first capitalistic industries were thrown back upon the exploitation of rural labor power in order to circumvent the guilds. The desire of the new capitalists to acquire land gave them a further interest antagonistic to the manorial system; the capitalistic classes wished to invest their newly acquired wealth in land in order to rise into the socially privileged landed class, and this required a liberation of the land from feudal ties. Finally, the fiscal interest of the state also took a hand, counting upon the dissolution of the manor to increase the taxpaying capacity of the farming country.[26]

It is therefore clear that Weber's analysis of declining feudalism converges strikingly with Marx's.

No less remarkable are the conceptual and substantive parallels that one finds in Weber's discussion of Eastern society. For it is indisputable, as we shall see, that Weber was familiar with Marx's characterization of the Asiatic mode of production and that he built on that concept in his own studies of Asiatic society and religion. Weber recognized that although landlords in all agrarian societies strove for independence from the political power above them, success in this endeavour was achieved only under feudalism. Feudalism was a decentralized political system in which the prince's officials were forbidden access to the lord's territory; or if permitted,

> had to come directly to the lord himself for the performance of his mission on behalf of the political authority, such as collection of feudal dues or serving of military summons.[27]

Under feudalism, there was a "division of powers," a multiplicity of comparatively autonomous domains. The *locus classicus* of feudalism, thus understood, was Western Europe and Japan. Weber agreed with Marx that the East had exhibited a fundamentally different socioeconomic and political structure.

THE ASIATIC MODE OF PRODUCTION: WEBER'S FRUITFUL ELABORATION OF MARX'S CONCEPT

Weber had a lifelong concern with the question of why rational capitalism emerged first in the West and not in the East. This led him to a systematic exploration of the basic structural and cultural differences between the two civilizations. It is beyond doubt, as we shall see, that Weber recognized the distinctive character of the Asiatic mode of production and that he was familiar with Marx's ideas on the subject. In his study of the religions and social structure of India before it was subjected to British rule, Weber pauses to make this observation:

> Karl Max has characterized the peculiar position of the artisan of the Indian village—his dependence upon fixed payments in kind instead of upon production for the market—as the reason for the specific "stability" of the Asiatic peoples. In this Marx was correct.[28]

Weber thus accepts Marx's characterization of the Asiatic mode, but expands and rounds out Marx's analysis by investigating religious as well as economic and political institutions.

Like Marx, Weber sees the roots of the Asiatic mode in the need to construct complex, artificial irrigation systems. Originating in the ancient Near East, riverine irrigation networks became the foundation of the entire economy of Mesopotamia and Egypt, the oldest centres of civilization.[29] "Every new settlement," writes Weber,

> demanded construction of a canal, so that the land was essentially a man-made product. Now canal construction is necessarily a large-scale operation, demanding some sort of collective social organization; … Here then is the fundamental economic cause for the overwhelmingly dominant position of the monarchy in Mesopotamia (and also in Egypt).[30]

That canals and irrigation networks had existed in the earliest historical centres, Sumer and Akkad, is evident from inscriptions. Building and maintaining the canals and dikes required the labour services of large numbers of people who laboured "under the direction of royal overseers, so that very soon the ancient city kingdom began to develop into a bureaucracy." The aggressive wars of Assyria and Babylonia were fought primarily with one aim in view: "to conquer subjects who would dig a new canal for a new city."[31]

In economic terms, Weber likens the Mesopotamian monarchy to an *oikos*, a huge household. The royal *oikos* derived its revenue from bondsmen and serfs on the one hand and from royal subjects who rendered labour services and paid taxes in kind. Weber writes:

> Like the pharaohs, the kings of Sumer and Akkad regulated the labor services of their subjects, provided them with food and drink, and then saw to it that they received payment in kind. There were all sorts of royal warehouses—for wagons, grain, spice, treasure—and all sorts of royal workshops…. Above all, everything needed for official building projects was produced in the royal *oikos*.[32]

Sumerian kings also engaged in commerce and monopolized trade at the river mouths.

> Ancient Egyptian institutions were likewise shaped by the necessity, arising from geography and climate, to develop a somewhat sophisticated bureaucratic administration and to mobilize the population for large-scale work on the irrigation system…. [T]he individual was above all a servant of the state. Thus when the pharaohs boast that they have established order and have visited every city of their realms, it is clear from the context that they are thinking of the irrigation system and its demands.[33]

The ancient Egyptian economy, also an enormous royal *oikos*, mainly occupied itself with the construction of systems for distributing, channelling, draining, and raising the waters of the Nile. The entire society was therefore shaped by the basic requirement of regulating the great river, to ensure the provision of society's economic needs.

The resulting political-administrative structure was a highly centralized bureaucratic state, or what Weber calls a "liturgy-state." In such states, writes Weber,

> every individual is bound to the function assigned him within the social system, and therefore every individual is in principle unfree.[34]

Every individual was an instrument of pharaonic power; the individual and his possessions were no more than entries in the royal cadaster. The typical peasant of the time is depicted in inscriptions as paying little rent for his land, and always ready to evade taxes:

> the officials arrived unexpectedly, the women began to cry, and soon a general flight and hunt began; those liable for taxes were hunted down, beaten, and tortured into paying what was demanded by the officials, who were themselves held responsible for quotas based on the official cadaster. This was the guise in which the state appeared to the peasants of the Near East.... The profound feeling of alienation from politics found among Near Eastern peoples had its origin in this repressive relationship.[35]

Thus Weber described the earliest forms of "Oriental despotism," based on forced labour and liturgies exacted from the population by a highly repressive, centralized bureaucracy. In the Near East, as elsewhere, the monarchy originally evolved with the expanding wealth and power of the military chieftain and his retinue. That the Egyptian monarch fed, equipped, and led the army and became the absolute landlord and all-powerful ruler, was causally bound up with the administrative requirements of river regulation and irrigation. The pharaoh's "retinue" was the entire army and bureaucracy. Little wonder that he was divinized.

In the East, then, political power belonged to no one but the Prince; for he, the ruler, had successfully "separated" the administrative officials from control over the key resources with which they worked. This Weber contrasted with a system in which the Prince granted land to the members of his retinue who paid their own costs and thus enjoyed considerable autonomy. "According to the dominance of one or the other of the systems," Weber observed, the political and social constitution of the state would be entirely different. *Economic considerations largely determine which form would win out.* The East and the West show in this respect the usual contrast. For oriental economy—China, Asia Minor, Egypt—irrigation husbandry became dominant, while in the West where settlements resulted from the clearing of land, forestry sets the type.[36]

To understand the fundamental structural differences between East and West, one must pay close attention to economic processes and how they conditioned other developments. For Weber, the differences between East and West extended to all the major institutions of the respective civilizations. The Asian "city," for instance, differed markedly from the Occidental one, for "Everywhere outside the West," writes Weber,

the development of the city was prevented by the fact that the army of the Prince is older than the city.

And in an apparent dialogue with the Marxists, Weber observes,

Whether the military organization is based on the principle of self-equipment or on that of equipment by a military overlord who furnishes horses, arms and provisions, is a distinction quite as fundamental for social history as is the question whether the means of economic production are the property of the worker or of a capitalistic entrepreneur.... In the west the army equipped by the war lord, and the separation of soldier from the paraphernalia of war, in a way analogous to the separation of the worker from the means of production, is a product of the modern era, while in Asia it stands at the beginning of historical development.[37]

The distinctiveness of the East rests on the fact that in Egypt, Western Asia, China, and India "irrigation was crucial." The "water question," Weber continues,

conditioned the existence of the bureaucracy, the compulsory service of the dependent classes, and the dependence of the subject classes upon the functioning of the bureaucracy of the king. That the king also expressed his power in the form of a military monopoly is the basis of the distinction between the military organization of Asia and that of the West.[38]

Thus Weber fully agrees that the requirements of water regulation and complex irrigation projects are crucial for an understanding of Asian social structure; just as he acknowledges that Marx was right in tracing the "stationary" character of Indian society to the peculiar position of the artisan in the Indian village. It is therefore undeniable that Weber's analyses of the East largely coincide with Marx's conception of the Asiatic mode of production.

What we find in Weber's analyses of Asian society is neither a belittling of economic conditions nor an attempt to refute Marx. On the contrary, what we find is a recognition of the centrality of economic conditions. Weber is nonetheless engaged in "rounding out" Marx's analysis by giving systematic attention to other salient conditions, notably the political, military, and religious. In Marx's and Engels's quite brief discussions of the Asiatic mode, they had little to say about Asian religions. But Weber wishes to show that in both China and India certain religious norms prevailed that positively precluded the spontaneous emergence of a western type of capitalism. In this case as in *all* others, Weber is certainly not arguing some sort of idealistic determination of history.

ASIAN RELIGIONS

The Religion of China

Here, as in his studies of India and ancient Israel, Weber is concerned with the question of why rational capitalism, as he defined it, emerged as an indigenous development only in the West. As he progressed in those studies, Weber came to view capitalism as an aspect of a much more comprehensive and general process, and he discovered fundamental differences between the civilizations of the East and the West.

Students of economic development in the West had stressed two factors that, among others, had contributed greatly to the rise of capitalism: the great influx of precious metals and a significant growth in population. Weber observes, however, that in the case of China, similar developments were evident. The great increase in the stock of precious metals led to a greater development of the money economy, particularly in state finance. Yet, that did not shatter traditionalism; if anything, it strengthened it. Likewise, the enormous growth in population "was neither stimulated by, nor did it stimulate, capitalist development. Rather, it was … associated with a stationary economy."[39]

In the West, Weber proffers, the cities of antiquity, the papal curia, the towns, and the emerging states of the Middle Ages "were vehicles of financial rationalization, of money economy, and of political capitalism" (p. 13). In China, in contrast, there were no cities like Florence, and the state failed to establish a money economy. The Chinese "city" was fundamentally different from the Occidental one; it did not become a centre in which capitalist relations and institutions could germinate, for it lacked political autonomy. Unlike the *polis* of antiquity and the commune of the Middle Ages, it had neither political privileges nor military power of its own, no "self-equipped military estate such as existed in Occidental antiquity" (p. 13). The Occidental city became sufficiently strong to repel an army of knights and was not dependent for its survival on any centralized bureaucracy. Political associations of merchant and craft guilds were nonexistent in the Chinese "city," and legal contracts, either economic or political, could not be made. In short, there did not emerge in China an independent bourgeois class centred in autonomous towns—which, in the West, was the fruit of prolonged struggles and revolts. Revolts were indeed common in the Chinese city, but they were organized to remove specific officials or to change specific practices, not to guarantee the freedom of the city. One of the reasons was that the Chinese city dweller never became a citizen in the Western sense, for he "retained his relations to the native place of his sib, its ancestral land and temple. Hence, all ritually and personally important relations with the native village were maintained" (p. 14).

The differences between the Occidental and Oriental cities can be traced to their different origins. The *polis* of antiquity was an overseas trading city, whereas in China, trade was predominantly inland. In order to preserve tradition, foreign trade and contact were limited to a single port, Canton. Furthermore, industrial development was not centred in the city where it could, as in the West, escape the control of traditional groups and interests. Thus the economic, political, and formal-legal foundations of an autonomous and rational organization of industry and commerce were absent.

Control of the rivers, in China as in Egypt and other ancient civilizations, led to some rationalization of the economy, but was greatly limited due to religious and other conditions:

> [The] laws of nature and of rites were fused into the unity of *Tao*. Not a supramundane lord creator, but a supra-divine, impersonal, forever identical, and external existence was felt to be ultimate and supreme. This was to sanction the validity of eternal order and its timeless existence. The impersonal power of Heaven did not "speak" to man. It revealed itself in the regimen on earth, in the firm order of nature and tradition which were part of the cosmic order, and, as elsewhere, it revealed itself in what occurred to man. The welfare of the subjects documented heavenly contentment and the correct functioning of the order. All bad events were symptomatic of disturbance in the providential harmony of heavens and earth through magical forces. (p. 28)

River regulation, the basis of imperial authority, was assured not by empirical-rational means alone but by the conduct of the emperor who had to abide by imperatives of the classical scriptures. If, for example, the dikes broke, this was evidence that the emperor did not have the qualities of charisma demanded by heaven and therefore had to do public penitence for his sins.

As in all large far-flung states with undeveloped systems of communication, administrative centralization remained relatively inefficient; nevertheless, that did not facilitate the growth of multiple centres of power. The central government employed various means to prevent officials from becoming independently powerful in their areas of assignment. The official was never assigned to his home province and had to shift every three years, either to another province or to another office. Not knowing the provincial dialect, he was dependent on interpreters, and not being familiar with the local laws and traditions, he became wholly dependent on assistants from the province, whom he paid from his own pocket.

> this resulted in actual power being vested in the hands of the unofficial, native subordinates. And the higher the rank of the authorized official the less was he able to correct and control their management. Thus the local and central government officials were not sufficiently informed about local conditions to facilitate consistent and rational intervention. (p. 50)

Yet, that did not lead to a Western-type feudalism either, for appointment to office was based on educational qualifications rather than criteria of birth and rank.

The dependence of the central government on its officials, and of the officials, in turn, on provincial assistants, enhanced traditionalism; even the "money economy" contributed to the strengthening of traditional structures. The officials became in effect "tax farmers," who extracted what they could from their provincial subjects, gave as little as they dared to their superiors, and kept the rest. They were prebendaries who had a paramount interest in maintaining the existing socioeconomic conditions and hence the profits from their prebends. Thus, as the money economy expanded so did prebendalization, a great obstacle to attempts at internal change. To become prebendaries they were dependent on the central government; once they became officials and received their assignments, however, they acquired only a very limited power, for they remained dependent on the indigenous elements of the provinces in which they were strangers. This is in sharp contrast with the West where

> there were strong and independent forces. With these, princely power could ally itself in order to shatter traditional fetters; or, under very special conditions, these forces could use their own military power to throw off the bonds of patrimonial power. This was the case in the five great revolutions which decided the destiny of the Occident; the Italian revolution of the twelfth and thirteenth centuries, the Netherland revolution of the sixteenth century, the English revolution of the seventeenth century, and the American and French revolutions of the eighteenth century. We may ask: Were there no comparable forces in China? (p. 62)

The Chinese were no less acquisitive than the Europeans, and their capacity for work and industry was unsurpassed; there were even powerful and autonomous merchant guilds, though not concentrated in the towns; there was a tremendous growth in population since the eighteenth century, and, finally there was a constant increase in precious metals. Yet, no capitalism. How does Weber explain that fact?

Though "private property" emerged, it never became truly private as in the West: The sib in China was so powerful that true alienation of land from it was impossible. Land was not unconditionally or permanently sold; rather, the sib always retained the right to repurchase. There were moneylenders and various forms of commerce, but they did not lead to modern rational, capitalistic enterprise. "There was no rational depersonalization of business," Weber writes, "comparable to its unmistakable beginnings in the commercial law of Italian cities" (p. 85). In China, the growth of wealth in the form of money led to different results. When officials retired, for instance, they invested their money in landholdings which enabled some of their sons to study so as to pass the state examinations and thus become eligible for "tax-farming" careers of their own. In that way the whole familial community had a vested interest in the examination system and other traditional institutions. The community was held together by powerful and rigid kinship bonds.

The power of the sib rested to a large degree on the ancestor cult; ancestral spirits acted as mediators between their descendants and the deities. The "city," then, never became a "hometown" but remained "typically 'a place away from home' for the majority of its inhabitants" (p. 90). Cities were mere urban settlements of farmers and "there remained only a technical administrative difference between city and village. A 'city' was the seat of the mandarin and was not self-governing; a 'village' was a self-governing settlement without a mandarin" (p. 91). The sib and other traditional elements were in the long run stronger than the rational bureaucracy. Illiterate old age, for example, carried a higher status and authority than the most learned mandarin, and Chinese justice, far from becoming formal, legal, and rational, remained patriarchal.

There were still other developments that contributed to the formation of capitalism in the West but were patently missing in China. After pacification of the empire, there was neither rational warfare nor even an "armed peace during which several competing autonomous states constantly prepared for war. Capitalist phenomena thus conditioned through war loans and commissions for war purposes did not appear" (p. 103). An additional handicap to capitalist development was the empire's lack of overseas colonies.

Administrative development in China also took a different form from that of the West. That is best seen in the bureaucracy composed of *literati*. To be sure, they had to qualify for office by passing examinations, which in turn required a certain education, but their education was based entirely upon the classical literature. They were therefore quite far from being bureaucrats in the Western sense, for their ideal, above all, was to be cultivated Confucian gentleman.

> The Chinese examinations [writes Weber] did not test any special skills, as do our modern national and bureaucratic examination regulations for jurists, medical doctors, or technicians.… The examinations of China tested whether or not the candidate's mind was thoroughly steeped in literature and whether or not he possessed the *ways of thought* suitable to a cultured man and resulting from cultivation in literature. (p. 121)

Rational administration depended on subordinates who were skilled in the required technical and administrative tasks, for the *literati* themselves rejected the one-sided thoroughness and specialization characteristic of Western civilization from Plato to its restatement in the "calling" of ascetic Protestantism. Yet, although the *literati* viewed the examinations as tests of their cultivation and general humanistic knowledge, the popular view was different:

> In the eyes of the Chinese masses, a successfully examined candidate and official was by no means a mere applicant for office qualified by knowledge. He was a proved holder of magical qualities, which, as we shall see, were attached to the certified mandarin just as much as to an examined and ordained priest of an ecclesiastic institution of grace, or to a magician tried and proved by his guild. (p. 128)

Orthodox Confucianism had renounced the beyond and in so doing had ignored the religious needs of the masses. Magic and animism, always strong among the peasants,

> had come under the patronage of a priesthood which was tolerated because it claimed to have originated with a philosophical personage, Laotzu, and his doctrine. Originally the meaning of this doctrine did not differ in the main from that of Confucianism. Later it became antagonistic to Confucianism and was finally considered thoroughly heterodox. (p. 177)

There were repeated power struggles between the *literati* and the priests, in which the former were always victorious. Yet, ironically, the *literati* constantly availed themselves of the Taoist's priestly and magical services, affording Taoist heterodoxy a recognized place in the religious practice.

The "victorious Confucians … never seriously aimed at uprooting magic in general and Taoist magic in particular. They only sought to monopolize office prebends" (p. 194).

Not only were magic and animism tolerated, but they were also systematized so as to become highly significant forces in Chinese life. All sciences that had empirical and naturalistic beginnings were organized as magical and supernatural practices and rituals. The Chinese world, despite its secular, rational-empirical elements, remained enchanted—a magic garden. The *literati* were to a notable degree secular or "this worldly," but not consistently so. They not only tolerated magic as a means of taming the masses—they themselves believed in it. Under those circumstances it is understandable why they never waged war against magic, never strove to divest Chinese culture of magical beliefs and practices.

"Demagification" of religion, Weber believed, was carried out in the West most consistently and thoroughly by ascetic Protestantism, but the process had begun with the ancient Jewish prophets. That does not mean, Weber emphasizes, that the Puritans did not retain superstitious beliefs; that they did is obvious from their witch trials. Rather, it means that they came to regard "all magic as devilish." For Weber, then, one criterion of the rationalization of religion is the degree to which it has rid itself of magic. But there is still another criterion: "the degree to which it has systematically unified the relation between God and the world and therewith its own ethical relationship to the world" (p. 226). Whereas Puritanism resulted in a "tremendous and grandiose tension with the 'world,'" Confucianism regarded this world as the best of all possible worlds. Above all, the Confucian was to adjust to the world; his conduct had implications for cosmic harmony so he exercised rational self-control and repressed all irrational passions that might disturb his poise. But such conduct did not weaken the powers of magic; quite the contrary, it took the use of magic for granted, for though the educated Confucian adhered, or submitted, to magical practice with some skepticism, the masses were altogether steeped in it. And the *literati* (unlike the Old Testament prophets), far from having demanded that the masses abandon such practices, even connived in them—for material as well as spiritual reasons. "Tension toward the 'world' had never arisen because, as far as is known, there had never been an ethical prophecy of a supramundane God who raised ethical demands" (p. 230). A true prophesy that raised such demands and which viewed the world as matter to be shaped according to ethical norms was unknown in Chinese history.

As we see, then, Weber counterbalances the conditions apparently favourable to the development of capitalism by other unfavourable conditions. As he repeatedly stresses, his treatment of an enormously complicated problem with innumerable conditions could hardly yield a simple answer. Yet his analysis strongly suggested that it was the prevailing religious mentality in China that constituted a major obstacle to the emergence of rational capitalism of the European type. Now as earlier, however, Weber acknowledges that the religious mentality was codetermined by economic and political conditions.

The Religion of India

In India, too, Weber saw many social and cultural conditions which, it would seem, should have given rise to modern rational capitalism. Warfare, finance, and politics, for instance, had been rationalized, and the last of these even in quite "Machiavellian" terms. Many of the older types of capitalist forms had at one time or another been in evidence: state creditors and contractors, tax farmers, and so on. Urban development also seemed to parallel that of the West at many points. In addition, what Weber called rationality was prominent in many aspects of Indian cultural life: the rational number system, arithmetic, algebra, rational science, and in general a rational consistency in many spheres, together with a high degree of tolerance toward philosophical and religious doctrines. The prevailing judicial forms appeared compatible with capitalist development; there existed an autonomous stratum of merchants; handicrafts as well as occupational specialization were developed, and, finally, a high degree of acquisitiveness and a high evaluation of wealth were notable aspects of Indian social life. "Yet," Weber writes,

> modern capitalism did not develop indigenously before or during English rule. It was taken over as a finished artifact without autonomous beginnings. Here we shall inquire as to the manner in which Indian religion, as one factor among many, may have prevented capitalistic development (in the Occidental sense).[40]

Here, again, we see Weber's distinctive methodological approach. He regards Indian religion as "one factor among many" which "may have prevented capitalist development." Because there was no way of quantifying or weighting the elements, all one could do was to make as strong and as cogent a case as possible. If Indian religion had taken another form—for example, equivalent to that of ascetic Protestantism—then, perhaps, a modern, rational type of capitalism might have developed there too. Because economic, urban, scientific, and other developments were somewhat equivalent in India and the West, and modern capitalism emerged autonomously only in the latter civilization, the different religious ethos that took shape there must have made a significant causal contribution to the origin of the modern economic system. Ultimately, however, Weber sees more operative there than just the Protestant ethic; what he sees as really crucial is that despite the rational, scientific elements in the East, and the existence there of economic strata and forms seemingly conducive to the emergence of a modern rational economy, the East remained an "enchanted garden." That meant that all aspects and institutions of Oriental civilization were permeated and even dominated by the magical mentality—which became a brake on economic developments in particular and on rationalization of the culture as a whole. In contrast, Occidental civilization, already in its early stages of development, had undergone significant *disenchantment*, which was increased almost as a unilinear development right to the present. Disenchantment or rationalization began with the scriptural prophets; but Christianity, Greek formal logic, Roman law, the medieval papal curia, cities and states, the Renaissance, the Reformation, the Enlightenment, and the various bourgeois revolutions all contributed to the process that has made Western civilization as a whole fundamentally different from that of the East.

Actually, Weber's studies of the world religions embrace much more than religious phenomena and institutions. In effect, he takes the entire social structure of the society in question into his purview. In the case of India, the caste system was clearly of fundamental importance. The origin of the four main castes or categories—Brahmans, Kshatriyas, Vaishyas, and Shudras—is shrouded in mystery; more, however, is known about the proliferation of groupings, so that literally thousands of subcastes crystallized in the course of Indian history. Basing himself on the best Indological sources, Weber sketches the process by which new castes form and others undergo schisms.

With the increasing wealth of some strata, numerous tasks were defined by them as "lower" and unclean so that eventually the native, resident population refused to engage in them. That made room for alien workers, whatever their origin, who moved into those occupations and became a "guest" people tolerated for the economic function they fulfilled. At first, they were not properly a part of the host village organization; they retained their own community organizations and had full jurisdiction over them. When, in addition, certain ritual barriers were raised against the guest peoples, Weber calls them a *pariah people*. (One example of this in the West was the Jews during the Middle Ages—except that in their case, as Weber shows, it was precisely the Jews who brought with them certain ritual practices that they voluntarily maintained against the host people.) Eventually, through a variety of forms of transition, a *pariah people*, having established itself in some of the formerly native Hindu occupations, develops an interest in maintaining its hold over those occupations and demands and receives certain Brahmanical services. The members of the pariah group, underprivileged anyway, come to prefer a legitimate status to that of an alien people since "caste organizations, like quasi-trade unions, facilitate the legitimate defense of both internal and external interests of the lower castes" (p. 17). The hope and promise which Hinduism held out to these negatively privileged strata helps to explain "their relatively minor resistance in view of what one would expect of the abysmal distance Hinduism established between social strata" (p. 17).

The caste system, to be sure, had essentially negative consequences for economic development, but not, as one might at first expect, primarily because it imposed restrictions and prohibitions on social interaction. Rather, it was because the caste system became totally traditionalistic and antirational in its effects. It is here that Weber takes time to acknowledge an insight which reveals that in these studies, as in others, he took leads from Marx. "Karl Marx," writes Weber:

> has characterized the peculiar position of the artisan in the Indian village—his dependence upon fixed payment in kind instead of upon production for the market—as the reason for the specific "stability" of the Asiatic peoples. In this, Marx was correct. (p. 111)

Weber adds, however, that "not only the position of the village artisan but also the caste order as a whole must be viewed as the bearer of stability" (p. 112). That order was quite flexible in the face of the requirements of the concentration of labour in large-scale enterprises; caste proscriptions on interactions with the ritually impure were not the main impediment to industrial development. All the great religions, he suggests, have placed such restrictions on modern economy. It was the traditional, antirational "spirit" of the whole social system which constituted the main obstruction; that, along with the "artisan's traditionalism, great in itself, was necessarily heightened to the extreme by the caste order" (p. 112).

The antirational spirit became manifest in the prevalence of magic and in the role of the Brahmans, whose very power was connected "with the increasing significance of magic in all spheres of life." This together with other religious developments had significantly modified the character of Indian economic strata. If, for example, there was an Indian "bourgeoisie," it was very weak for at least two reasons:

> first, was the absolute pacifism of the salvation religions, Jainism and Buddhism, which were propagated, roughly, at the same time as the development of the cities.... Second, there was the undeveloped but established caste system. Both these factors blocked the development of the military power of the citizenry; pacifism blocked it in principle and the castes in practice, by hindering the establishment of a *polis* or *commune* in the European sense. (pp. 88–89)

The merchants as well as the guilds had no independent military organizations and therefore could be repressed whenever a prince found it expedient to do so. The Indian town enjoyed no true self-government or autonomy.

Also, apart from the implications that the sacred cow had for Indian animal husbandry, magico-religious practices retarded technical-industrial development. Often, "tools were worshipped as quasi-fetishes" and along with "other traditional traits, this stereotyping of tools was one of the strongest handicaps to all technical development" (p. 99).

Indian religions, including Buddhism, had attained a highly technical virtuosity that resulted in an extreme devaluation of the world; none of them enjoined the adherent to prove himself or his grace through action or work. Quite the contrary, the highest good was a contemplative flight from the world. Indian asceticism never translated itself into a methodical, rational way of life that tended in its effects to undermine traditionalism and to change the world.

Thus, India, like China, remained an "enchanted garden" with all sorts of fetishism, and animistic and magical beliefs and practices—spirits in rivers, ponds, and mountains, highly developed word formulas, finger-pointing magic, and the like. In contrast to the Hebrew prophets, who never made peace with the magicians, the Brahmans (a distinguished, cultivated, and genteel stratum like the Mandarins), in the interests of their power position, not only recognized the influence of magic but rationalized it and made numerous concessions to the unclassical magicians (p. 295)—despite the fact that ideally, according to the Classic Vedas, magic was to be suppressed, or at least merely tolerated among the masses.

The general character of Asiatic religion, Weber concluded (on the basis of his studies of China, India, Korea, Ceylon, and so on), was a particular form of gnosis—that is, positive knowledge in the spiritual realm, mystically acquired. Gnosis was the single path to the "highest holiness" and the "highest practice." Such "knowledge," far from becoming a "rational and empirical means by which man sought with increasing success to dominate nature," became instead "the means of mystical and magical domination over the self and the world … by an intensive training of body and spirit, either through asceticism or, and as a rule, through strict, methodologically ruled meditation" (p. 133). This gave rise to a redemption aristocracy, for such mystical knowledge was necessarily esoteric and charismatic, hence not accessible or communicable to everyone. The holy and godlike was attained by an "emptying" of experiences of this world. Psychic peace, not restlessness, was godlike; the latter, being specifically creature-like, was illusory, transitory, and valueless.

Hence, in contrast to the soul-saving doctrines of Christianity, no emphasis was placed on "this life"; Asiatic religion led to an otherworldliness. "In Asia generally," writes Weber, "the power of a charismatic stratum grew." In sharp contrast to the Hebrew prophets, however, that stratum

> succeeded in breaking the dominion of magic only occasionally and only with very temporary success.
>
> Not the "miracle" but the "magical spell" remained, therefore, the core substance of mass religiosity. This was true above all for peasants and laborers, but also for the middle class. (p. 335)

That this magical, antirational mentality had a profound impact on economic conduct and development could not be doubted. Magic was employed

> for achieving all conceivable sorts of inner-earthly values—spells against enemies, erotic or economic competition, spells designed to win legal cases, spiritual spells of the believer for forced fulfillment against the debtor, spells for securing of wealth, for the success of undertakings. (p. 336)

The depth and tenacity of the magical mentality created conditions in which the "lust for gain" never gave rise to the modern economic system Weber called rational capitalism. What was notably absent from Asiatic religion therefore was the development that in the Occident ultimately broke the hold of magic over the minds of men and gave rise to a "rational, inner-worldly ethic." That historical process began

> with the appearance of thinkers and prophets who developed a social structure on the basis of political problems which were foreign to Asiatic culture; these were the political problems of civic status groups of the city without which neither Judaism nor Christianity nor the development of Hellenic thought is conceivable. (p. 338)

The ancient Jewish prophets then were fundamental, since it was to them and to the early Greek thinkers that the roots of the *Rationalisierungsprozess* (that is, the "rationalization process") in the West could be traced.

Ancient Judaism

For Weber, the development of Judaism was important for the profound impact it had on the beginnings of Western civilization. According to the Jewish religious conception, God created the world and intervened in history; the world in its present form was a result of God's response to the actions of humanity and particularly the Jews. The present condition of toil, trouble, misery, and suffering, the opposite of that promised for the future, was temporary and would "give way again to the truly God-ordained order. The whole attitude toward life of ancient Jewry was determined by this conception of a future God-guided political and social revolution."[41] For the attainment of the future order, everything depended on the worldly actions of the Jews and their faithful devotion to the Commandments of God (Yahweh). In addition to ritual correctitude, there was

> a highly rational religious ethic of social conduct; it was free of magic and all forms of irrational quest for salvation; it was inwardly worlds apart from the paths of salvation offered by Asiatic religions. To a large extent this ethic still underlies contemporary Mideastern and European ethic. World-historical interest in Jewry rests upon this fact. (p. 9)

The historical importance of Judaism, apart from its being the source of Christianity and Islam, lies in its rational-ethical character, and for this reason:

> Only the following phenomena can equal those of Jewry in historical significance: the development of Hellenic intellectual culture; for western Europe, the development of Roman law and of the Roman Catholic church resting on the Roman concept of office; the medieval order of estates; and finally, in the field of religion, Protestantism. (p. 5)

In this remarkably painstaking study, Weber defined the historical status of the Jews as that of a "pariah people"—a term that has been subject to considerable misunderstanding. The term refers primarily to the social segregation of the Jews that resulted to a large degree from the ritualistic requirements of their religion. Weber understands the segregation of the Jews in that sense as self-imposed and long antedating their forced ghettoization in medieval Europe for economic and other reasons. Weber is intent upon showing that general social and historical conditions, though important, were not sufficient to explain how Jewry developed into a people "with highly specific peculiarities," because Jewry's distinctiveness never would have come about in the absence of the specific Jewish ritual and religious commandments. Here again, Weber is exploring the influence of religious ideas on social existence and development—but always against the background of social, economic, and political structures which he examines fastidiously.

Weber shows, for instance, how the older stratification system in ancient Israel changed and how in its place there soon emerged a wealthy urban patriciate on the one hand and a number of impoverished and indebted strata on the other. Ancient Israel, situated as it was in the midst of the great and powerful states and along major trade routes, became a centre of trade with many cities. Evidence of class conflict between "indebted peasants and urban creditors existed from the beginning of recorded history" (p. 61).

Conflict between the rich and the poor was exacerbated with the emergence of the monarchy, particularly under Solomon; Weber calls attention to the ambivalence with which Jewish tradition has regarded the third king of Israel. It was against the background of the basic transformation of Israelite society that the prophets of social justice emerged. Now, increasingly, the kings, whose oppressive consequences Samuel had prophesied, were making of Israel a *corvée* state, a "house of bondage" like the Egyptian state the Jews despised as an abomination. The prophets spoke out against this trend and voiced sharp criticism of the monarchs, their private sins as well as their public practices. The prophets, though not out of political motives per se, thus expressed the sentiments of the peasants and other oppressed groups who remembered that they had fought for freedom against the privileged strata, and that God had brought their forefathers out of the land of Egypt. Now the people saw themselves increasingly subject to debt bondage, taxes, and *corvée* duties.

It would be wrong to suppose, Weber emphasizes, that when the prophets rebuke the monarchs or speak out against the rich, they are direct ideological spokesmen of the oppressed. There is no doubt that the political content of their messages was drawn from the actual events of the day and from reflecting on the condition of the oppressed. But the real inspiration and meaning of their message, Weber insists, were purely religious. Yahweh and his commandments were being forsaken and his Covenant violated. It was that primarily, if not exclusively, that motivated the prophets to say what they did and to foretell doom. They increasingly deprecated the patricians and their riches, and the kings and their chariots, and "hallowed the time when Yahweh himself as war leader led the peasant army, when the ass-riding prince did not rely on horses and chariots and alliances, but solely on the God of the Covenant and his help" (p. 111).

Here, we may pause to note how Weber conceives the relationship between religious ideas and socioeconomic conditions. The prophets were a relatively autonomous stratum in Israelite society; they were religious practitioners with strictly religious interests. However, their political orientation, which became evident in a specific period, was clearly related to changes in social stratification and to the institutionalization of the monarchy. "It is no accident," Weber writes,

> that the first appearance of the independent, politically oriented seers, who were succeeded by these prophets, coincided almost exactly with that great transformation which kingship under David and Solomon brought about in the political and social structure of Israel. (p. 110)

Although the prophets were religious thinkers, and comprised a relatively autonomous stratum, their message, and the various forms it assumed, could not be explained in strictly immanent terms. There was a definite relationship between the prophetic movement and other aspects of the social structure, and the fact that prophecy acquired a political character in a given historical period can be understood only by viewing it in relation to the general social changes that had come about. The relative independence of the prophets was facilitated by the fact that in Israel the king was not a priestly dignitary at the apex of a hierocratic order and that the prophets received support and protection from wealthy and powerful Yahwistic families whom the monarchy could not suppress. However, if, in Weber's view, "rationalization" was a consequence of the prophets' unceasing war against magical and orgiastic practices, that was not out of any rational, secular, or political considerations on their part; rather, it had to be explained on the basis of their unswerving devotion to Yahweh.

This devotion was based on the unique relation of Israel to its God, expressed and guaranteed in a unique historical event—the conclusion of a covenant with Yahweh. The prophets and the antiroyalist Yahwistic nobles always hearkened back to that great and miraculous event in which God kept his promise, intervened in history, and liberated the Jews from Egyptian bondage. That was proof not only of God's power but of the absolute dependability of his promises. Israel, then, as the other party to the Covenant mediated by Moses, owed a lasting debt of gratitude to serve and worship Yahweh and to have no other gods before him. This rational relationship, unknown elsewhere, created an ethical obligation so binding that Jewish tradition regarded "defection" from Yahweh as an especially fatal abomination (p. 119). Moreover, the markedly rational nature of the relationship lay in the worldly character of God's promises to Israel; not some supernatural paradise or utopia was promised, but

> that they would have numerous descendants, so that the people should become numerous as the sand of the seashore, and that they should triumph over all enemies, enjoy rain, rich harvests, and secure possessions. (p. 119)

To Moses was held out the hope of leading his people out of Egypt and into the Promised land—here on Earth and, in fact, just across the border, despite the circuitous route required to reach it. "The god," writes Weber, "offered salvation from Egyptian bondage, not from a senseless world out of joint. He promised not transcendent values but dominion over Canaan which one was out to conquer and a good life" (p. 126).

Of course, the conception of Yahweh, as well as the degree of devotion to him, varied through time and with the different social strata. The richness of Weber's analysis cannot be conveyed here. The main point is that the eminently rational character of Judaism could be explained by the convergence of a number of circumstances: (1) The Jews loathed everything that emanated from Egypt, including the cult of the dead; (2) Bedouin practices were also rejected, for Amalek was a traditional enemy of Israel; (3) as for Baal, once the Jews became a settled agricultural people in Canaan, the attributes of Baal and other functional deities were soon syncretized with those of Yahweh, so that he was no longer merely the "war god of the confederacy" but could bring rain and assure a good harvest. In addition, however, and perhaps most important, was Israel's peculiar relationship to God and his Covenant. When, in Weber's words,

> [Yahweh] was angry and failed to help the nation or the individual, a violation of the *berith* with him had to be responsible for this. Hence, it was necessary for the authorities as well as for the individual from the outset to ask which commandment had been violated? Irrational divination means could not answer this question, only knowledge of the very commandments and soul searching. Thus, the idea of *berith* flourishing in the truly Yahwistic circles pushed all scrutiny of the divine will toward an at least relatively rational mode of raising and answering

the question. Hence, the priestly exhortation under the influence of the intellectual strata turned with great sharpness against soothsayers, augurs, day-choosers, interpreters of signs, conjurors of the dead, defining their ways of consulting the deities as characteristically pagan. (p. 167)

In ancient Israel, the relation of priests to prophets was quite fluid so that the Levites, for example, gained their prestige less by their special skills in offering sacrifices than by their rational knowledge of Yahweh's Commandments. Oracular and magical means were systematically reduced to a minimum, and "became less and less important as against the rational case study of sins, until the theological rationalism of Deuteronomy (18:9–15) in substance discredited lot casting altogether or at least ceased to mention it" (p. 179). All forms of sexual and alcoholic orgiasticism were consistently opposed until they became anathema to the various advocates and defenders of Yahwism—the Levitical Torah teachers, the prophets, and the wealthy and politically influential, pious Yahwistic families. Thus, although magic was never eliminated from popular practice, it was dislodged from its position of dominance in ancient-Judaism—a fact that contrasts with all other ancient religions.

In Weber's view, classical prophecy acquires its most characteristic form when the great powers of the area, Egypt and Mesopotamia, resumed their expansionist policy. The classic scriptural prophets—for example, Amos, Isaiah, Jeremiah, Ezekiel—despite their purely religious motives, were in effect political demagogues and even pamphleteers. It would be wrong, however, to view prophecy, exclusively or even primarily, as a response to internal developments and conflicts—as the expression of the interests and sentiments of the "people" who were now oppressed by the overlords and the monarchy. Prophecy in its classical form, Weber insists, never would have arisen in the absence of the great-power conflict that constituted a threat to the existence of Israel. When the monarchy was strong or protected by a great power, the prophets "remained silent—or rather [were] reduced to silence. With the decreasing prestige of the kings and the growing threat to the country, the significance of prophecy again increased and the scene of the prophet's activities moved closer and closer to Jerusalem" (p. 269).

They spoke in the streets and addressed their publics directly; their inspiration was spontaneous and their major concern was "the destiny of the state and the people. This concern always assumed the form of emotional invectives against the overlords" (p. 269). When they prophesied doom and a catastrophe actually befell the country, they showed no sign of personal jubilation; instead they mourned but also expressed hope for better times now that God's wrath had passed. Objectively, they were involved in conflicting political interests and party antagonisms, but they had no personal political interests or motives. They were mere mouthpieces through which Yahweh spoke. In Weber's words:

> according to their manner of functioning, the prophets were objectively political and above all, world-political demagogues and publicists, however, subjectively they were no political partisans. Primarily they pursued no political interests. Prophecy had never declared anything about a "best state" (disregarding Ezekiel's hierocratic construction in the Exile) nor has it ever sought, like the philosophical *aisymnete* or the academy, to help translate into reality social-ethically oriented political ideals through advice to power holders. The state and its doings were, by themselves, of no interest to them. Moreover, unlike the Hellenes they did not posit the problem: how can man be a good citizen? Their question was absolutely religious, oriented towards the fulfillment of Yahweh's commandments. (p. 275)

Thus Weber demonstrates the enormous complexity of prophecy in Israel and implicitly argues that no simple formula is sufficient for an understanding of the phenomenon. Their pronouncements on internal affairs must not be understood as direct ideological manifestations of class relationships and conflicts. The prophets did not stem from the oppressed and disadvantaged strata; most of them were wealthy and came from distinguished families. Even Amos, who was described as a poor stockbreeder, was an educated man; like Isaiah (who was wealthy and distinguished), he cursed the rich and the great but "yet pronounced the rule of the uneducated, undisciplined demos as the worst of all curses" (p. 277). They were therefore neither defenders of democratic ideals nor spokesmen for the "people," and their main support came not from the oppressed but from individual, pious, and distinguished families in Jerusalem. That their motives were purely religious becomes clear, in addition, from their condemnation at one and the same time of both debt slavery and the fertility cults and shrines of Baal "which meant much to the rural population for economic as well as ideal reasons" (p. 279).

The prophets and the Torah teachers were of major importance in the rationalization of Judaism. However, the documentation of the radical "disenchantment" of Judaism was only one of the tasks Weber set himself in this extraordinary study. Another important problem was how the Jews came to constitute a pariah community. That, Weber shows, must be viewed as the result of both prophecy and the special ritual requirements of Judaism that the Jews took with them into exile and held to stubbornly and tenaciously.

With the destruction of the Temple and the exile of the Jews, sacrifice, permissible only in Jerusalem, became impossible. Hence, it became all the more essential to preserve the tradition in other ways. Jews were to remain ritually pure and guard themselves against any and all pagan practices and worship. That was particularly important since the *Diaspora* was regarded as a temporary situation and the hope of returning to the homeland remained alive. Slowly, there emerged a distinctive religious community organization with new institutions peculiar to the Exile.[42]

Weber thus traced the "rationalization process" in the West to its roots in ancient Judaism. In his late writings on China, India, and Israel, in his posthumously published *General Economic History*, and in the introduction he wrote, just before he died, to the book edition of *The Protestant Ethic*, he views capitalism and Protestantism, as well as many other distinctive Western institutions as the products of a long process of "rationalization." Weber's last pronouncements on the subject therefore reveal a wider and more complex conception than the earlier one conveyed in the *The Protestant Ethic*. It is Weber's illumination of the distinctive character of Western civilization as a whole that must be regarded as his most important substantive contribution.

The true importance of Weber's writings on religion should now be altogether clear. His fastidious examination of Asian religions (and the contrast they present to Judaism and Christianity) may be viewed as a masterly analysis of what Marx might have called the religio-cultural "superstructure" of the Asiatic mode of production. Nothing in Weber's analysis contradicts Marx's conception. On the contrary, Weber's penetrating insights provide a fuller grasp of the social totality—the "foundation" and the "superstructure."

Religion, for Weber, was neither an epiphenomenon nor a prime mover of history. Religion was rather a significant element in a complex constellation of factors. Moreover, Weber nowhere proposed a general theory of the relation of religion to other conditions. Weber's theories, like Marx's, were historically specific: If Eastern religion placed obstacles before the development of industrial capitalism, that was true only in a specific historical epoch. Weber observes that when the Western powers began to build railroads and factories in China, the geomancers demanded that in locating structures on certain mountains, forests, rivers, and cemetery hills, foresight should be exercised in order not to disturb the peace of the spirits."[43] Then in a footnote Weber adds this observation:

> as soon as the Mandarins realized the chances for gain open to them, these difficulties suddenly ceased to be insuperable; today [1920] they are leading stockholders in the railways. In the long run, no religious-ethical conviction is capable of barring the way to the entry of capitalism, when it stands in full armor before the gate; but the fact that it is [now] able to leap over magical barriers does not prove that genuine capitalism could have originated in circumstances where magic played such a role.[44]

It remains for us to examine one more instance of Weber's convergence with Marx.

WESTERN CAPITALISM: WEBER'S COMPLEMENTARY ANALYSIS

A major presupposition of industrial capitalism, Weber agreed, is "free" labour in Marx's sense. Persons have to be free from bonds of servitude such as chattel slavery and serfdom and free, that is, separated, from their means of production. A large mass of free labourers had first emerged in the West, in England, the classical land of peasant evictions. The Enclosure movement created a giant mass of vagabonds, so that "as early as the 16th century there was such an army of unemployed that England had to deal with the problem of poor relief."[45] This huge labour reservoir made the factory system possible. In the earliest phases of that system, the concentration of workers in shops was compulsory. The poor, the homeless, and the criminals, writes Weber,

> were pressed into factories, and in the mines of Newcastle the labourers wore iron collars down into the 18th century. But in the 18th century itself the labour contract everywhere took the place of unfree work. It meant a saving in capital, since the capital requirement for purchasing the slaves disappeared; also a shifting of the capital risk onto the worker,

since his death had previously meant a capital loss for the master. Again, it removed responsibility for the reproduction of the working class, whereas slave-manned industry was wrecked on the question of family life and reproduction of the slaves. It [the labour contract] made possible the rational division of labour on the basis of technical efficiency alone, and … freedom of contract first made concentration of labour in the workshop the general rule. Finally, it created the possibility of exact calculation, which again could only be carried out in connection with a combination of workshop and free worker.[46]

Like Marx, then, Weber stresses free labour as a precondition of the modern economic system. "Persons must be present," he writes,

who are not only legally in the position, but are also economically compelled, to sell their labour on the market without restriction…. [T]he development of capitalism is impossible if such a propertyless stratum is absent, a class compelled to sell its labour services to live; and it is likewise impossible if only unfree labour is at hand. Rational capitalistic calculation is possible only on the basis of free labour; only where … workers who in the formal sense voluntarily but actually under the compulsion of the whip of hunger, offer themselves, the costs of products may be unambiguously determined by agreement in advance.[47]

Industrial capitalism, as it emerged in eighteenth-century England, entailed "*the concentration of all the means of production* in the hands of the entrepreneur."[48] Note the italicized phrase, the Marxian expression that Weber employs. For Weber, as for Marx, industrial capitalism rested on the "appropriation of all physical means of production—land, apparatus, machinery, tools, etc., as disposable property of autonomous private industrial enterprises."[49]

Weber thus accepts the basic Marxian presuppositions of the capitalist mode of production. Now, however, as in the case of the Asiatic mode, Weber proceeds to supplement Marx's analysis by proposing an "elective affinity" between the ethos of ascetic Protestantism and the values (spirit) of modern, rational capitalism. Parenthetically, it is worth noting that both the "rational" dimension of capitalism in Weber's sense, and the "affinity" of capitalism with Protestantism were anticipated by Marx. The "bondless greed after riches," wrote Marx, this passionate chase after exchange-value, is common to the capitalist and the miser; but while the miser is merely a capitalist gone mad, the capitalist is a *rational* miser. The never-ending augmentation of exchange-value, which the miser strives after, by seeking to save his money from circulation, is attained by the more acute capitalist, by constantly throwing it afresh into circulation.[50]

And in another context Marx writes,

[F]or a society based upon the production of commodities, in which the producers in general enter in social relations with one another by treating their products as commodities and values, whereby they reduce their individual private labour to the standard of homogeneous human labour—for such a society, Christianity with its *cultus* of abstract man, more especially in its bourgeois developments, Protestantism, Deism, etc., is the most fitting form of religion.[51]

From one of his last pronouncements on the subject of the relation of Protestantism to capitalism, it becomes certain that no so-called religious determinism was intended by Weber. That the *economic* and *political* interests of the Puritans had been salient could not be doubted. Weber reviews the situation in seventeenth-century England in which at first mercantilism prevailed, and the monarchy granted fiscal and colonial privileges and monopolies. This type of capitalism Weber describes as nonrational; it was *not* the system out of which modern industrial capitalism developed. Rather the modern form of capitalism was pioneered by

a stratum of entrepreneurs which had developed in independence of the political administration [and] secured the systematic support of Parliament in the 18th century, after the collapse of the fiscal monopoly policy of the Stuarts.

The capitalism of these entrepreneurs, Weber continues, was oriented

to market opportunities which were developed from within by business interests themselves on the basis of saleable services.

The two types of capitalism collided here for the last time, and the

> point of collision of the two types was the Bank of England. The bank
> was founded by Paterson, a Scotchman, a capitalist adventurer of the type
> called forth by the Stuarts' policy of granting monopolies. But Puritan
> businessmen also belonged to the bank.… [W]e can trade step by step
> the process by which the influence of Paterson and his kind lost ground
> in favor of the rationalistic type of bank members who were all directly
> or indirectly of Puritan origin or influenced by Puritanism.…
>
> …In England it [mercantilism] finally disappeared when free trade
> was established, an achievement of the Puritan dissenters Cobden and
> Bright and their league with the industrial interests, which were now in
> a position to dispense with mercantilist support.[52]

So in this case too, it is undeniable that Weber took into account economic
and political interests.

It is essential, in this connection, to understand what Weber is *not*
asserting. Neither here nor anywhere else in his writings does Weber set
forth a general theory of the relation of "religion" to "economics." Nor
does he argue that the Puritan ethic is a permanent prerequisite or element
of capitalism. On the contrary, just as his treatment of the influences of
Eastern religion applied only to a specific epoch, so did his assessment of
the impact of ascetic Protestantism. For once capitalism established itself,
the religious roots of that system were dead. The Puritan concept of the
"calling" became a *caput mortuum*.[53]

SOCIAL CLASS AND OTHER ASPECTS OF SOCIAL ORGANIZATION: WEBER'S REVISION OF MARX'S CLASS THEORY

In the last chapter of the third volume of *Capital*, Marx begins a very
promising discussion of classes. That is one of the contexts in which Marx
speaks of the wage labourers, capitalists, and landowners as the three big
classes in England of his time. But Marx barely begins his analysis (it
lasts a mere page and half), when it is interrupted by the words: "[Here
the manuscript breaks off.]" Marx never completed what appears to have
been intended as a systematic analysis of social classes. As a result, scholars

have had to imagine how Marx might have completed that chapter following his logic and piecing together the references to class scattered throughout his work.

It is quite evident that Weber developed his own conception of class in a critical dialogue with Marx. In *Economy and Society*, Weber notes, "The unfinished last part of Karl Marx's *Capital* apparently was intended to deal with the issue of class unity in the face of skill differentials."[54] Weber's highly sophisticated discussion may be regarded as an attempt to complete Marx's final chapter in the light of twentieth-century conditions.

Weber concurs in many essential respects with Marx's characterization of capitalism. Although capitalist forms existed in premodern periods of history, Weber agrees that capitalism as described by Marx is a modern phenomenon, and that it has become the dominant mode of production since the middle of the nineteenth century. Weber also agrees that modern capitalism presupposes "the appropriation of all physical means of production—land, apparatus, machinery, tools, etc., as disposable property of autonomous, private industrial enterprises."[55] Like Marx, Weber stresses, in addition, a free market and "free labour." "Persons must be present," he writes, "who are not only legally in the position, but are also economically compelled, to sell their labor on the market without restriction." On the face of it, workers hire themselves out voluntarily, but actually it is "under the compulsion of the whip of hunger."[56] Thus "free labour," for Weber as for Marx, is a precondition of modern industrial capitalism. For both thinkers "free labour" has a double meaning: It refers to the fact that workers are free of slavery and other forms of forced servitude, and it refers to the fact that they have been separated from any and all means of production.

Weber employs all of Marx's major class concepts: class consciousness, class conflict, class interest, and so on. For Weber, the main social classes were

1. the working class as a whole—the more so, the more automated the work process becomes;
2. the petty bourgeoisie;
3. the propertyless intelligentsia and specialists (technicians, various kinds of white-collar employees, civil servants—possibly with considerable social differences depending on the cost of their training);
4. the classes privileged through property and education.[57]

In that list, we can begin to see Weber's departure from Marx, and why he saw the need to revise Marx's theory. Earlier, we saw that Marx anticipated the "sinking" of the petty bourgeoisie (small producers and small businessmen) into the working class. But Weber and others, writing early in the twentieth century, noted that that was not in fact happening as dramatically as Marx had supposed it would. At the same time, Weber witnessed the phenomenal growth of the "new middle class"—specialists, technicians, and other white-collar employees. That was a development that Marx never explicitly anticipated. Yet the remarkable growth of that class touched the very heart of Marx's theory, for in his scheme of things, the fact that the members of the new middle class were propertyless—that is, nonowners of the means of production—meant that they shared with the manual workers a common relationship to the means of production. At least, that is the way many Marxists after Marx looked at the matter. It followed that blue- and white-collar workers have common interests and that they would develop a common class consciousness. But it became increasingly clear in the early twentieth century that white-collar employees did not look upon manual workers as class brothers and sisters at all.

Under nineteenth-century conditions, Marx may have been justified in ignoring "status" distinctions among various types of workers, but for Weber, the theorist par excellence of growing bureaucratization, it was obvious that differences in education, training, and property other than means of production all played a considerable role in shaping social psychology and, hence, class identification.

Thus, what we find in Weber is a refinement of Marx's categories. Accordingly, he stressed that the control of all types of wealth—not only the means of production—was a source of power, and that social honour or prestige based upon property, education, or whatever, might also be transformed into power. For Weber, then, classes, status groups, and political parties "are phenomena of the distribution of power." "We may speak of a class," writes Weber,

> when (1) a number of people have in common a specific causal component of their *life-chances*, insofar as (2) this component is represented exclusively by economic interests in the possession of goods and opportunities for income, and (3) is represented under the conditions of the commodity or labor markets.[58]

Although Weber is intent upon analytically separating "class" from "status group," his intention is by no means a watering down of the class concept. Class situation, he emphasizes, tends to determine "life-chances"; members of a class tend to share a common fate. In those terms, Weber's view of the class situation is not as remote from Marx's as some commentators have suggested. "It is the most elemental fact," writes Weber,

> that the way in which the disposition over material property is distributed among a plurality of people, meeting competitively in the market for the purpose of exchange, in itself creates specific life chances. According to the law of marginal utility, this mode of distribution excludes the non-owners from competing for highly valued goods; this favors the owners and, in fact, gives to them a monopoly to acquire such goods. Other things being equal, the mode of distribution monopolizes the opportunities for profitable deals for all those who, provided with goods, do not necessarily have to exchange them. It increases, at least generally, their power in the price struggle with those who, being propertyless, have nothing to offer but their services.... This mode of distribution gives to the propertied a monopoly on the possibility of transferring property from the sphere of use as a "fortune," to the sphere of "capital goods," that is, it gives them the entrepreneurial function and all chances to share directly or indirectly in returns on capital. All this holds true within the area in which pure market conditions prevail. *"Property" and "lack of property" are, therefore, the basic categories of all class situations.*[59]

At the same time, Weber goes on to show that within the broad categories of propertied and propertyless, other important distinctions exist, not only in income, but in prestige, or social honour, as well. Prestige, for Weber, is associated with the *style of life* of a *status group*. Within any given class, one will find several status groups. The relative prestige accorded them may rest on the size and source of their income, their political positions in the community, their education, their specialized training, or other evaluated social characteristics. Among the wealthy and propertied, we find old and new rich and other status distinctions based on the source of one's wealth; among the propertyless, we find status gradations based upon occupation, education, skill, size of income, expertise, the colour of one's collar, and so on. Status differences, Weber maintains, must be taken into account in class analysis because those differences give us an idea of how certain social groups within a class regard themselves and how they are regarded by others.

There is another facet of social structure Weber brought into relief. Marx had neglected noneconomic forms of power—power not directly derived from wealth and property. But Weber, living in the early twentieth century, saw more clearly the bureaucratization of modern society. Large, formally rational, complex organizations were becoming more and more common. "Power," for Weber, referred to the ability to realize one's will despite and against the resistance of others. It was crystal clear that those who occupied the command posts of bureaucratic organizations had little trouble in realizing their will, whether they were personally wealthy or not.

Thus Weber argued that the concentration of power was not confined to the economic sphere. There were several strategic areas of social life in which one could observe: (1) the concentration of the means of power in the hands of small minorities and (2) the consequent separation of the majority of the people from those means. Such was the inevitable meaning of advancing bureaucratization. For Marx and the Marxists, the essential question was: Who controls the means of production? For Weber, it was necessary to ask, in addition, who disposes over the other strategic means of controlling and dominating human beings?

Weber does not deny that the control of key economic resources is decisive; but that in itself, he holds, is insufficient for an understanding of the structure of social power in general. He therefore elaborates Marx's theory, arguing that control of the means of political administration, means of violence, means of scientific research, and so on, are also major means of dominating men. He writes:

> Organized domination which calls for continuous administration, requires that human conduct be conditioned to obedience towards those masters who claim to be the bearers of legitimate power. On the other hand, … organized domination requires the control of those material goods which in a given case are necessary for the use of physical violence. Thus, organized domination requires control of the personal executive staff and the material implements of administration.[60]

In this way, Weber convincingly observes that Marx's "separation" of the worker from the means of production is only one facet of a general social process. If "separation" is one side of the coin, concentration of power is the other. Marx's concentration of the means of production is generalized by Weber to other means of power—notably, the administrative, military, and scientific-technical. In that light, Weber's analysis of bureaucracy is not so much a refutation as it is an adaptation of Marx's theory to twentieth-century conditions.

BUREAUCRACY

For Weber, bureaucracy was becoming more and more characteristic of twentieth-century society. Growing bureaucratization was one more powerful manifestation of formal and technical rationality, of the "rationalization process" in the West. Hence, it was essential, Weber believed, to understand the nature of bureaucracy.

Conceived as a pure type, the modern bureaucratic organization has several distinctive characteristics.[61] A "bureau," or office, is an official jurisdictional area regulated by definite administrative rules. The activities of a typical bureaucrat are regarded as duties for which he has been trained and which he is qualified to carry out thanks to his specialized training. Bureaus are arranged in a *hierarchy*, a system of superordinate and subordinate offices in which the lower have less authority than the higher, and are, accordingly, supervised by them. Each bureau or office contains a body of official records or "files." The underlying administrative rules of this type of organization are quite *general*, enabling the official to regulate matters abstractly. That is, the people outside the organization are not treated as individuals whose unique situations must be dealt with case by case, but rather as members of categories. The typical bureaucrat is supposed to be impartial and disinterested. That attitude is intended to ensure that all clients in a given category will be treated in the same manner.

Weber emphasized that office holding in a bureaucracy is not just a "job." Rather it is looked upon as a "vocation" or profession requiring specialized training and examinations. The official fulfills his tasks in a dutiful manner and owes his allegiance to the office, not to individuals. He obeys orders and follows the rules not as a personal servant of his superior, but because he is devoted to the organization.

Typically, such an official attains an elevated social esteem by virtue of his holding office. Historically, that has been more true in Europe than in the United States. In Europe, status conventions, the trained expertise of the incumbents, and the fact that they were drawn from economically privileged strata all contributed to the high esteem associated with office holding in the State bureaucracy. In the United States, such status conventions were comparatively weak throughout its history. Since the end of World War II, however, the rapid growth of governmental bureaucracies has brought with it some "European" characteristics.

There are still other important features of a modern bureaucracy. Normally, the official, after a short qualifying period, acquires *tenure*— that is, he holds the position for life. Furthermore, he earns a salary, not a wage, and becomes entitled to an old-age pension. A wage is measured in terms of work done; but a salary is associated with one's status or rank in the organization. Officials aspire to move up from lower to high positions and thus to earn a higher salary. Modern bureaucracy presupposes a money economy. Officials are compensated in money, not in kind. Salaries in the form of money tend to place officials in a state of extreme economic dependence.

The increasing expansion of bureaucracy in modern society may be accounted for by both the quantitative and qualitative development of administrative tasks. As Weber noted,

> The decisive reason for the advance of bureaucratic organization has always been its purely *technical* superiority over any other form of organization. The fully developed bureaucratic apparatus compares with other organizations exactly as does the machine with the non-mechanical modes of production. Precision, speed, unambiguity, knowledge of the files, continuity, discretion, unity, strict subordination, reduction of friction and of material and personal costs—these are raised to the optimum point in the strictly bureaucratic administration, and especially in its monocratic form.[62]

Speed, precision, and other forms of cost reduction are among the main reasons why we find that the typical, modern capitalist enterprise is a large, complex corporation. However, in both the private and the public spheres, it is not merely considerations of efficiency but rather of *power* that have accounted for growing bureaucratization. The bureaucratic tendency has been promoted by power politics, warfare, the creation of large standing armies, and by the immense budgets required for those purposes. At the same time, the social welfare policies of the modern state have also contributed to the enormity, complexity, and costliness of its administrative apparatus.

One of Weber's most illuminating observations with respect to modern bureaucracy was made by elaborating on a central idea of Marx's. Marx, it will be recalled, traced the roots of modern capitalism to the *separation* of the producers (peasant-proprietor) from their means of production. Marx was among the first to demonstrate that capital was becoming increasingly *concentrated* and *centralized*. His argument was, in brief, that the accumulation of capital in the economy as a whole assumed the form of competition among firms, with some winning and others losing. The latter were either destroyed or absorbed by the victors. The growth of capital in one enterprise was facilitated by the failure of others. Those who remained in the race had successfully reduced their production costs by making larger investments in machinery and the like. As the costs of investment increased, entry into the field of production was restricted to fewer and fewer, but larger, capitals. Capital thus became increasingly concentrated in large-scale corporate organizations.

Weber agreed that the concentration of economic power was, in fact, a powerful tendency of capitalism. But he hastened to add that Marx had centred attention on only one aspect of a much more general historical trend. That is, one could witness parallels to the separation of the producer from the means of production and the concentration of those means in several other social spheres. Thus, Weber argued that historically the soldier had been separated from the means of violence and the civil servant from the means of administration, while those means have also undergone continual concentration. At one time, fighting men owned their own weapons and were economically capable of equipping themselves. That was true of tribal levies, the armed citizens of the ancient city-states, the militias of early cities, and all feudal armies. But modern warfare is a "war of machines," writes Weber, "and this makes centralized provisioning technically necessary, just as the dominance of the machine in industry promotes the concentration of the means of production and management."[63] Historically, army service had shifted from the shoulders of the propertied to those of the propertyless.

Similar processes have occurred in other spheres as well, notably scientific research. If, for example, we think of scientists and inventors as recently as the beginning of the twentieth century, someone like Thomas Edison comes to mind. Edison was a "tinkerer" who worked alone in his cellar and produced a highly significant invention. Today's science is a different matter altogether. In order to become a "scientist," one must first successfully pass the examinations of a university or some other large educational organization, and obtain the required degrees. One is then enabled to engage in scientific activities by gaining employment in the laboratory of some governmental, corporate, or university organization, all of which are big bureaucratic enterprises. The means of research are large and expensive, and they are controlled by the administrative heads of those organizations, not by scientists. Thus, as Weber observed, "Through the concentration of such means in the hands of the privileged head of the institute the mass of researchers and instructors are separated from their 'means of production,' in the same way as the workers are separated from theirs by capitalist enterprises."[64] The concentration of power is characteristic of several major institutional spheres of modern society and not just the economy. It is not just the blue-collar worker who has become "proletarianized." Almost everyone has become a paid labourer, working in a large complex organization, and depending upon it for a livelihood.

Once such bureaucratic structures are established, they are practically indestructible, Weber believed, because a bureaucracy is a power instrument of the first order for those who occupy its command posts. It facilitates the domination and control of large numbers of people. The individual bureaucrat is chained to his specialized activity and is only a small cog in the total operation. His entire mind and body have been trained for obedience and those who rule such organizations expect compliance as a matter of course. Thus, Weber makes a strong argument for the inevitable growth of bureaucracy. The vested power interests in it, the social control and discipline it facilitates, the specialization of work and the accompanying requirements of expertise—all these factors would make the dismantling of bureaucracy extraordinarily difficult. Indeed, bureaucracies are rarely, if ever, dismantled; they are merely taken over. The bureaucratic state apparatus can be "made to work for anybody who knows how to gain control over it. A rationally ordered officialdom continues to function smoothly after the enemy has occupied the territory; he merely needs to change the top officials."[65] Weber's analysis therefore led him to the conclusion that "revolution," in the sense of transcending bureaucracy and creating a new, nonbureaucratic society, was becoming more and more unlikely.

Weber viewed the bureaucratization of modern society with apprehension. The immense concentration of power in fewer and fewer hands was bound to endanger liberal-democratic institutions and to diminish individual freedoms. Increasingly the individual was subjected to an organizational discipline that drastically reduced his initiative; increasingly he was subjected to a *formally* rational regimen that eliminated any opportunities for autonomous and genuinely rational conduct. In Weber's words, bureaucratic "discipline is nothing but the consistently rationalized, methodically prepared and exact execution of the received order, in which all personal criticism is unconditionally suspended and the actor is unswervingly and exclusively set for carrying out the command."[66] What all formally rational, large-scale organizations have in common are regimentation and discipline. A bureaucracy, no less than a factory, tends to mould a person's psychophysical being in an effort to adapt it to the demands of the organization. In short, bureaucracy "functionalizes" human beings. It is "horrible to think," wrote Weber "that the world could one day be filled with nothing but those little cogs, little men clinging to little jobs and striving towards bigger ones."[67]

THE CHARISMATIC POLITICAL LEADER: WEBER'S ERROR

The challenge that bureaucratization poses for democracy is a formidable one. To meet this challenge Weber placed his faith in "leaders." Whether in business, politics, or military affairs, great leaders had to be created as an antidote to bureaucracy. After World War I, he was asked by a student about his political plans and he replied that he had none "except to concentrate all my intellectual strength on one problem, how to get once more for Germany a great general staff."[68] It seems, therefore, that Weber's political concerns penetrated his scholarship in this important respect, and that his theoretical ideas on charismatic leadership crystallized in the course of his reflections on post-war Germany and the embattled Weimar Republic. In the debates of 1919–1920 on the new constitution, Weber vigorously supported provisions for a popularly elected president. Describing Weber's attitude in this regard, Wolfgang J. Mommsen writes:

by virtue of his direct links with the will of the masses the *Reichspräsident* was to be an opening for the rise of political leaders over and above party machines and parliaments. In this way Weber hoped to assist a "leader democracy" to come to the fore in Germany, in which charismatically qualified politicians with a sense of foresight but also with a sense of proportion are at the helm, instead of a "leaderless democracy of professional politicians without a calling."[69]

Like Nietzsche and most likely under his influence, Weber assigned considerable weight to the role of the outstanding individual in history. Only such individuals could make history by setting new goals and thus imparting new energy to the people. There was, however, no Nietzschean contempt for the masses here. "In contrast to Nietzsche's ethic of the Master," writes Mommsen, "which culminated in the outright rejection of all democratic politics, Weber adhered to the fundamental principles of liberalism which hold sacrosanct the dignity of the individual and aspire to see society organized in such a way that all individuals may preserve a maximum of free initiative" (p. 27). It was on the basis of such principles, and certainly not in opposition to them, that Weber formulated his ideas on charismatic leadership. What Weimar Germany needed in particular, Weber believed, were leaders of quality who could persuade the masses to follow them voluntarily. For Weber, great leaders emerged in response to an inner "calling"; they lived *for* politics, not off politics. In the competition of such leaders for mass followings, however, Weber approved of demagogy and emotional appeals designed to bind the masses to the leader.

A careful examination of Weber's writings reveals that he viewed charismatic leadership in a purely positive light. He was blind, somehow, to the anti-democratic and tyrannical potential of charismatic leadership. Only by keeping the charismatic principle alive could the world (Germany?) be saved from the mediocrity accompanying the inexorable advance of bureaucracy. Not too long after he died, however, the charismatic and bureaucratic principles were fused in his homeland into a horrendous synthesis. In that light, Weber's concept of personal charisma, insofar as it was purely positive, was also misleadingly one-sided. Where Weimar Germany is concerned, it is easy to see why Weber recognized the need for strong leadership, but it is difficult to understand why he failed to anticipate the possibility of anti-liberal fusion of the charismatic and bureaucratic principles, for he fully recognized the political immaturity and weakness of the German middle classes. Given their economic power, they should have supported the strengthening of liberal-democratic institutions. Instead, they sought the protection of the old-regime elements against the working classes. Yet, for Weber, the unrestrained will of the masses and their demands for equality were by far the greatest threat to the foundations of freedom in the Western world. "By contrast," writes Mommsen,

> he [Weber] regarded as comparatively negligible the danger that the rule of the *Führer*, legitimized through personal plebiscite, could turn into a dictatorial (or even fascist) regime, even though Weber himself had pointed out that in general "leader democracies" were characterized by a highly emotional type of devotion to and trust in the leader, and that this accounted for a tendency to follow as a leader the type of individual who is most unusual, who promises the most or who employs the most effective propaganda measure. (p. 34)

Under modern conditions, according to Weber, a "leader democracy" requires a bureaucratic administrative apparatus as well as a bureaucratic party organization. Their role is to serve as "obedient servants" ensuring that the leader's decisions are efficiently carried out. Here, again, it is noteworthy that the dangers and risks Weber perceived in this connection were the gradual undermining of a leader's charisma by the bureaucrats. The opposite danger, that the leader would succeed in wielding the entire State and Party apparatus as an instrument of cold-blooded tyranny and genocide, Weber failed altogether to foresee. So although Weber had never intended his theory of the charismatic political leader to be constructed in an anti-democratic manner, his theory nevertheless lent itself to such an interpretation, for it gave pre-eminence to the political leader as opposed to the mass of citizens.

If one compares Weber with Robert Michels, a Weber disciple of sorts, one sees clearly that Weber's conception of the charismatic political leader was in fact construed in an anti-democratic fashion. Michels, as we shall see, decried the oligarchical tendency in democratic organization in which leaders employed the administrative apparatus to preserve their own status and interests. The leaders of the German Social-Democratic Party, for example, behaved in a manner reminiscent of the Sun King, each thinking of himself, "*Le Parti c'est moi!*" As Mommsen reminds us, however, Weber

> drew very different conclusions from the evidence of an increasing bureaucratization within modern parties. Not only did he consider the trend towards "plebiscitarian democracy," which inevitably involved a substantial enhancement of the role of political leaders at the expense of the "ruled," to be irreversible; he saw it also as a *positive* development, in that it served as a counterweight to the bureaucratization of the apparatuses of power. (p. 100, italics added)

To support his contention that Weber's conception of leadership could be construed in an anti-democratic manner, Mommsen cites the fact that

> Michels justified his decision to support Mussolini and the Italian fascist *Füher-staat* by express reference to Max Weber. Among other things, Michels was able to invoke Weber's explicit claim that the emotional attachment of the broad masses to the leader constitutes the specific characteristic of charismatic authority, and that the leader determines the content of policy on his own ultimate authority alone, while the assent of his supporters resides purely in their trust in the leader's charismatic leadership-qualities as such, rather than in their concurrence with the particular objectives he lays down. (p. 102)

It seems indisputable, then, that a frank examination of Weber's theory of charismatic political leadership discloses the dangers to democracy that its one-sidedness entails.

THE HISTORICAL-SOCIOLOGICAL METHOD

We have pointed out many substantive parallels in the writings of Marx and Weber. We have observed a wide area of convergence in their respective analyses of what Marx called the major modes of production in history, and where those analyses did not precisely converge, they proved to be complementary and compatible.

But there are methodological parallels as well. For we have seen that Marx's method, interpreted nondogmatically, makes no attempt to reconstruct history to fit some a priori conception. His method is revealed not as an effort to impute causal priority to economic conditions, but rather to determine the relationship between the economic and other orders of society. That being the case, we can see a definite methodological affinity between Marx and Weber, since much of the latter's work was also a study of "economy and society." Indeed, one might say that Weber took over Marx's method as a heuristic principle, and applied it with great skill.

So far as social science research is concerned, the really important lesson to be learned from Marx and Weber is the importance of history for an understanding of society. Though they were certainly interested in grasping the general and universal, they concerned themselves with the concrete circumstances of specific periods, and the similarities and contrasts of diverse geohistorical areas. They clearly recognized that an adequate explanation of social facts requires a historical account of how the facts came to be; they recognized that comparative-historical analysis is indispensable for the study of stability and change. In a word, it is these two extraordinary thinkers in particular who stand out as the architects of a historical sociology well worth emulating, for both of them subscribed to an open, historically grounded theory and method.

NOTES

1. The debate with the Marxian legacy includes Max Weber, Vilfredo Pareto, Gaetano Mosca, Robert Michels, Émile Durkheim, and Karl Mannheim (Chapters 8–13).

2. Talcott Parsons, "Capitalism in Recent German Literature," *Journal of Political Economy*, 37, 1929, p. 40.

3. See his introduction to *The Theory of Social and Economic Organization* (Glencoe, Ill.: The Free Press, 1947), p. 6.

4. Jonathan H. Turner and Leonard Beeghley, *The Emergence of Sociological Theory* (Homewood, Ill.: The Dorsey Press, 1981). The quoted passages may be found on pp. 257, 245, and 243, respectively.

5. See Albert Salomon's article in Georges Gurvitch and Wilbert E. Moore, *Twentieth-Century Sociology* (New York: The Philosophical Library, 1945), p. 596.

6. H. H. Gerth and C. Wright Mills, eds., *From Max Weber: Essays in Sociology* (New York: Oxford University Press, 1946), p. 63.

7. George Lichtheim, *Marxism: An Historical and Critical Study* (New York: Frederick A. Praeger, 1961), p. 385.

8. Irving M. Zeitlin, *Ideology and the Development of Sociological Theory* (Englewood Cliffs, N.J.: Prentice-Hall, 1968), p. 112.

9. Reinhard Bendix and Guenther Roth, *Scholarship and Partisanship: Essays on Max Weber* (Berkeley: The University of California Press, 1971), p. 238.

10. Ibid., p. 240.

11. *Verhandlungen des Ersten Deutschen Soziologentages* (Tübingen: Mohr, 1911), p. 101. Cited in Bendix and Roth, *Scholarship and Partisanship*, pp. 242–43.

12. Cited in Bendix and Roth, *Scholarship and Partisanship*, pp. 242–43.

13. Marx, *The Poverty of Philosophy* (Moscow: Foreign Languages Publishing House, n.d.), p. 127.

14. Bendix and Roth, *Scholarship and Partisanship*, p. 227.

15. Max Weber, *The Methodology of the Social Sciences* (Glencoe, Ill.: The Free Press, 1949), p. 65.

16. Ibid., p. 68.

17. Max Weber, *The Protestant Ethic and the Spirit of Capitalism* (New York: Charles Scribner's Sons, 1958), p. 25. (Hereafter all page references to this work will be indicated in parentheses immediately following the quoted passage.)

18. Engels, *The Origin of the Family, Private Property, and the State,* p. 131.

19. Ibid., p. 139.

20. Weber, *The Agrarian Sociology of Ancient Civilizations*, tr. R. I. Frank (London: NLB, 1976), p. 349. Hereafter the title of this book is cited as *ASAC*.

21. Ibid., pp. 349–50.

22. Weber, *GEH*, pp. 54–55.

23. Ibid.

24. Ibid., p. 67.

25. Ibid., p. 82.

26. Ibid., pp. 82–83.

27. Ibid., p. 63.

28. Max Weber, *The Religion of India*, trans. and ed. Hans H. Gerth and Don Martindale (Glencoe, Ill.: The Free Press, 1958), p. 111.

29. Weber, *ASAC*, p. 38.

30. Ibid., p. 84.

31. Ibid.

32. Ibid., p. 85.

33. Ibid., p. 106.

34. Ibid., p. 109.

35. Ibid., p. 131.

36. Weber, *GEH,* pp. 57–58, italics added.

37. Ibid., p. 237.

38. Ibid.

39. Max Weber, *The Religion of China,* trans. and ed. Hans H. Gerth (Glencoe, Ill.: The Free Press, 1951), p. 12. (Hereafter all page references of this work will be indicated in parentheses immediately following the quoted passage.)

40. Weber, *The Religion of India*, p. 4. (Hereafter all page references to this work will be cited in parentheses immediately following the quoted passage.)

41. Max Weber, *Ancient Judaism,* trans. and ed. Hans H. Gerth and Don Martindale (Glencoe, Ill.: The Free Press, 1952), p. 4. (Hereafter all page references to this work will be cited in parentheses immediately following the quoted passage.)

42. A critical examination of the state of biblical scholarship since the publication of Weber's *Das Antike Judentum* (1921) may be found in Irving M. Zeitlin, *Ancient Judaism; Biblical Criticism from Max Weber to the Present* (Cambridge: Polity Press, 1984).

43. Weber, *GEH*, p. 265.

44. Ibid., p. 276, n. 4.

45. Ibid., p. 129.

46. Ibid., p. 137.

47. Ibid., pp. 208–09.

48. Ibid., p. 227.

49. Ibid., p. 208.

50. Karl Marx, *Capital*, Vol. 1 (Moscow: Foreign Languages Publishing House, 1954), p. 153, italics added.

51. Ibid., p. 79.

52. Weber, *GEH*, p. 258.

53. Ibid., p. 270.

54. Max Weber, *Economy and Society,* ed. Guenther Roth and Claus Wittich, 3 vols. (New York: Bedminster Press, 1968), I, 305.

55. Max Weber, *General Economic History*, trans. Frank H. Knight (New York: Collier Books, 1961), p. 208.

56. Ibid., p. 208–09.

57. Weber, *Economy and Society,* I, p. 305.

58. Ibid., Vol. II, p. 927.

59. Ibid.

60. Max Weber, "Politics as a Vocation," in H. H. Gerth and C. W. Mills, eds., *From Max Weber: Essays in Sociology* (New York: Oxford University Press, 1958), p. 80.

61. The present discussion is based on Weber, *Economy and Society*, Vol. III, pp. 956–1005.

62. Ibid., p. 973.

63. Ibid., p. 981.

64. Ibid., p. 983.

65. Ibid., p. 989.

66. Ibid., p. 1149.

67. Cited by J. P. Mayer, *Max Weber and German Politics* (London: Faber and Faber, 1944), p. 127.

68. Mayer, *Max Weber and German Politics*, p. 107.

69. Wolfgang J. Mommsen, *The Political and Social Theory of Max Weber* (Cambridge: The University of Chicago Press/Polity Press, 1989), p. 22. (Hereafter all page references to this work will be cited in parentheses immediately following the quoted passage.)

CHAPTER 9

Vilfredo Pareto (1848–1923)

Pareto, Mosca, and Michels have been called Neo-Machiavellians because their theories were profoundly influenced by the ideas of Niccolo Machiavelli (1469–1527), who viewed the human being as driven by self-interest and ruled by the insatiable desire for material gain. For Machiavelli, selfishness is an eternal trait of human nature that is constant and immutable. However, this rather negative view of human nature led Machiavelli to a positive assessment of human possibilities through the study of history. For if human actions are motivated by a selfish nature, and if that constant nature tends to produce similar and recurring types of action, then the actions of the past, as recorded in history, may be studied and used as a basis for anticipating the future. Hindsight provides a serviceable degree of foresight! The study of history supplies us with a vast reservoir of guidelines as we step into the future. Machiavelli thus rejected all utopias that envision a future radically different from the past. In this respect as in others Pareto, Mosca, and Michels followed in his footsteps.

Machiavelli never said that the end justifies the means. He did not argue that *all* means are justified in the pursuit of any end; nor did he completely separate moral standards from political actions, as some scholars have alleged. He did, however, maintain that the use of evil means, such as violence, is often necessary. When violence is clearly in the public interest, the prince, or political leader, should not shy away from using it. Force, as a last resort, is essential in some circumstances if the prince is to fulfill his two primary responsibilities of ensuring the State's internal stability and external independence.

Machiavelli proposed that violent conflict, invasions, and wars were permanent attributes of the human condition. But he stressed that conflict can produce beneficial results if it is dealt with by a properly organized and stable government which, for Machiavelli, is a mixed government. It was precisely the social strife between the plebeians and aristocrats of Rome that contributed to its greatness and liberty. One cannot get rid of conflict, and attempts to suppress it create only apparent stability. The wise prince will therefore strive to create a dynamic equilibrium between the diverse and competing social forces of his society.

Machiavelli has no sympathy for governments that fail to defend their societies with resoluteness and boldness. He prefers a free, republican form of government and insists that a citizens' militia is the strongest bulwark against tyranny. A militia of citizen-soldiers is always superior to standing professional armies or mercenary forces. The internal stability and external independence of a society demand of the wise prince that

> he should learn from the fox and the lion; because the lion is defenseless against traps and a fox is defenseless against wolves. Therefore one must be a fox in order to recognize traps, and a lion to frighten off wolves. Those who simply act like lions are stupid. (*The Prince*, chapter 18; and see *The Discourses*, II, 13)

As a fox, the prince must be a skilful pretender. It is best if he possesses the virtues of good faith, charity, humanity, and religion; but if he lacks such virtues, he should certainly *appear* to possess them. As a lion he must be prepared to use force when necessary. Cruelty, employed economically, may be more merciful than clemency; for while the former injures only a few and retrains the rest by fear, the latter breeds disorder and rebellion, which injures the entire body politic.

The incidence of force could never be lessened in the international arena because it lacked a prince—a Leviathan, as Hobbes later argued. Domestic violence could, however, be reduced by means of law, appropriate political institutions, and civility. The greater the cruelty, the weaker the regime, since increased cruelty shows that the prince has lost the consent of the governed.

The aim of the wise prince, then, is to maintain the republic by the force *of* the people; and this is best accomplished by fulfilling three basic responsibilities:

1. ensuring that the people's material needs are met;
2. protecting them and their possessions; and
3. eliminating dangerous inequalities.

The existence of conflicting interest groups and classes being inevitable, the prince must mediate between them so that order and justice and the overarching interests of the commonwealth are maintained. It is the well-being of the community as a whole, not merely of individuals and factions, that makes a State great. Moreover, the wise prince will foster the free and open pursuit of power, thus ensuring a continual supply of fresh political talent.

As we read the upcoming chapters on Pareto, Mosca, and Michels, we will see how they adapted and applied Machiavelli's ideas to early twentieth-century conditions.

PARETO'S REPUDIATION OF THE ENLIGHTENMENT'S LEGACY

The work of Vilfredo Pareto is an exceedingly ambitious attempt at rebutting and discrediting the principles of the Enlightenment in both its eighteenth- and nineteenth-century forms. His voluminous writings may be viewed as a sustained onslaught upon liberal-democratic, socialistic, and Marxian theories. Whereas Marx had viewed man as a rational and perfectible creature, Pareto portrayed him as essentially nonrational and unchanging, and advanced his theory of "residues" with the aim of demonstrating that proposition. And while Marx viewed class conflict in history as increasing man's potential for freedom, Pareto regarded history as essentially cyclical. As a direct antithesis to Marx's theory of class struggle, Pareto advanced his theory of elites. The circulation of elites, the real stuff of history, had few, or perhaps no, positive consequences for the "people."

PARETO AND SCIENCE

For Pareto, there were basically two independent and mutually exclusive domains of human conduct: that of science and logic on the one hand and of sentiment on the other. Science involves logic, observation, and objective experience, and "truth" rests on those processes. The other domain is "nonlogico-experimental"—which is just the beginning of

Pareto's cumbersome vocabulary. There are two independent domains, and science has nothing to say about "reasoning" that leaves its realm. Pareto denies that rationality can ever replace the other realm or even make serious inroads upon it. In fact, *sentiment* is the fundamental and predominant force in society, *the determining factor* of human conduct (outside the very restricted sphere in which Pareto arbitrarily confined logico-experimental norms).

Pareto's first task as he saw it was to distinguish carefully between scientific and nonscientific propositions. Objective experience is the sole criterion of scientific theory, which is arrived at inductively by describing the relations among facts; in short, scientific theories are "logico-experimental." Other "theories," which he calls "nonlogico-experimental," add something to experience and seek to dominate the "facts." Pareto subscribed to the methodological view that treated "laws" as strictly heuristic devices, not necessarily as the workings of "reality." When uniformities, or relationships among phenomena, become evident, "law" is the name one gives to such patterns; "law" is not some *force* to which the facts are actually subject. The scientist selects certain observable phenomena and organizes them according to some scheme in which the phenomena appear to be subject to a certain "law." There are no "necessary" laws; rather, phenomena behave "as if" there were, and the scientist states the degree of probability with which the phenomena in question will follow a specified pattern. Scientific relatively, then, was for Pareto, as for others, such as Vaihinger, Mach, and Poincaré, a basic assumption.

Pareto's sole aim, he assures us again and again, is scientific truth, which can be attained in the social realm by applying the methods of the physical sciences. In all his works, he stresses that he is not interested in improving or changing the world; he is not concerned with providing theoretical guidance for practical affairs. Rather, he has one single and exclusive aim in view: to study the uniformities phenomena present, their "laws." Like many economists before him, Pareto advocated the method of successive approximations. Since no concrete phenomenon can be known in all its details, some sort of abstraction always becomes necessary. What aspect one singles out for study depends on one's interests. One begins with some simplifying assumptions, taking into account additional complicating factors as one proceeds—a method equally applicable to natural and social phenomena.

There is, however, an important characteristic of social phenomena Pareto is intent upon accentuating: The utility of an idea and its truth are not necessarily identical in the social sphere. As a matter of fact, they are often independent of each other. He reminds his reader periodically that when he argues for the absurdity of an idea, that does not necessarily mean that it is injurious to anyone; and when he argues that an idea has utility, the reader should not assume that it is experimentally true. Clearly, a great many ideas that are patently false, or whose relative truth is not known, have currency among men. Who holds those doctrines and why? What are the consequences of holding those beliefs and for whom? Those are the questions, Pareto tells us, that interest him and that he wants to answer by means of scientific sociology.

LES SYSTÈMES SOCIALISTES

In this two-volume critique of socialist and communist doctrines, from the earliest schemes of antiquity through the so-called "utopian socialists" and concluding, finally, with the theories of Marx, one clearly perceives the outline of the theoretical framework that Pareto later elaborated in his general sociology. An examination of the *Systèmes* leaves no doubt as to the polemical nature of Pareto's "sociological" concepts and propositions. After examining the various socialist theories Marx himself had regarded as "pre-scientific" and finding them all wanting, Pareto is prepared for a scrutiny of so-called "scientific socialism." The last two chapters, in many respects the most interesting, deal with Marx's thought.

Pareto came to the study of sociology through his critique of socialism, which in effect contains all the ideas one later meets in his *Traité de Sociologie*. His explicit critique of Marx may be found first of all in the *Systèmes*, but also in a number of articles in his introduction to *Capital*. In his *Systèmes* he promises us a rather interesting study:

> On the one hand, we shall inquire into the real facts which have favored the establishment of certain social systems, or the appearance of certain projects for social systems; in other words, what are the things or facts which reveal themselves to us in these forms; on the other hand, we shall examine the "reasonings" which have been employed to justify these systems or projects for systems and we shall see to what extent the premises are drawn from experience and from logical deductions.[1]

Pareto acknowledges, in passing, the limited validity of Marx's socio-logical theory: "This research will show us often that there are economic facts which modify social institutions and doctrines and which are thus reflected in the consciousness of men, as in the view of the 'materialist conception of history'" (Tome V, vol. I, pp. 26–27). But he never uses its guidelines to assess its fruitfulness as an analytical tool and in fact never returns to it except to "refute" it by assertion. Socialism in general and Marxism in particular are regarded by Pareto as religions that emerged and gained popularity because they appealed to certain "sentiments" (a term, as previously mentioned, that has a special meaning in Pareto's system: a nonlogical principle of conduct). Never in this work does he relate doctrines and beliefs to social conditions, for that in effect would have taken him back to Marx's conception; nor does he ask whether and to what degree rational interests, rather than blind sentiments, might better explain the popularity in a given period of socialism or Marxism. Pareto rarely pauses to analyze the social conditions of men, but speculates instead about their sentiments and instincts.

Whereas classes and class conflict were transient historical phenomena for Marx, Pareto insists that class conflict is destined to continue forever. Its forms may change, but the substance remains the same. He writes:

> Suppose collectivism to be established, and that "capital" no longer exists; then only a particular form of class struggle will have disappeared and new ones will emerge to replace it. New conflicts will appear between the different kinds of workers and the socialist state, between the intellectuals and the non-intellectuals, between the various politicians, between the politicians and those they administer, between innovators and conserva-tives, etc. Are there really such people who imagine seriously that with the advent of socialism the sources of social innovation will be dried up? That men will no longer envision new projects, that interests will not push some men to adopt these projects in the hope of acquiring a dominant place in society? (Tome V, vol. II, p. 455)

Why, in Pareto's view, is class conflict destined to be an eternal human condition? Not so much because a complex, heterogeneous society is bound to have a variety of groups with different and conflicting interests; but rather because it is rooted in the nature of men and is a form of their struggle for life:

> The struggle for life or well-being is a general phenomenon for living things, and everything we know about this leads us to recognize it as one of the most powerful forces for the conservation and amelioration of the race. It is therefore extremely improbable that men will be able to transcend this condition.… All our efforts can never result in a fundamental change of this condition, only slight modifications of its forms. (Tome V, vol. II, p. 455)

Pareto thus views class conflict as an inseparable aspect of men's struggle with nature, and hence as inevitable and unending. Social conflicts are rooted in natural conditions, not least in the very nature of man, who is pushed into action by essentially "natural" and therefore "nonlogical" forces. That is the substance of Pareto's theory of human conduct as he later elaborates it in his "sociology."

As he develops his critique of socialism and shows us how one must "scientifically" analyze the phenomenon, he presents us with all the notions we shall later meet in the obscure and awkward terms of his sociological treatise. First, he discusses a number of concepts to illustrate that one cannot employ them logically. Take, for example, "liberty" and "constraint"; the first is associated with agreeable feelings and the second with disagreeable ones. All one has to do to get people to accept constraint is to give it the name of liberty. Why?—because those and similar concepts advanced by the socialists and optimistic liberals draw their force from sentiments and not from logic. Is there then anything salvageable in the general socialist idea? Any worthwhile elements?

Inheritance, he grants, is a very "imperfect" means of distributing the wealth of a society. The way is therefore open to reformers of goodwill, but they must take care not merely to criticize the existing system but rather to bring forth preferable alternatives. But Pareto still sees a number of problems—reformers ought to use clear and precise terms, and more important, the new social arrangement must be compatible with the character of men. "Every human society," argues Pareto, "includes some elements unadapted to the conditions of life of the particular society, and if the actions of these elements are not confined to certain limits, the society will be destroyed" (Tome V, vol. II, p. 131). This poses a difficult problem for socialists, because humanitarian sentiments (which he grants are "useful" up to a point) oppose the "necessity" of selecting and eliminating unadaptable elements. So Pareto sees two problems requiring solution: (1) Can the birth of unadaptable elements be reduced? (2) If not, can they be eliminated with a minimum of error in choice, with a minimum of suffering, and without violating humanitarian sentiments too much? Pareto thus offers us a "scientific" approach to the problem of selecting and eliminating the "poorly adapted," the "misfits."

Throughout his *Systèmes,* as in his later work, Pareto maintains that sentiment is the dominant and overwhelming force of social conduct, and that logic and rationality are of minimal significance. One must not stop at the "reasonings" of men—which are anything but reasonable—but go on to examine the underlying sentiments; sentiment for Pareto is an unchanging entity. Only the "reasonings" (or what he later calls "derivations") that justify and "explain" human conduct vary, not the sentiments. Just what are those sentiments or real forces that are masked by, among other things, socialist rhetoric?

Pity, says Pareto, is one such prevalent sentiment, which impels men to sympathize with their fellows who suffer wrongs or pain and to seek a remedy. That is a very "useful" sentiment, he assures us, for it is the cement of society and the real basis of all ameliorative social doctrines. In the lower classes, there exists a sentiment that "has its sources in the suffering which those in these strata endure and in the desire to try to put an end to it by getting hold of the means which men in the higher strata enjoy, or quite simply by coveting what the other has" (Tome V, vol. II, p. 64). So, Pareto argues, "pity" manifests itself in socialist doctrine and men accept the doctrine for that "reason" and not for the "logico-experimental validity" of the doctrine. Why does socialism appeal mainly to the proletariat? Does the proletariat have a monopoly on the sentiment of pity? It has not escaped Pareto that socialist ideas have also appealed to individuals of the upper classes so he "explains" that fact as a result of the degeneration of the sentiment of pity, corresponding to a general degeneration of those classes (Tome V, vol. II, p. 65). In all epochs, humanitarian sentiments have given rise to sentimental reveries. When there is but a faint echo of that attitude in poetry or literature, that is a sign that the elite is strong, vigorous, and self-assured, but as the elite "decays," the expression of humanitarian sentiment grows. This, then, is Pareto's first major idea: the theory of sentiment, the manifestations of which he will later call "residues" and "derivations." His second major idea also appears for the first time in his *Systèmes.*

Sentiments change little or not at all. What does change is the form of appeal to certain sentiments and/or the justifications of certain actions motivated by sentiments. But here, to anticipate our later discussion somewhat, Pareto sees a distinction between the *elite* and the *nonelite*. The elite acts primarily on the basis of enlightened self-interest, whereas the lower, subject classes are moved largely by sentiment. To further its interests, the elite finds it expedient to appeal for support to the sentiments of the lower classes. Thus, the nonelite, the mass, is impelled into action by blind force, while the elite conducts itself according to a rational understanding of its situation.

Elites and aristocracies do not last. They degenerate rather rapidly. Every elite therefore has the need to reinvigorate itself with reinforcements from the lower classes, its best elements. The decadence of the elite expresses itself in an outburst of sickly humanitarianism, while a new elite full of *strength* and *vigour* forms in the midst of the lower classes. "Every élite," writes Pareto, "that is not ready to fight to defend its position is in full decadence; there remains nothing for it to do but to vacate its place for another élite having the virile qualities which it lacks. It is by means of force that social institutions are established and it is by means of force that they are maintained" (Tome V, vol. II, p. 40). The struggle and circulation of elites is the stuff of history; therefore, popular uprisings are of no real consequence for the people. They serve merely to facilitate the fall of the old elite and the rise of the new. The elites use the lower classes, by paying lip service to their sentiments, in order to retain or to take power. "Most historians," writes Pareto, "do not see this movement. They describe the phenomenon as though it were the struggle of an aristocracy or oligarchy, always the same, against the people, always the same" (Tome V, vol. 22, pp. 35–36). In reality, however, two aristocracies are struggling for power. The various revolutions of history, for example, the triumph of the bourgeoisie over the feudal aristocracy, achieved nothing for the people and neither will they do so in the future. There will be no definite liberation of the human being.

PARETO'S SOCIOLOGY

Pareto defined sociology as the study of human society in general, and his declared aim in this work[2] was a general theory of society. More precisely, he wanted a theory of human conduct and chose as his point of departure an examination of the norms of scientific conduct, which is "logico-experimental," as is the typically rational conduct of *homo economicus*. Economic man acts on the basis of observation, experience, and logical reasoning. Do the logico-experimental norms so characteristic of scientific and economic conduct carry over into other areas? Do they guide man's other actions? There can be little doubt that Pareto had settled those questions in his own mind long before he undertook this copious study whose ostensible purpose was to answer them scientifically. His conclusions were not, contrary to what he would have us believe, the result of any inductive method.

Man's actions in general are nonlogical. That is the "hypothesis" Pareto wants to prove and account for in his sociology. How does he proceed? He does not ask whether, to what degree, and under what social circumstances man's general conduct is either logical or nonlogical. Rather, he defines logico-experimental conduct, confines it more or less exclusively to scientific and economic actions (though he might include certain military and political arts), and then by means of his residual definition classifies all other actions as nonlogical. He then proceeds to inundate us with illustrations of man's nonlogical or nonrational actions. Having convinced himself that all of man's acts that are "nonscientific" and "noneconomic" are also nonlogical, he needed a scientific explanation. Apparently he believed he was providing one in his concepts of "sentiments" and "residues," which he occasionally uses as synonyms for "values" but more often than not as unchanging, instinctual, biopsychic forces.[3]

The latter is also implied throughout Pareto's work in his treatment of residues (soon to be defined) as "constants." It makes no difference to Pareto whether it is a matter of worshipping fetishes or idols, saluting a flag, examining a creature's entrails to foretell the future, supporting universal suffrage, voting socialist, and so on—they are all manifestations of the unchanging psychic state of man. All those actions, different as they may appear, are motivated essentially by the same force, the same constant. What varies historically are the "explanations," "reasons," and theoretical justifications men provide for their actions. But those, the "derivations" as Pareto calls them (apparently because they are, in his view, derived from the sentiments), are to be regarded under all circumstances as the effects of the sentiment, *the ultimate cause* of both the nonlogical action and the nonlogical explanation. Only the action ("residue") and the rhetoric provided to justify it ("derivation") are observable, and both are the manifestations of a nonobservable, unchanging force—namely, the "sentiment." *How* the "constant" determines a variety of actions and how, according to any logic, constants can determine variables, Pareto never takes pains to tell us. Furthermore, he does not attempt anywhere in his work to determine scientifically whether in fact man's conduct is predominantly nonrational, but rather asserts it again and again, as he does his "purely scientific" intention. "We have no preconceptions, no a priori notions," he says somewhat naively and then proceeds, after he has distinguished the logical from the nonlogical, to give examples *only* of the latter. Logical or rational action is the appropriate linking of means to ends, appropriate not subjectively but objectively—that is, from the standpoint of an informed outside observer. Such rationality, Pareto would have us believe, is minimal if not altogether absent from most human conduct. He does occasionally grant, somewhat inconsistently, that logical actions are "very numerous" among "civilized" peoples, thereby implying that they are few and far between among the "noncivilized"; one is forced to wonder how man survived with little or no rationality and how the "primitives" survive if they have as little rational knowledge as Pareto suggests.

As for "logical actions," even among the civilized, Pareto drops them unceremoniously, never to weigh the proportion of them in man's total conduct. By means of the rather dubious "method" of citing examples of nonlogical conduct, Pareto believed that he had *demonstrated* the nonrationality of human conduct and that man is *by nature* nonrational and moved primarily, if not exclusively, by nonlogical forces. "Nonlogical actions," writes Pareto, "originate chiefly in definite psychic states, and sentiments, subconscious feelings, and the like. It is the province of psychology to investigate such psychic states. Here we start with them as data of fact without going beyond that."[4]

In Pareto's system, A = sentiments, B = nonlogical conduct, and C = pseudo-logical theory or rationale. People imagine that it is C that impelled them to act. In actuality, A determines both B and C, so that the causal relationship is AB, AC. Pareto is, however, prepared to assign some influence to C: The "existence of the theory C reacts upon the psychic state A and in many cases tends to reinforce it. The theory consequently influences B, following the line CAB" (Vol. I, p. 89). Actions can also have influence "upon the psychic state A and consequently upon the theory C, following the line BAC," and so on. A few paragraphs later, although he describes the psychic state very much as an effect of various social conditions, Pareto continues for some arbitrary reason to treat it as the main underlying cause of conduct:

> For example, C is the theory of free trade; D, the concrete adoption of free trade by a country; A, a psychic state that is in great part the product of individual interests, economic, political, and social, and of the circumstances under which people live. Direct relations between C and D are generally very tenuous. To work upon C in order to modify D leads to insignificant results. But any modification in A may react upon C and upon D. D and C will be seen to change simultaneously, and a superficial observer may think that D has changed because C has changed, whereas closer examination will reveal that D and C are not directly correlated, but depend both upon a common cause, A. (Vol. I, p. 91)

Here, clearly, social conditions, and economic, political, and other *interests* are assigned some importance. Do such interests and conditions conduce to rational conduct? Apparently not! In the very next paragraph, Pareto ignores the sociological implications of the previous one and proceeds as Pareto the psychologist to make a number of assertions that are never substantiated by the scientific empirical method he so celebrated:

> Theoretical discussions, C, are not, therefore, very serviceable directly for modifying D; indirectly they may be effective for modifying A. But to attain that objective, appeal must be made to sentiments rather than to logic and the results of experience. The situation may be stated, inexactly to be sure, because too absolutely, but nevertheless strikingly, by saying that in order to influence people thought has to be transformed into sentiment. (Vol. I, p. 91)

Inexact as the proposition is, Pareto nonetheless remains wedded to it: Sentiments, not rational interests, determine human conduct.

Throughout his exposition as, for example, in his discussion of magic and religion, he regards magical beliefs and practices as just so much nonsense. His approach is neither historical nor sociological, for he never stops to relate social conditions to certain beliefs and practices in various times and cultures. Since he is determined to show just how nonrational man is, he has nothing to say about the "scientific" knowledge and rational actions which play, no doubt, an essential role even in the most "primitive" of societies. Magic, religion, and so on, are regarded by Pareto as effects of "sentiments in which they originate (and which) are fairly common throughout the human race," not as correlates of the conditions under which men interact with each other and with the natural environment. The emphasis throughout is on institutionalized conduct as a manifestation of a psychic state, never vice versa. When he notes, for instance, the marked prominence of *law* in Roman culture, he "explains" it solely by reference to the prevailing *psychic state*. So important to him is that concept that he compares whole societies on that basis: "Among modern peoples, the English, at least down to the last years of the nineteenth century, have more than any other people resembled the Romans in their *psychic state*" (Vol. I, p. 168, italics added). And that is all he has to say on the subject.

This, therefore, is the heart of the Paretian system, already adumbrated in his *Systèmes Socialistes*: Men are essentially nonlogical because they are impelled into action by nonlogical forces, namely, *sentiments*. But men also have a persistent "need" to "rationalize" their conduct, which they do by means of pseudo-logical formulas. Together with his theory of elites, which occupies a very minor portion of his treatise, this constitutes the major theme of Pareto's work.

SOCIETY, ELITES, AND FORCE

Social differentiation, for Pareto, refers primarily to the fact that individuals are "physically, morally, and intellectually different." More, some individuals are "superior" to others. Pareto uses the term *elite* to refer to "superiority"—in intelligence, character, skill, capacity, power, and so on. Although he allows for the possibility that some people are given the label of elite without in fact possessing those qualities, on balance he sticks to the proposition that those who possess elite qualities become elites. One can measure the degree of excellence in every human endeavour, in prostitution and theft as well as in law and medicine, and assign to the individuals in each an index ranging from 0 to 10. A grade of 10 may thus be assigned to the very best in each field, reserving 0 for the man who is a good-for-nothing or an "out-and-out idiot." Napoleon, he says, "was certainly not an idiot, nor a man of little account, as millions of others are. He had exceptional qualities" (Vol. III, p. 2029). Thus the elite of a society consists of those with the highest indices in their branches of activity. This Pareto divided into two: a *governing elite,* that is, those "who directly or indirectly play some considerable part in government, and a *nongoverning élite,* comprising the rest" (Vol. III, p. 2032). Together they constitute the higher stratum, or class, of the society. The lower stratum or nonelite, in contrast, are those with whose political influence "we are not just here concerned"—and whose influence turns out to be practically nil from Pareto's standpoint. To the rulers and the ruled, Pareto relates his residues—but only the first two classes of residues, for he has nothing more to say about the remaining four.

There is, according to Pareto, a predominance of class I residues in the higher stratum, and a predominance of class II in the lower. More precisely, in the higher stratum "Class II residues gradually lose in strength, until now and again they are reinforced by tides upwelling from the lower stratum." Revolutions are in fact great religious tides, the upward thrusts of lower classes strong in class II residues. Residues are also invoked to explain why "history is the graveyard of aristocracies;" for the elite decays in quantity and quality—that is, in the requisite residues that "enabled them to win their power and hold it. The governing class is restored not only in numbers, but—and this is the more important thing—in quality, by families rising from the lower classes and bringing with them vigor and the proportions of residues necessary for keeping themselves in power. It is also restored by the loss of its more degenerate members" (Vol III, p. 2054). If the circulation ceases, the governing class collapses and "sweeps the whole of a nation along with it. Potent cause of disturbance in the equilibrium is the accumulation of superior elements in the lower classes and, conversely, of inferior elements in the higher classes" (Vol. III, p. 2055). Thus the rudiments of Pareto's theory of revolution. But the "theory" includes another important element, *force,* which for Pareto, may be the more important one. "Superior elements" are not only those "fit to rule" but those willing to use force. Inferior and decadent elements are unfit and fear its use. The "decaying" elite, shying away from the use of force, tries to buy off its adversaries; it becomes less the lion and more the fox and, therefore, increasingly vulnerable to the new lions.

"Societies in general subsist," writes Pareto in one of his typical "explanations," "because alive and vigorous in the majority of their constituent members are sentiments corresponding to residues of sociality (class IV)." A gregarious instinct in men binds them together. "But," he adds, "there are also individuals in human societies in whom some at least of those sentiments are weak or indeed actually missing." Whether the society will subsist or dissolve depends on the relative proportion and strength of social sentiments within it. Corresponding to the distribution and intensity of such sentiments (that is, individuals holding them), one will find a society either more or less "uniform" or inclined to change: The greater the proportion and intensity of the residues of sociality, the greater the uniformity, and conversely, the weaker they are, the greater the tendency toward change. Societies are essentially "heterogeneous," says Pareto, in the distribution of residues; "the requirement of uniformity is very strong in some individuals, moderately strong in others, very feeble in still others, and almost entirely absent in a few." And "one may add as a datum of fact that the number of individuals in whom the requirement of uniformity is stronger than the average requisite of the intermediate state in which the society is stated is much greater than the number of individuals in whom the requirement is weaker than the average, and very, very much greater than the number in whom it is entirely missing" (Vol. IV, p. 2172). Why is that a "datum of fact" for Pareto? Because "if the requirement of uniformity [apparently his term for unity and solidarity] were to fail, society would not hold together, and each individual would go his own way, as lions and tigers, birds of prey, and other animals do." So societies hang together due to the predominance in them of individuals with strong social instincts; the "proof" lies in the fact that societies do not dissolve.

That is not all. What Pareto calls derivations, theologies, and so on, correspond to the "greater or lesser potency of the sentiments of uniformity." Thus one theology "will glorify the immobility of one or another uniformity, real or imaginary, the other ... will glorify movement, progress, in one direction or another" (Vol. IV, p. 2173). That is what actually happened in history. Men have sought merely to justify whatever sentiments they have held; moved by those blind forces, they "explain" and justify their practice post hoc by talk. The same is true with respect to force, which "is used by those who wish to preserve certain uniformities and by those who wish to overstep them. And when each says he abhors the use of force, he means by the other."

Pareto goes on to suggest that the question of whether "the use of violence to enforce existing uniformities is beneficial to society, or whether it is beneficial to use force to overstep them," can be solved by a kind of utilitarian (functional) calculus. The various uniformities have to be distinguished to see which of them are beneficial and which deleterious to society. Nor, indeed, is that enough; for it is further necessary to determine whether the utility of the uniformity is great enough to offset the harm that will be done by using violence to enforce it, or whether detriment from the uniformity is great enough to overbalance the damage that will be caused by the use of force in subverting it; in which detriment and damage we must not forget to reckon the very serious drawback involved in the anarchy that results from any frequent use of violence to abolish existing uniformities, just as among the benefits and utilities of maintaining frankly injurious uniformities must be counted the strength and stability they lend to the social order. So, to solve the problem as to use of force, it is not enough to solve the other problem as to the utility in general, of certain types of social organization; it is essential also and chiefly to compute all the advantages and all the drawbacks, direct and indirect. (Vol. IV, p. 2175)

But this calculus, to determine what is "beneficial to society," we now learn is best left to the scientific elite and to the ruling class, for "social utility is oftentimes best served if the members of the subject class, whose *function* it is not to lead but to act, accept one of the two theologies according to the case—either the theology that enjoins preservation of existing uniformities, or the theology that counsels change" (Vol. IV, p. 2175, italics added). In spite of the cautious wording, what we have here is a thinly veiled assumption of the incompetence of the "people" to decide for themselves what is or is not good for them; "social utility" is best served if they follow passively and accept the judgments of the various elites.

When the rule of the governing elite is threatened, and out of humanitarian (or other) sentiments it declines to meet force with force, even a small group can impose its will upon it. If the governing class shies away from the use of force for reasons of expediency, and resorts instead to fraud and deceit in order to outwit its adversaries, that eventually brings about a change in its composition—power passes "from the lions to the foxes." Foxiness, resting on the residues of the combinations instinct (class I), becomes preponderant and intensified in that class while class II residues decline. It is precisely the increase of class I residues supplying the "artistry and resourcefulness" now needed to outsmart one's opponents, that makes the governing class increasingly vulnerable to those willing and able to use force—the lions—either from within that class or from the subject one.

The leaders of the subject class, ready, willing, and able to employ force, topple the governing class; that is accomplished all the more easily if it is moved by humanitarian sentiments and if it has found few or no ways of assimilating into its midst the elite of the subject class. A closed aristocracy is most vulnerable and insecure. On the other hand, the more adept is the governing class in absorbing those subject elements who are skilled at "chicanery, fraud, and corruption," the more secure is its rule, for it undercuts the possibility that the "talented" elements will "become the leaders of such plebeians as are disposed to use violence. Thus left without leadership, without talent, disorganized, the subject class is almost always powerless to set up any lasting regime" (Vol. IV, p. 2179). There will always be a subject class. That is inevitable because it has no real leadership; its elite elements are consistently coopted by the governing elite.

Although the governing elite, being small, is greatly strengthened by the influx of class I residues (that is, individuals holding them who are inclined to rule), the subject class is enfeebled not only by the loss of those elements, but also by the fact that though it

> is still left with many individuals possessed of combinations-instincts, [they] are applied not to politics … but to arts and trades independent of politics. That circumstance lends stability to societies, for the governing class is required to absorb only a small number of new individuals in order to keep the subject class deprived of leadership. However, in the long run the differences in temperament between the governing class and the subject class become gradually accentuated, the combinations-instincts tending to predominate in the ruling class, and instincts of group-persistence in the subject class. When that difference becomes sufficiently great, revolution occurs. (Vol. IV, p. 2179)

That is Pareto's theory of revolution, based on residue, sentiments, and temperament. The general formula, he tells us, can be applied to nation-states. Those who have not lost "the habit of applying force" will win over those who have lost the "habit"; in the long run, the latter situation "leads a country to ruin" (Vol. IV, p. 2179).

As for the oppressed, or those who think they are, derivations, such as humanitarianism, are used to arouse them or to bring the neutrals over to their side, or to get them to condemn or otherwise weaken the governing powers. Pareto has nothing but contempt for "those whose spinal columns have utterly rotted from the bane of humanitarianism" (Vol. IV, p. 2186). The temptation is irresistible to present just a few examples of Pareto's "scientific-sociological" approach to "force." In a country where the ruling class, A, out of humanitarian or other considerations, "is becoming less and less capable of using force," it is "shirking the main duty of a ruling class. Such a country is on its way to utter ruin." But then the B's, the subject class, "apply force on a far-reaching scale, and not only overthrow the A's but kill large numbers of them—and, in so doing, to tell the truth, they are performing a useful public service, something like ridding the country of a baneful animal pest." Owing to that, "the social fabric is acquiring stability and strength. The country is saved from ruin and is reborn to a new life." Again, "slaughter and rapine are external symptoms indicating the advent of strong and courageous people to places formerly held by weaklings and cowards." Commenting on the French Revolution of 1789, if the governing class "had had the faith that counsels use of force and the will to use force, it would never have been overthrown and, procuring its own advantage, would have procured the advantage of France." Failing in its function, however, it "was a good thing that power should pass into the hands of people who showed that they had the faith and the resolve requisite for the use of force" (Vol. IV, p. 2191). He has much to say about force, about the spineless and the courageous, but one finds nothing more than that in his functional calculus for determining what is good for "society."

Pareto occasionally reminds us, contrary to his practice, that residues are not to be regarded as the only determining factor. However, Pareto can explain almost any problem in terms of the proportion of class I and class II residues. If, for instance, Alcibiades persuaded the Athenians "against the better judgment of the conservative Nicias, to undertake the Sicilian expedition," that was due to the preponderance among them of class I residues. And Pareto adds: "Had sentiments of group-persistence been at all strong in the Athenians, they would have followed the view of Nicias, or would at the most have been satisfied with sending a small expedition that would have been no great tax on their resources (Vol. IV, p. 2421). That is typical of what Pareto considers to be "explanation."

After recounting some of the historical events in very superficial terms, he concludes: "It is plain enough that what was lacking in Athens was such a balance between the combinations-instincts and the residues of group-persistence that while the combinations-instincts encouraged to adventure, the group-persistences would supplement them with the perseverance and firmness of resolve required for success in the schemes imaged" (Vol. IV, p. 2424). More, the fact that Alcibiades could be more effective leading the "slow-thinking" Spartans than the natives of his own city, "demonstrates how desirable it is that combination-instincts should predominate in the leaders and the instincts of group-persistence in subordinates." It is desirable, in other words, that the "masses," in any case predominantly nonrational, blindly follow and leave to the elite the work of making ingenious combinations. Both Sparta and Athens would have been easily defeated had they fought "with a people possessing ability to innovate combined with ability to make the proper use of novelties, a situation that arises in countries where our class I residues predominate in the leaders and class II residues in the subject classes" (Vol. IV, p. 2429). Pareto's "proof": Thebes and Macedonia were equally endowed in a number of respects—both made improvements simultaneously in the arts of war, both had leaders with highly developed combination-instincts who commanded people with "the group-persistences required for steadfastness of purpose." Why then did the Macedonians fare better? This is Pareto's reply: "Through a greater intensity in their class II residues, the Macedonians stood by their leaders more consistently than the Thebans did" (Vol. IV, p. 2429).

In effect, the combination-instinct, for Pareto, is the intelligence of the elite to take advantage of the superstitions of the masses but never to believe the absurdities themselves. He relates how Nicias, when commanding the Athenians, "was induced by his group persistences to place his trust in oracles and so led the army under him to complete ruin." He concludes

> that oracles are good things if they are used by rulers, who perhaps have no faith in them, as means of persuading their subordinates, but harmful if they are taken at face value by rulers and used as an end in themselves, not as means of persuasion. To make the proposition general, and so applicable to times that know no oracles, one need merely replace the term "oracles" with the term "group-persistences." (Vol. IV, p. 2440)

Pareto goes on to say that the elite will achieve its end all the more efficiently, the more the masses are kept unaware of that doctrine, suggesting thereby that they are able to learn of their deliberate manipulation and, given such knowledge, could prevent it. He thus leaves himself open to the inference that the "stupidity" and acquiescence of the "people" need not be permanent. Explicitly, however, this is his formula for success: A people's prejudice (class II residues) should be strong enough to assure its obedience to the leader, but not so strong as to prevent certain innovations. It is this "scientific-sociological" proposition which explains victory in war and prosperity and progress in peace.

Forms of government do have some influence on social events and development, Pareto acknowledges, but such forms are themselves "products of the character traits of the peoples involved, the traits, therefore, being far more important as causes of the social phenomena" (Vol. IV, p. 2445). He quotes Von der Goltz's remarks about conditions in Prussia before the battle of Jena to the effect that in France the civil authority always defers to the military "whereas in Germany the prevailing spirit in the civil government, as well as in the public at large, is always to block the military authority" (Vol. IV, p. 2447). Pareto notes parenthetically that in his time the situation has reversed itself. The "constant" character traits have *not only changed* but have also switched places—with no further light thrown on the phenomenon.

Having the right traits and using force will ensure the maintenance of the governing class. How might a governing class best defend itself and eliminate those who threaten it? "The infliction of death," replies Pareto, "is the surest means, but also the most harmful," since it could lead to a destruction of society's best individuals. Persecution is also not very practical since that tends to create martyrs, who are even more dangerous to the elite. In general, then, he leaves one effective formula for rulers: "One may say … that a governing class offers effective resistance only as it is disposed to go to the limit in resistance, without hesitation, using force and resorting to arms whenever necessary" (Vol. IV, p. 2480).

PARETO AND FASCISM

It is not known how much direct influence Pareto had upon Mussolini, or even whether there was any direct contact between the two men when the latter was a political refugee in Lausanne. Before the march on Rome, Pareto had a very reserved and occasionally even hostile attitude toward the fascist movement. It is indisputable, however, that once the Italian dictator had established himself in power, Pareto gave his wholehearted approval to what he apparently regarded as the "moderate form" fascism assumed in its early phase. Later, he maintained his support and approval of the regime but, according to his biographer, G. H. Bousquet, underscored "the necessity of safeguarding a number of liberties."[5]

Fascism, for Pareto, seemed not only to confirm his theories but also to hold out hope for a "new era." That he identified with the new order is borne out by the fact that on March 23, 1923, he accepted an appointment as senator—a position he had declined to accept in the pre-fascist govern-ment. In a letter to an acquaintance at the time of acceptance, he wrote: "I am happy to see that you are favorably disposed to the new regime, which, in my opinion, is the only one capable of saving Italy from innumerable evils."[6] And, in the same vein, "France will save herself only if she finds her own Mussolini."[7]

In general, Pareto's attitude seems to have been that because the pre-fascist regime did not, or could not, save the country from "anarchy" by legal means, fascism had to do it by force. Having accomplished that, however, the regime should have strived to establish a "new legality." Fascism would be good for Italy if it avoided wars and if it refrained from imposing "exaggerated" restrictions on freedom. In short, fascism would be good if it were not fascism! His call for "liberties," however, was typically Paretian: What is most essential is that the new elite govern "effectively"—and that requires that it concede a "certain dose of liberty" to the people. Reflecting on fascism a year or so before he died, Pareto wrote, "We have arrived today at a point where there appears, among … the clouds of the future, the beginning of the transformation of democracy, of parliamentarism, of the cycle of demagogic plutocracy; and Italy which formerly was the mother of so many forms of civilization, could very well have a grand role to play in bringing into the world another."[8]

In his attitude toward fascism, then, we have a clearer view of Pareto's own firmly held sentiments, whose manifestations may also be found throughout his work.

NOTES

1. Vilfredo Pareto, *Oeuvres Complètes,* Tome V, *Les Systèmes Socialistes,* 2 volumes (Geneva: Giovanni Busino, Librarie Droz, 1965), p. 25. (Hereafter all page references to this work will be indicated in parentheses immediately following the quoted passage.)

2. Pareto, *Mind and Society.*

3. I find it very difficult to understand how Talcott Parsons, in his *Structure of Social Action,* could interpret residues as values; this interpretation may suit his thesis that the works of Weber, Pareto, Durkheim, and others converged conceptually and theoretically, but it can be upheld only by means of a very selective reading of Pareto's work.

4. Pareto, *Mind and Society*, Vol. I, 88. (Hereafter all page references to this work will be indicated in parentheses immediately following the quoted passage.)

5. See Bousquet, *Pareto,* p. 89.

6. Ibid., p. 193.

7. Ibid., pp. 193–94 n.

8. Ibid., p. 197. See also H. Stuart Hughes, *Consciousness and Society*, rev. ed. (New York: Vintage Books, 1977), pp. 270–74.

CHAPTER 10

Gaetano Mosca (1858–1941)

Mosca, like Pareto, conceived of his life's work as an effective repudiation of the prevailing democratic and collectivistic theories, particularly Marxism. Those theories, elements of which could be traced to ancient Greece, were given a more explicit formulation by the representatives of the Enlightenment in the eighteenth century; in the nineteenth century, they were logically extended by Karl Marx and thus given a renewed impetus. Rousseau, in those terms, was the real parent of Marx, and Marx the true heir of the Enlightenment. Though Marx is regarded as the founder of modern socialism, writes Mosca, its "first intellectual and moral parent was undoubtedly Rousseau."[1] The various doctrines emanating from those sources are precisely the ones Mosca is "combating all along in these pages" (p. 152). Like Pareto, he wants once and for all to destroy the Rousseauian-Marxian fantasy "that once collectivism is established, it will be the beginning of an era of universal equality and justice, during which the state will no longer be the organ of a class and the exploiter and the exploited will be no more" (p. 447). Mosca's entire output, in particular *The Ruling Class*, is intended as a refutation of that "utopia" against which he advances his own theory: There will always be a ruling class!

To support his thesis, Mosca relies ultimately, as did Pareto, on the assumption of "constant psychological tendencies determining the behavior of the human masses" (p. 1). Yet, what emerges from this total work is a theory which is, on balance, less dogmatic and less rigid as well as more *sociological* than Pareto's—though he prefers to describe his work as political science rather than sociology. His sociological view is evident not only in his rejection of geographic, climatic, social Darwinian, and racial theories, but especially in his explicit use of concepts such as "social structure," "social types," and "social forces." It is, he writes, "social structure, upon which after all, decision as to whether a people is to rule or to be ruled depends" (p. 61). Those concepts lead him to the view that it is not categories such as race, topography, climate, struggle for existence, and so on, which account for the relative cultural backwardness of certain groups, but definite social relationships: "We are obliged to agree … that European civilization has not only hindered but actually thwarted any effort toward progress that Negroes and Indians might have made of their own accord" (p. 23). Given identical social and cultural conditions, there is no reason to believe that blacks could not distinguish themselves as well as whites. When black children recognize their condition, that is, "realize that they belong to a race that is adjudged inferior, and that they can look forward to no better lot than that of cooks and porters, they lose interest in studying and lapse into apathy" (p. 24).

Mosca is also aware that "every individual is wont to adopt the ideas, the beliefs, the sentiments that are most current in the environment in which he has grown up" (p. 26). His more consistently sociological approach may be further illustrated in this insistence that it is not any alleged organic differences among peoples that determine "the differences in social type that they have adopted, but rather the differences in social contacts and in historical circumstances to which every nation … is fated to be subject" (p. 28). The doctrine which has mechanically transposed the Darwinian view from the natural to the social realm is also erroneous: It is not primarily a struggle *for existence* which prevails in society but a struggle for *preeminence;* that is "a constant phenomenon that arises in all human societies" (p. 29).

Struggle for preeminence is Mosca's term for the social competition and conflict over wealth, power, and prestige, for "control of the means and instruments that enable a person to direct many human activities, many human wills, as he sees fit. The losers, who are of course the majority in that sort of struggle, are not devoured, destroyed, or even kept from reproducing their kind, as is basically characteristic of the struggle for life. They merely enjoy fewer material satisfactions and, especially, less freedom and independence" (p. 30). In opposition to the various nonsociological doctrines, Mosca emphasized that it is the accumulation of experience and positive knowledge which accounts for the advance in civilization, and that the rise and decline of societies must be viewed as the effects of "changes in their types of social structure" (p. 35). If Frenchmen, for example, are different today from what they were one hundred years ago, then that is due to the radical changes that have taken place in "the economic and political situation in France" and to the different intellectual atmosphere now prevailing there.

Mosca gives so much attention to social and cultural conditions that his so-called "constant psychological laws" are relegated to a relatively subordinate position. In Pareto's system, as we have seen, "sentiments" and the basic irrationality of man play so fundamental a role as to virtually exclude a consideration of sociocultural conditions. Mosca, on the other hand, keeps those conditions constantly in view. The "great psychological laws," he writes, "reveal their operation … in administrative and judicial institutions, in religions, in all the moral and political customs of the various nations; and it is therefore upon these last categories of facts that we must concentrate our attention" (p. 46). Although his general argument rests somewhat less than Pareto's on psychological laws, Mosca, too, ultimately falls back upon such "laws" for his explanation of why the struggle for preeminence, as well as the ruling class, must be eternal phenomena.

THE RULING CLASS

The observation that rulers and ruled have existed throughout history obviously did not originate with Mosca, as he readily acknowledged. Plato, for example, had given considerable attention to the rulers and the ruled of his Ideal State. It was, however, only in the work of Saint-Simon, Mosca believed, that one could see a definite and clear-cut anticipation of his own doctrine: That once a society reaches a certain stage of development, "political control in the broadest sense of the term (administrative, military, religious, economic, and moral leadership) is exercised always by a special class, or by an organized minority" (p. 239). Saint-Simon had not only asserted "the inherent necessity of a ruling class. He explicitly proclaimed that that class has to possess the requisites and aptitudes most necessary to social leadership at a given time and in a given type of civilization" (pp. 329–30).

In 1883, in his first work, *Teorica dei Governi e Governo Parlamentare*, Mosca elaborated on Saint-Simon's view and argued "that even in democracies the need for an organized minority persists, and that in spite of appearances to the contrary, and for all the legal principles on which government rests, this minority still retains actual and effective control of the state" (p. 331). To emphasize that he was the *first* among his contemporaries to give that thesis explicit form, he adds: "In years following came the first edition of the present work, *Elementi di scienza politica*, and, among others, works by Ammon, Novikov, Rensi, Pareto and Michels" (p. 331).[2]

Mosca's thesis—that under all systems, including politically democratic ones, a ruling class prevails—was obviously one with which Marx or the Marxists would not have disagreed. They knew very well that the "history of all hitherto existing society is the history of class struggles." That was, after all, the first observation Marx and Engels made in the *Communist Manifesto*. Three paragraphs later, they also state quite clearly that modern bourgeois society "has not done away with class antagonisms. It has but established new classes, new conditions of oppression, new forms of struggle in place of the old ones."[3] If Marx had stopped there, his thesis would have been identical with Mosca's. But, of course, Marx did not stop there and went on to argue that classes (including ruling classes) and class conflict rest on definite socioeconomic conditions and that the elimination of those conditions could lead to a society in which a ruling class would be superfluous and unthinkable. What was inevitable under some conditions was altogether avoidable under others. The point for Mosca, in contrast, was that history gives us no realistic basis for such a vision, since it is a fundamental and inexorable psychological law, and not primarily social conditions, which determines man's nature. What has been true "of all hitherto existing society" will continue to be true in all future societies. In that way Mosca reversed the implications of Marx's thesis and transformed it into a conservative one. The ruling class is a permanent attribute of society, as is the struggle for preeminence. In all societies there have been and will continue to be two classes: one that rules and the other that is ruled. In Mosca's scheme, however, the ruled are assigned a somewhat less passive role than in Pareto's.

The ruled masses, Mosca acknowledges, are able to bring pressures to bear upon the rulers. The "pressures arising from the discontent of the masses who are governed, from the passions by which they are swayed, exert a certain amount of influence on the policies of the ruling, the political class" (p. 51). Popular discontent may even result in the overthrow of a ruling class, but another such class would inevitably emerge from the "masses themselves to discharge the functions of a ruling class. Otherwise all organization, and the whole social structure, would be destroyed" (p. 51). The ruling or political class assumes "preponderant importance in determining the political type, and also the level of civilization, of the different peoples" (p. 51).

The power of the ruling class as well as the inevitability of its dominion rests on the fact that it is an *organized minority*, which is accompanied in Mosca's system by an *unorganized majority*. The unorganized state of the majority renders each of its individual members quite powerless before the organized might of the minority. Precisely because it is a minority, a relatively small group, it can achieve what the majority cannot: mutual understanding and concerted action. "It follows," writes Mosca, "that the larger the political community, the smaller will the proportion of the governing minority to the governed majority be, and the more difficult will it be for the majority to organize for reaction against the minority" (p. 53).

Not only difficult, perhaps even impossible. There is an inexorable social law rooted in the nature of man which makes it inevitable that the representatives of the people—whether elected or appointed—will transform themselves from servants into masters. Appointed to represent and defend the common interests of the group as a whole, they soon develop special interests of their own; in their zealous pursuit of those interests they become a well-organized, powerful, and dominant minority. The ruling minority is strengthened not only by its organization but by the superior qualities—material, intellectual, moral—which distinguish it from the mass. Members "of a ruling minority regularly have some attribute, real or apparent, which is highly esteemed and very influential in the society in which they live" (p. 53).

The basic psychological law which impels men to struggle for preeminence always results in the victory of the minority, which by virtue of its organization and other superior qualities gains decisive control over certain "social forces." Control of any one social force—for example, military, economic, political, administrative, religious, moral, and so on—may lead to control of others. The military power of warrior lords, for instance, enabled them to demand and receive "the community's whole produce minus what was absolutely necessary for subsistence on the part of the cultivators; and when the latter tried to escape such abuses they were constrained by force to stay bound to the soil, their situation taking on all the characteristics of serfdom pure and simple" (p. 55). That has been true generally of societies in which land was the chief source of wealth: Military power led to wealth just as later wealth in the form of money led to political and military power. When "fighting with the mailed fist is prohibited whereas fighting with pounds and pence is sanctioned, the better posts are inevitably won by those who are better supplied with pounds and pence" (p. 57). In all societies, including, of course, representative democracies, the rich have readier access to agencies of social influence than the poor. In some societies during specific periods, control of "religious forces," as might be the case with priests, leads to wealth and political power; in other societies, specialized scientific knowledge becomes an important political force.

The various advantages of the ruling minority—organization, superior qualities, and control of social forces—conduce to the situation in which "all ruling classes tend to become hereditary in fact if not in law." There "is no eliminating that special advantage in favor of certain individuals which the French call the advantage of *positions déjà prises*." Among others, those advantages are the "connections and kinships that set an individual promptly on the right road, enabling him to avoid the gropings and blunders that are inevitable when one enters an unfamiliar environment without any guidance or support" (p. 61).

Arguing against social Darwinism and against the racial theories of Gumplowicz, Mosca adamantly insists on the social and cultural basis of the "superiority" of the various aristocracies and ruling classes in history. They "owe their special qualities not so much to the blood that flows in their veins as to their particular upbringing, which has brought out certain intellectual and moral tendencies in them in preference to others." And again, "the truth is that social position, family tradition, the habits of the class in which we live, contribute more than is commonly supposed to the greater or lesser development of the qualities mentioned" (p. 63).

Thus, Mosca rejects any attribution of organic superiority to the members of the ruling class, but he rejects equally the sociological implications of his statement that "social position, family tradition, and habits of class" determine the character of men. He is unwilling to seriously entertain the possibility that the psychology of men could be changed by changing social conditions and institutions. For Mosca, the existing institutions, notably the ruling class, though owing their existence in part to other sociocultural conditions, are ultimately the result of a basic, unchanging psychological nature in man. Only by clinging to that assumption can he support his theory: Men under all conditions will struggle for preeminence, and this must result in the basic dichotomy of rulers and ruled.

Although the organized minority has superior might and can therefore repel challenges to its rule by force, it does so only as a last resort. Generally, it succeeds in stabilizing its rule by making it acceptable to the masses. That is done by means of a "political formula," a term roughly equivalent to Marx's ruling-class ideology, Weber's "legitimation" of power, Sorel's "myths," and Pareto's "derivations." Every governing class, writes Mosca, "tends to justify its actual exercise of power by resting it on some universal moral principle" (p. 62).

The "political formula" is not invented and employed "to trick the masses into obedience" (p. 71). It is a "great superstition" or illusion that, at the same time, is a great social force; without it, Mosca maintains, it is doubtful that societies could persist. "Political formula," then, is a broader concept than the term suggests; it includes the common values, beliefs, sentiments, and habits that result from a people's community of history, making that people receptive to the fictions employed by the governing class to legitimize its rule.

Nationalism is an obvious example in the modern era of such a formula: "a man feels, believes, loves, hates, according to the environment in which he lives" (p. 73). In previous eras, rule by "divine right" was the prevalent formula. Formulas change with the sociohistorical circumstances, but under all circumstances the consent of the governed is based on a formula of some kind:

> The majority of a people consents to a given governmental system solely because the system is based upon religious or philosophical beliefs that are universally accepted by them. To use a language that we prefer, the amount of consent depends upon the extent to which, and the ardor with which, the class that is ruled believes in the political formula by which the ruling class justifies its rule. (p. 97)

Every successful regime rests on the careful cultivation of the beliefs of the lower classes in the ruling political formula. Failure to develop such all-embracing, general beliefs means that the rulers have failed to unify the different social groups and classes of the society.

Ruling ideas cannot depart too far from the culture of the governed without resulting in conflict and antagonism that threaten the very survival of the society. The principles underlying the formula must be rooted in the "consciousness of the more populous and less well educated strata of society" (p. 107). When such principles have sunk deeply enough into the consciousness of the poorly educated, the governing class, however corrupt and oppressive, gets remarkable results: the unswerving devotion of the poor, exploited, and oppressed masses. Nationalistic political formulas, properly cultivated, can effectively counter the internationalist doctrine of social democracy; Mosca saw a vivid demonstration of that thesis during World War I. It is of interest to note in this connection that nationalism was a greater social force than even he had believed. Before the war he wrote,

> These theories [proletarian internationalism] might have a certain practical efficacy in the event of a war between the Germans and the French, or between the Italians and the English, since all these nations belong to approximately the same social type. But if it were a question of repelling a serious Tatar or Chinese invasion, or merely a Turkish or Russian invasion, we believe that the great majority of proletarians even in countries where they are most strongly imbued with doctrines of worldwide collectivism would eagerly cooperate with the ruling class. (p. 115)

Thus, even Mosca was probably astonished to see that it took less than a Tatar invasion to mobilize and unite the workers behind their respective governments. In that instance, narrow-minded nationalistic sentiments had overwhelmed the peoples of Europe and had brought upon them a terrible carnage. Must, however, the ruling "political formula"—for example, nationalism leading to war—always win out? Mosca grants that such formulae gain acceptance among the masses primarily because they have so little education and so little understanding of their condition. But he does not envisage the possibility of raising the general level of their consciousness to the point where they might reject political formulas obviously not to their interest.

Another major social process to which Mosca calls attention is the emergence within the lower classes of a "directing minority," a kind of plebeian ruling class, which is often "antagonistic to the class that holds possession of the legal government" (p. 116). The directing minority becomes a state within the state, wielding more influence over the masses than the legal government. The greater the isolation of the classes from one another, and the greater the discontent of the lower classes, the greater, too, is the likelihood that they will support the overthrow of the existing legal government. One ruling class then replaces the other, but that avails the masses little or nothing. The really great danger in the growing cultural differences among classes, and in their mutual cultural isolation "is a decline in energy in the upper classes, which grow poorer and poorer in bold and aggressive characters and richer and richer in 'soft,' remissive individuals" (p. 117). The more closed the upper classes are to aspiring individuals from the lower classes, the greater their vulnerability and degeneracy, for it is only from the lower classes that the vigorous and strong elements may be recruited. In those classes, "the hard necessities of life, the unending and carking scramble for bread, the lack of literary culture, keep the primordial instincts of struggle and the unfailing ruggedness of human nature, alive" (p. 119). Here we recognize an idea Pareto formulated in a much less simple and straightforward fashion.

For Mosca, the fate of a ruling class depends on its energy, wisdom, and political sophistication. It has considerable control of its destiny. A ruling class of some sort is a permanent institution, and efforts to abolish it will always remain quixotic. The point, therefore, is to devise the best political system possible in the light of that fact; one could learn much in that regard from the great political thinkers of the past.

ARISTOTLE AND MONTESQUIEU

In 1908, Mosca became a Liberal-Conservative member of the Italian Chamber of Deputies. Thus, unlike Pareto, who had isolated himself from political life and had produced a correspondingly rigid system, Mosca was actively engaged in Italian politics. That, perhaps, contributed in his case to the formation of a more flexible political theory, which was reflected in his official party affiliation. Though he was indeed an elitist in some sense, he advanced what may be more precisely termed a liberal-aristocratic theory of politics.

He was a liberal in the sense that he had great respect and admiration for liberal principles, traditions, and institutions. The liberal principle, he believed "has had a more brilliant record than the autocratic principle" (p. 409). Political systems based on liberal principles have been more successful than others precisely because they have rested "upon the consent of the majority of citizens," but, he is quick to add, "though only a small fraction of the inhabitants may be citizens" (p. 409). The models for his "good polity," therefore, were the ancient city-state of Greece, about which Aristotle had written, and the English system before the institution of universal suffrage—the system Montesquieu had so much admired.

Liberalism is the proper mediation between two fundamental principles forever at work in all political systems, vying with each other for hegemony: aristocracy and democracy. Liberalism is best in the sense that it allows both principles to work side by side with neither overpowering the other. Officials are appointed or elected from "below"—that is, directly or indirectly by their subordinates; they are drawn, however, from a limited pool of wise, experienced, responsible, and devoted men who are best fit to rule—the aristocratic minority. They have authority but not unlimited power, since definite limits are imposed upon their powers in relation to "individual citizens and to associations of citizens." Those limits—checks and balances—are the essence of liberalism; they are the fundamental elements of what Mosca calls "juridical defence," which in turn is the real criterion of the advance of civilization.

> Such limits [writes Mosca] were not entirely unknown to classical Greece and ancient Rome. They are almost always recognized in modern constitutions. They relate to such things as freedom of worship, of the press, of education, of assembly, and of speech. They guarantee personal liberty, private property, and inviolability of domicile. (pp. 409–10)

The liberal principle does not preclude the existence of an aristocratic minority or even closed cliques within it. In fact, a certain degree of closure is essential and good. On the other hand, too much closure results in *autocracy*, something to be eschewed since it leads to the isolation of rulers and eventually to their downfall. The proper balance may be found in liberal systems which "steer the inclinations of at least the whole second stratum of the ruling class, which, if it does not in itself constitute the electorate, at least supplies the general staffs of leaders who form the opinions and determine the conduct of the electing body" (p. 410). The "second stratum" to which Mosca alludes here, though varying with the society, corresponds to Aristotle's great middle class, the basis of political moderation. For Mosca, too, it "forms the backbone of all great political organization" (p. 413). The existence of a large and stable second stratum makes it possible for a government to succeed without "paying homage to the beliefs and sentiments of the more ignorant classes. Only under such circumstances can one of the chief assumptions of the liberal system be made, we do not say complete, but not wholly illusory—namely, that those who represent shall be responsible to the represented" (p. 413).

In those terms, Mosca regards it as essential to preserve and properly balance the aristocratic and democratic tendencies present in varying degrees of strength in all political organizations. "If it is confined within moderate limits," he writes, "the democratic tendency is in a sense indispensable to what is called 'progress' in human societies" (p. 415). Excessive suppression of that tendency results in social stagnation: If the aristocracies of Homeric times, for example, had remained closed and stationary, then civilization never would have advanced beyond that stage.

Class conflict, Mosca acknowledges to the Marxists, has been a major force in the development of civilization. "The struggle between those who are at the top and those who are born at the bottom but aspire to climb has been, is, and will ever be the ferment that forces individuals and classes to widen their horizons and seek the new roads that have brought the world to the degree of civilization that it attained in the nineteenth century" (p. 416). Now, however, the democratic tendency has gotten out of hand; if it could be brought under control, then it would again become the conservative force that it ought to properly be.

> When the democratic tendency does not exert too great an influence, to the exclusion of other tendencies, it represents a conservative force. It enables ruling classes to be continually replenished through the admission of new elements who have inborn talents for leadership and a will to lead, and so prevents that exhaustion of aristocracies of birth which usually paves the way for great social cataclysms. (p. 416)

The best system, then, is one in which the democratic tendency is appropriately bridled and curbed. But the principle of balance and moderation is constantly being threatened and undermined in practice by the

Rousseauian-Marxian dogma of equality—a fantastic utopia; "every time the democratic movement has triumphed, in part or in full, we have invariably seen the aristocratic tendency come to life again through efforts of the very men who had fought it" (p. 417).

If, therefore, Mosca was combating the ideas of the Enlightenment, it was specific aspects of that intellectual movement that he opposed. He admired Montesquieu but rejected Rousseau. The former had asserted the need for checks and balances, in short—moderation. A system based on a balance of powers was more realistic and hence superior to the unbridled democratic theory of Rousseau. Although the latter had called for popular sovereignty and absolute equality, he had also recognized, Mosca alleges, the need for a ruling class. In Rousseau's *Social Contract*, Mosca found the following statement: "Taking the term in its strictest sense there has never been a real democracy and there never will be. It is against the natural order that the great number should rule and the small number be ruled" (p. 391). But as Meisel has shown, that passage was quoted out of context, and it was only by so doing that Mosca could have used it for his purposes. Rousseau goes on to say: "It is inconceivable that the People should be in permanent session for the administration of public affairs."[4] The real point Rousseau was making in that context was, in Meisel's words, "that *government* by all would be as much against 'the natural order' (since the result would be anarchy) as would be *sovereignty* (which is and remains inalienable) if possessed by less than all the people."[5] What Mosca feared most was "a demagogic dictatorship by a few experts in mob leadership" (p. 417) and he used the passage from Rousseau just quoted to show that he had also recognized the dangers of that kind of "democracy."

From Mosca's standpoint, then, Montesquieu and *even* Rousseau had admitted the necessity of a ruling class. Greatly impressed by the English system of restraining the ruling class, Montesquieu had extolled that system and suggested it be adopted as a model. But, after all, long before him, the basis of political balance and moderation, and their virtues, had been explored by Aristotle, that great thinker of antiquity whose ideas on the subject were still viable.

Aristotle's "classification of governments," writes Mosca, "into monarchies, aristocracies, and democracies (a classification that might now be judged superficial and incomplete) was certainly the very best that the human mind could contrive in his day."[6] It was an "extraordinary intellectual feat."

The genius of Aristotle, in Mosca's view, was to anticipate what modern scholarship has increasingly established as fact—namely, "that democratic, monarchical, and aristocratic principles function side by side in every political organism" (p. 52). The philosopher had recognized that good government is "mixed" government—that is, one in which the monarchy, the landed aristocracy, and the monied classes were properly balanced. In Mosca's terms, there "were so many political forces, the interplay of which, so long as any one of them did not prevail to the exclusion of others, was such as to provide a type of political organization in which due process of law was, in ordinary times, relatively secure" (p. 137).

Aristotle had maintained, moreover, that the stability and efficacy of a political organization depend on the existence of intermediate strata sufficiently large, prosperous, and independent to mediate between the extremes at the top and the bottom. To assure that, and thus the proper functioning of the Greek city-state, moderate property ownership was essential. Aristotle had thus intuited a principle which held true not only in his own time but in Mosca's as well. For Mosca had observed that wherever and whenever the middle strata have declined economically, and thus politically, "the modern representative system has yielded its worst results" (p. 391).

What Mosca liked particularly about Aristotle's system was that in it "not even the working classes, let alone slaves and metics, would be admitted to public office" (p. 427). Furthermore, he had already perceived clearly in his time what certainly could not be doubted in the twentieth century: that it is human selfishness, that basic psychological trait, which makes private property inevitable. That is something which extreme democrats and collectivists deny, asserting instead the precise opposite: Man is not inherently selfish; it is the institution of private property which has engendered selfish conduct in him.

One must follow Aristotle and adapt his teachings to present conditions: Make whatever economic concessions to the lower and more populous classes that are absolutely necessary without, however, "impairing the inviolability of private property too seriously and without laying unbearable burdens upon large and moderate fortunes. Among these concessions one might mention shorter working hours, insurance against old age, illness, unemployment and accidents, and restrictions on labor by women and children" (p. 472). Concessions may be made but they must not be carried "too far." They must be sufficient to assure political stability; toward that end it has become evident that "improved economic conditions have on the whole made the laboring classes less prone to resort to desperate and violent acts" (p. 472).

Mosca was thus reviving the "old doctrine of the golden mean" first found in Aristotle and later elaborated by others, notably Montesquieu. Although the latter had replaced Aristotle's classification with his own—despotic, monarchical, and republican governments—he retained the theory of balance. Looking to England, he advocated a modified monarchy in which the executive, legislative, and judicial powers were separate, independent, and reciprocally checked and balanced. Those principles could be found in their classic form in the English constitution whose advantages he described enthusiastically. Montesquieu had thus placed less emphasis than Aristotle on the role of social strata and forces and more on political, constitutional safeguards. Mosca therefore criticized Montesquieu and especially his followers who stressed the formal or legalistic aspect of the problem "rather than [its] substantial or social aspect. They have often forgotten that if one political institution is to be an effective curb upon the activity of another it must represent a political force—it must, that is, be the organized expression of a social influence and a social authority that has some standing in the community, as against the forces that are expressed in the political institution that is to be controlled" (p. 138).

It is the "social forces" and the relationship among them that are of primary importance in maintaining a social equilibrium, but the formal and legal political devices, though only secondary, are nonetheless essential. Montesquieu's theory was perhaps incomplete but not "mistaken in any substantial respect." "To make his doctrine complete," writes Mosca, "one need add that a controlling and limiting political institution can be effective only when it represents a section of the political class that is different from the section represented by the institution to be limited and controlled" (p. 475). Building in that way on the work of two great predecessors, Mosca develops the view that a ruling class is inevitable and the most one can hope for is a system of properly balanced social forces. Such balances have yielded the best political systems characterized by what he calls "juridical defence." The extension of juridical defence is the real meaning of progress.

JURIDICAL DEFENCE

The level of moral conscience of a people, as expressed in public opinion, religion, and law, is an indication of how far it has advanced from, say, barbarism to the various stages of civilization. In common with other nineteenth-century thinkers, Mosca accepted the evolutionary hypothesis—human history is an account of man's development from lower to higher cultural stages. A study of history shows that morality, justice, social order, and the like cannot be assured without instituting definite mechanisms to discipline the individuals and groups of society and to regulate the relations among them. The extent to which those mechanisms to assure respect for law have been developed determines the level of *juridical defence* and therefore the level of civilization a given society has achieved.

Men have instincts which are refractory to social order and discipline, and the control of those instincts cannot be entrusted to morality and religion alone. Adequate control requires a whole legislative system. The more a society succeeds in developing such effective systems, the better it is. In opposition to Rousseau (and Marx), then, who believed "that man is good by nature but that society makes him wicked and perverse," Mosca believed "that social organization provides for the reciprocal restraints of human individuals by one another and so makes them better, not by destroying their wicked instincts, but by accustoming them to controlling their wicked instincts" (p. 172).

That religion alone is insufficient for the control of those instincts is proved by the fact that "if we place side by side two peoples of the same degree of barbarism, one of which has embraced Christianity and the other not, it will be found that in practice their behaviors are very much the same, or at least there is no appreciable difference between them" (p. 218). Religious and moral sentiments are in themselves inadequate to afford the weak the protection they need. One sees, for example, that in "very religious countries, where the lower classes are completely at the mercy of the higher, it is no unusual thing to see masters beating their servants or other subordinates" (p. 129). The conclusion is inescapable, therefore, that institutionalized juridical and legal means of defence are required if a society is to achieve some semblance of justice. The class structure of society and the consequent social inequalities and injustices will always be with us; such injustices can only be mitigated under an adequate political, legal, and juridical system. In Mosca's words,

> The political organization proper, the organization that establishes the character of the relations between the governing class and the governed and between the various levels and various sections of the ruling class, is the factor that contributes more than any other to determining the degree of perfection that juridical defense, or government by law, can attain in a given people. (p. 130)

Ultimately, such a system can prevail only where several "social forces" mutually balance one another and where no single one of them is omnipotent or almost so. The absence or presence of such a balance explains, respectively, the difference between the system under the Czars, for instance, and the system in "England, where every arrest of an individual has to be legalized in earnest and very promptly" (p. 132). For Mosca, as for Montesquieu, England was the model. There, juridical defence was more highly developed than elsewhere; classes and other social forces were reciprocally balanced, and government by law, civil liberties, and due process were firmly established principles. Moreover, the honesty and integrity of English governmental officials were beyond question. The more a political system departed from that model, the less just and moral it was.

Whatever the "political formula," whether it is divine right or popular sovereignty, "when no other organized social forces exist apart from those which represent the principle on which sovereignty over the nation is based, then there can be no resistance, no effective control, to restrain a natural tendency in those who stand at the head of the social order to abuse their powers." In the absence of resistance, the ruling class "undergoes a real moral degeneration, the degeneration that is common to all men whose acts are exempt from the restraint that the opinion and the conscience of their fellows ordinarily impose" (p. 134). The absence of resistance leads to despotism or to what one might today call totalitarianism.

Juridical defence depends on the ability of social forces to check and balance one another and on the separation of powers in the political system. Equally important is the separation of the ecclesiastical and temporal authorities and that the "political formula" should "have nothing sacred and immutable about it." If the rulers rule in the name of a formula which has a monopoly on truth and justice, then "it is almost impossible that its acts should be debated and moderated in practice" (p. 139).

But there are still additional conditions on which juridical defence depends: (1) the distribution of wealth in a society and (2) the organization of its military forces. From his discussion of the first point, it becomes clear that Mosca felt that the issues raised by the socialists could not be ignored. The distribution of wealth had much to do not only with the social stability he desired, but with justice as well. Here important differences between his approach and Pareto's emerge even clearer than before.

Whereas Pareto's elites seem to be floating above society, without roots in its class structure, Mosca gives explicit attention to the phenomenon of class. Political power is always rooted in definite "social forces," and the economic is among the most important of such forces. Although he does not arrange them in any permanent hierarchy of importance, since that would vary according to time and place, he does regard the economic, political, legal, and military as the major social forces. In those terms, he generalized Marx's theory, much as did Weber, and argued that the control of the means of production, of political administration, of violence, and so on are all important in determining the structure of a society and its processes of change. Mosca also seems to have a greater concern with the issue of justice than Pareto, whose sociology often reads like a handbook for rulers. In the following passage, Mosca's treatment of the issue was not unlike that of the socialists in general and of the Marxists in particular:

> Laws and institutions that guarantee justice and protect the rights of the weak cannot possibly be effective when wealth is so distributed that we get, on the one hand, a small number of persons possessing land and mobile capital and, on the other, a multitude of proletarians who have no resource but the labor of their hands and owe it to the rich if they do not die of hunger from one day to the next. In that state of affairs to proclaim universal suffrage, or the rights of man, or the maxim that all are equal before the law, is merely ironical; and just as ironical is it to say that every man carries a marshal's baton in his knapsack, or that he is free some day to become a capitalist himself. (p. 143)

Clearly, then, *real* juridical defence and just relationships require more than formal, legal mechanisms; to the degree that liberal democracy ignores that fact, it connives in the perpetuation of sham liberalism and injustice. On the other hand, public ownership of the means of production is also no solution, for it may result in something worse than the present system. Raising an objection to socialism not unlike Weber's, Mosca writes: "Insofar as the state absorbs and distributes a larger and larger portion of the public wealth, the leaders of the ruling class come to possess greater and greater facilities for influencing and commanding their subordinates, and more and more easily evade control by anybody" (p. 143). Neither socialism nor sham liberalism is the answer; the only real solution is to follow the leads of Aristotle and to work out a system based on the proper balance of liberal-democratic and aristocratic principles.

That means, first of all, that the distribution of wealth should be such as to eliminate the great extremes resulting in haves and have-nots. The good polity, or what Mosca calls "a relatively perfect political organization," is one that "contains a large class of people whose economic position is virtually independent of those who hold supreme power." At least some of the members of that class must

> have sufficient means to be able to devote a portion of their time to perfecting their culture and acquiring that interest in the public weal—that aristocratic spirit, we are almost tempted to say—which alone can induce people to serve their country with no other satisfactions than those that come from individual pride and self-respect. In all countries that ever have been, or now are, in the lead as regards juridical defense—or liberty, as it is sometimes called—such a class has been prominent. (p. 144)

Thus a large middle class and an aristocratic spirit are among the essential preconditions of the good society; when they are lacking, "parliamentary government bears its worst fruits, as would any other political system" (p. 144).

There are social forces that militate against the establishment of a juridical equilibrium, chief among them being nationalism, the Church, large monied interests, and finally, social democracy. Any political system organized primarily on the basis of any single one of those forces, and its corresponding principles, makes it "difficult for all social forces to participate in public life, and more difficult still for any one force to counterbalance another. That is as true when power is in the hands of elected officials who are said to be chosen by the people as it is when power is entrusted exclusively to employees who are assumed to be appointed by a prince" (p. 147). For Mosca, then, government in the name of the "people" may become as autocratic as any other.

UNIVERSAL SUFFRAGE

"Popular sovereignty" as a result of universal suffrage is a myth—a very dangerous myth, moreover, because through it the people are led to believe that they rule and that the elected officials are mere servants. In reality, however, the officials are just as much masters under that system as they are in all others. That, in essence, is Mosca's view of representative democracy; of course, it did not originate with him. The entire thesis was anticipated almost verbatim by Marx and Engels, as Mosca knew very well. On the twentieth anniversary of the Paris Commune, Engels wrote,

> Society had created its own organs to look after its common interests, originally through simple division of labor. But these organs, at whose head was the state power, had in the course of time, in pursuance of their own special interests, transformed themselves from the servants of society into the masters of society. This can be seen, for example, not only in the hereditary monarchy, but equally so in the democratic republic. Nowhere do "politicians" form a more separate and powerful section of the nation than precisely in North America.[7]

But for Engels the process by which servants are transformed into masters was inevitable only under certain social conditions. The point of the Marxian analysis was to specify what those conditions were and, by abolishing them, to create new conditions of freedom. In Mosca's hands, however, Marx's *historically specific* thesis becomes a universal law: The transformation of servants into masters is inevitable in all systems, past, present, and future. Moreover, the so-called "servants" of the people under the representative system were never servants to begin with.

In actuality, Mosca asserts the "representative" "has himself elected"; if that sounds "too inflexible and too harsh to fit some cases, we might qualify it by saying that *his friends have him elected*."[8] Elections do not change the fact that "those who have the will and, especially, the moral, intellectual, and material means to force their will upon others take the lead over the others and command them" (p. 154). It is unavoidable in all social organizations that a minority will gain control of those *means* and thus over the lives and fate of the majority of men. Elections give the people no real freedom of choice "and the only ones who have any chance of succeeding are those whose candidates are championed by groups, by committees, by *organized minorities*" (p. 154). What are the criteria by which such minorities choose and support certain candidates? Mosca's reply, not unlike one Marx and Engels would have given, is that "as a rule they are based on considerations of property and taxation, on common material interests, on ties of family, class, religion, sect, or political party" (p. 155).

But would Mosca go so far as to deny any and all influence on the part of the people? No! As was indicated in a previous comparison with Pareto's work, Mosca allows for some measure of influence on their part. The representative system, writes Mosca, "results in the participation of a certain number of social values in the guidance of the state, in the fact that many political forces which in an absolute state, a state ruled by a bureaucracy alone, would remain inert and without influence upon government become organized and so exert an influence on government" (p. 155). After all, the candidates and other representatives of the ruling minorities cannot altogether ignore the various organized publics nor even the unorganized voters. They must win over their goodwill. The "sentiments and passions of the 'common herd' come to have their influence on the mental attitudes of the representatives themselves, and echoes of a widely disseminated opinion, or of any serious discontent, easily come to be heard in the highest spheres of government" (p. 155).

Even the most despotic of regimes cannot ignore the sentiments of the masses or offend them with impunity. The representative system, however, allows for greater sensitivity to their discontent, since each incumbent knows that the grumblings and dissatisfaction of all the people could easily lead to his ouster and to the victory of another organized minority.

In Mosca's various discussions, the "people" is occasionally portrayed as a "common herd" whose behaviour is governed by "sentiments" and "passions"—by irrational forces. There is some resemblance here between his conception and Pareto's, but Mosca remains, by and large, more consistently sociological. If the people generally have little or no rational understanding of their existential conditions and interests, it is because they are "poor and ignorant." They are uneducated, culturally impoverished, unorganized, and powerless. Normally they have no means of control over the powerful. "In these circumstances," Mosca writes, "of the various organized minorities that are disputing the field, that one infallibly wins which spends more money or lies most persuasively" (p. 156). The recurring emphasis on social conditions leaves the door open to the *possibility* of changing them—a point to which we shall later return.

Disposition over social forces is what gives the various organized minorities their political significance. One of them will always win out, become the *political class*, and fulfill the political function. The point, then, is not to dream of a day when classes and ruling classes will be no more, but to devise, under the given circumstances, the best political system possible. Returning once more to Aristotle, Montesquieu, and the English political system, Mosca writes that such a system "enables all the elements that have a political significance in a given society to be best utilized and specialized, best subjected to reciprocal control and to the principle of individual responsibility for the things that are done in the respective domains" (p. 159). In England, though it is true that officials are elected or appointed, it is nonetheless true that it is the "prominent people" who fulfill the main political functions, and without pay. Such persons have that aristocratic spirit expressed so well in the French saying, *noblesse oblige*, which is so essential for the good polity.

PARLIAMENTARISM

In Mosca's discussion of parliaments, one sees some similarities to Pareto's treatment of representative government, but the similarities are superficial, because despite Mosca's criticisms, he regards parliamentary institutions as an essential aspect of liberal government—an opinion Pareto, judging from his later writings, did not share. It is true, Mosca acknowledges, that particularly the elective, lower houses of parliaments are often characterized by "prattlings," "long-winded speeches," and "futile bickerings." It is also true, as the socialists and anarchists allege, that it is not the majority's interests, opinions, and aspirations that are there represented, "but the interests of the wealthy ruling classes" (p. 255). Finally, there is no denying the excessive interference on the part of individual members in the workings of the administration generally and in the distribution of wealth through taxation and other devices. These main defects of parliament as an institution had become so conspicuous by Mosca's time that they came to be designated by the pejorative term "parliamentarism."

Yet, those defects are as nothing in their evil consequence compared with the situation that would result from the abolition of parliament and other representative institutions. Under prevailing conditions, Mosca insists, "the suppression of representative assemblies would inevitably be followed by a type of regime that is commonly called 'absolute.'" Suppression would result in a totalitarian system in which all social forces and values were subordinated to the ruling group and its bureaucracy. A disgust with "parliamentarism" and a fear of the revolutionary fervour of social democracy could lead, Mosca prophetically observes, to an "absolutely bureaucratic" order. "What we cannot admit is that such a step would be a wise one. We need give no long demonstration of that thesis in view of all that we have been saying as to the dangers and drawbacks involved in giving absolute predominance to a single political force that is not subject to any limitation or discussion whatever" (p. 256).

Thus Mosca is unequivocally opposed to the weakening of the representative system. The repeatedly pronounced emphasis he places on the vital importance of liberal institutions is altogether absent from Pareto's later works. The collapse of those institutions, Mosca maintains, would lead to "moral ruin," to the violations of "juridical defense, of justice, of everything that we commonly call 'liberty'; and those violations would be far more pernicious than any that can be laid to the charge of even the most dishonest of parliamentary governments, let alone of representative governments" (p. 257).

Mosca is thus directing his argument in two opposing directions. Against the more zealous opponents of democracy and socialism he is arguing that the destruction of representative and liberal government would result in something far worse. And to the socialists, Marxian and others, he is saying that they ought to abandon their utopian dogmas about the abolition of classes—including the ruling class. The best system (and best, too, because capable of realization) is not the classless society but the one advocated by Aristotle, Montesquieu, and himself—namely a system permitting the various organized social forces to moderate and balance one another. The socialists would resign themselves to that if they were to realize that even under the most equalitarian of systems a ruling class would inevitably arise, since the people still have to choose their representatives "from among candidates who would be put forward by groups, or committees, and these groups would be made up of persons who by taste and by interest would be actively devoted to political life" (p. 259).

The primary evil of the parliamentary form of government is that more often than not it is the members of the lower, elected chamber who control the bureaucracy; it is precisely those men who have only one eye on their professional responsibilities, the other being on the electorate. That makes for a situation in which their desire to govern well is "effectively thwarted by their no less natural desire to serve their own personal interests, and the sense of professional duty in ministers and representatives is always balanced by all sorts of ambitions and vanities, justified and unjustified" (p. 259). What Mosca is suggesting here, once more, is that the "evil" results from the inadequate assertion of the aristocratic tendency, so necessary for sound and healthy government. If ministers were sufficiently independent of the electorate, they would be less subject to pressures of personal ambitions and party interests and hence more concerned with their professional responsibilities. What is required is that the "governors" be drawn from that stratum of citizens who are both wealthy enough to be incorruptible and educated enough to govern wisely.

Mosca was calling for the development of a public-spirited, non-bureaucratic civil service, "a special class of volunteer unsalaried officials," as it once prevailed in England. Eventually, the "democratic current" swept away that institution, revealing pointedly, again, the main dangers and evils of the democratic philosophy: It "recognizes no political act, no political prerogative, as legitimate unless it emanates directly or indirectly from popular suffrage" (p. 270). The democratic principle has successfully suppressed the aristocratic, and with very undesirable results. Historically, it was a mistake to grant universal suffrage, but now it is too late to "go back on it without committing a second mistake which might have unforeseeable consequences of a very serious nature" (p. 492). One must therefore make the best of the existing situation by strengthening the aristocratic principle. That, together with a large middle class, a system of balanced forces, and institutions of juridical defence, makes for the best system possible. But the system requires still another condition which, strange as it may sound, is a standing army.

STANDING ARMIES

History teaches, writes Mosca, "that the class that bears the lance or holds the musket regularly forces its rule upon the class that handles the spade or pushes the shuttle" (p. 228). This was also true of premodern Europe, where the class that controlled the means of violence acquired economic and political power as well. What Mosca found altogether intriguing, then, was the contemporary situation where the military was successfully subordinated to the civil authority. That became possible "only through an intense and widespread development of the sentiments on which juridical defense is based, and especially through an exceptionally favorable sequence of historical circumstances" (p. 229). Ironic as it may appear, Mosca asserts, the control by the civil authority of the military and other groups with access to means of violence was facilitated by the institution called the *standing army*.

Mosca's reasoning rests on the assumption that in every society there are those who have a greater inclination than others toward adventure, belligerence, aggression, and violence. They make up the bands of armed men who in some societies, the "loosely organized," rule and terrorize every village and town. In other societies, the "better organized," they become a ruling class, "lords and masters of all wealth and political influence," as they did in medieval Europe. In bureaucratic states, finally, the standing army, being unrestrained and unchecked, has "no difficulty in dictating to the rest of society" (p. 228). In none of these types of society is the military controlled by a civil authority. Only in those societies, therefore, in which (1) *the standing army is combined with* (2) *institutions of social balance and juridical defence* does one find the hegemony of the civil authority. One without the other would not have produced that result.

Before the standing army was institutionalized, it was the adventurers and criminals who were recruited as needed. But by the beginning of the eighteenth century, the "necessity of keeping many men in arms and the difficulty of paying wages large enough to attract volunteers brought on conscription in most countries on the European continent. That system meant that common soldiers no longer came from the adventurous and criminal classes but were recruited from among peasants and workingmen" (p. 232). It meant, too, that now the class structure of the society as a whole became the basis of the military structure—that is, that the authority of the upper classes as well as the submissiveness of the lower were transferred to the military sphere. Officers were recruited almost exclusively from the upper strata and common soldiers from the lower. The men at the top of the military hierarchy retained "close ties with the minority which by birth, culture, and wealth [stood] at the peak of the social pyramid" (p. 233). That, together with the deeply rooted institutions of juridical defence, explains, according to Mosca, why in England and the United States, for example, the army did not become "a tool for coups d'état." In those countries and others with similar conditions, "the standing army has so far stripped the class of persons who have natural tastes and capacities for violence of their monopoly of the military function." It follows, Mosca reasons, that enduring peace would bring with it the dissolution of the standing army and, hence, a regression to the state in which the bold and violent oppressed "the weak and peaceful." Therefore, he concludes, "war itself—in its present forms the root of so many evils, the parent of so many barbarities—becomes necessary every now and again if what is best in the functioning of our Western societies today is not to decline and retrogress to lower types of juridical defense" (p. 243). Ultimately, Mosca was led to that pessimistic conclusion, which he himself called "grave and terrible," by his view of human nature as essentially *base, selfish,* and *brutish.*

We see, then, that although Mosca argued the necessity of a ruling class, he nevertheless qualified his thesis rather severely. He recognized that a good society requires (1) the elimination of extreme inequalities and (2) the creation of a balance of social forces in which none could aggrandize to itself sufficient power to tyrannize over all the rest. It is precisely such qualifications, however, that tend to undermine Mosca's central thesis. What really emerges from his brilliant analysis is not the necessity of a ruling elite or even the necessity of a plurality of competing elites. Rather, it is that a good polity presupposes the existence of many different social groups (not elites) capable of checking and limiting one another's powers and especially the power of the state. Mosca understood very well that democracy requires the diffusion of power in a wide range of social and political organizations which can set limits on the powers of the leadership. A society that fails to institutionalize a division of powers along those lines will unavoidably become totalitarian.

Thus interpreted, Mosca's theory appears in a new light, and his work may be read quite differently from the way it has been in the past. For his analysis, far from proving the necessity of a ruling class, effectively shows how the traditional gap between rulers and ruled can be significantly reduced.

NOTES

1.   Gaetano Mosca, *The Ruling Class*, trans. (from *Elementi di Scienza Politica*) Hannah D. Kahn, ed. and rev. Arthur Livingstone (New York: McGraw-Hill Book Company, 1965), p. 170. (Hereafter all page references to this work will be indicated in parentheses immediately following the quoted passage.)

2. For an account of the dispute over who had priority in this regard, see James H. Meisel's *The Myth of the Ruling Class* (Ann Arbor: University of Michigan Press, 1962), pp. 170–89.

3. Karl Marx and Frederick Engels, *Selected Works* (Moscow: Foreign Languages Publishing House, 1950), Vol. I, p. 438.

4. Quoted in Meisel, *Myth of the Ruling Class,* p. 254.

5. Ibid., p 255.

6. Mosca, *Ruling Class*, p. 43. (Hereafter all page references to this work will be indicated in parentheses immediately following the quoted passage.)

7. Marx and Engels, *Selected Works*, p. 438.

8. Mosca, *Ruling Class*, p. 154. (Hereafter all page references to this work will be indicated in parentheses immediately following the quoted passage.)

CHAPTER 11

Robert Michels (1876–1936)

In common with Weber, Pareto, and Mosca, Robert Michels devoted a large part of his intellectual labours to the challenge of Marxism. It was primarily the ideas of those antecedent thinkers that Michels employed and elaborated in the development of his own critique. Yet, despite certain criticisms of Marx's social thought, he remained something of a reconstructed Marxist himself; rejecting what he regarded as the utopian aspects of the Marxian vision, he retained elements of the Marxian method of analysis.

In 1927, sixteen years after *Political Parties* first appeared, Michels delivered at the University of Rome a series of lectures on political sociology. In those lectures, published under the title *Corso di Sociologia Politica*, he concerned himself with what he considered to be a major theoretical issue: the relative validity of Marx's conception of society and history. Noting a fact Marx himself was the first to acknowledge—that aspects of his economic interpretation of history had been anticipated by many thinkers before him—Michels writes: "The Arab philosopher, Ibn Kaldun, who lived in the fourteenth century, may have been the earliest scientific exponent of the economic conception of history."[1]

As for classes and class conflicts, those phenomena were also observed before Marx placed them at the centre of his investigation. Michels cites Benjamin Disraeli, who had portrayed in his novel entitled *Sybil* the great cultural chasm that lay between the upper and lower classes. So great was the chasm, in fact, that English society could be viewed as *two nations*. In his novel, Disraeli "repeated the idea that had caused him in his parliamentary discourse of 1840 to declare that the recognition of the proletariat's rights to its political emancipation and the betterment of its economic conditions was the only way to close the abyss that already separated the 'two nations.'"[2] Other thinkers—English, French, and German—had also anticipated elements of Marx's general conception, but that is not to deny, Michels emphasizes, the originality of the Marxian synthesis. It "is an indisputable merit of Marx and Engels to have been the first not only to erect as a system the particular part that the productive forces play in the historic process, but also to have assigned to them, with the creation of a new philosophy, their place in science."[3]

To underscore this point, Michels shows that even Pareto, a major opponent of Marxism, appreciated the scientific aspects of Marx's system. "Historical materialism," wrote Pareto in his *Trattato di Sociologia Generale*,

> has been a notable scientific advance because it has helped to clarify the contingent character of certain phenomena, such as moral phenomena and religious phenomena, to which was given, and is given yet by many, an absolute character. Besides it certainly has an element of truth in insisting on the interdependence of economic phenomena and other social phenomena; the error stands in having changed this interdependence to a relationship of cause and effect.[4]

Pareto also acknowledged the value of Marx's sociological principles which "discredited the unreal notion of those who want to explain facts with the ideas that men hold."[5]

This general attitude towards Marxism, shared in varying degrees by Pareto, Weber, and Benedetto Croce, was Michel's as well. There are invaluable principles and insights to be found in Marx's "materialist conception" which can be incorporated into a scientific sociology minus the "subversive flavor" of Marxism. Michels thus agreed with Croce who observed that

> historical materialism, deprived of the elements of finality or inevitable utopia which Marxist socialism wanted to confer upon it, cannot give any support to socialism or to any other practical way of life. The economic conception of history is a doctrine that explains the reasons, the genesis, but does not help to illuminate socialism, which is a wishful vision of the future. It is silent on the outcome of the struggle it has traced through history.[6]

In the remainder of his lectures, Michels seeks "to mark the boundaries within which historical materialism conforms to historical truth, and above all to examine its place in political science."[7]

Following Weber, Pareto, and Mosca, Michels reconstructs Marx's method and calls for a more pluralistic approach: "The complete view of things results from the action of several forces of dissimilar nature."[8] He fully acknowledges the fundamental importance of economic developments for social change; in that Marx was right. But what Marx had overlooked was that there were other forces or tendencies at work sufficiently strong to preclude the realization of democracy and socialism as he had envisioned it. For Michels, these tendencies were "dependent: (1) upon the nature of the human individual, (2) upon the nature of the political struggle; and (3) upon the nature of organization."[9] What Marx had not seen, according to Michels, was that as a result of those tendencies, "democracy leads to oligarchy, and necessarily contains an oligarchical nucleus." That is the central thesis which Michels develops in his classic study, *Political Parties.*

The most effective documentation of this thesis could be made, Michels reasons, by describing the structure and tendencies of the various social-democratic parties in Europe. The aristocratic and oligarchical character of the various *conservative* parties was indisputable. But that, after all, was to be expected and proved nothing since they had no commitment to democracy and based themselves quite frankly on conservative principles. If, on the other hand, oligarchical phenomena could be found "in the very bosom of the revolutionary parties," which professed to represent or to be working toward the negation of those phenomena, then that would constitute "conclusive proof of the existence of immanent oligarchical tendencies in every kind of human organization which strives for the attainment of definite ends" (p. 11).

Ultimately, the "immanence" of those tendencies rests, for Michels, on certain innate human tendencies which urge man to transmit his material possessions to his legitimate heir or other kin. The same applies to "political power [which] comes also to be considered as an object of private hereditary ownership" (p. 12). Those tendencies prevail due to "the peculiar and inherent instincts of mankind," but they are also "vigorously nourished by the economic order based upon private property in the means of production" (p. 12). Herein lies the theoretical dilemma Michels never managed to resolve: Is the quest for power and material goods to be regarded as a function of the socioeconomic order in which men live, or is it a result of an immutable human psychology? By his own admission, an ideal democracy is impossible under "the existing economic and social conditions" (p. 12). But if he followed that logic to the end, there could be no "iron law," since oligarchic and other social tendencies are contingent upon the existing social system. Michels therefore places great emphasis on so-called innate psychological laws.

Like Pareto and Mosca before him, Michels rested his general argument as to the inevitability of oligarchy on a conception of human nature precisely the opposite of that held by Marx. It is man's *inherent* nature to crave power and, once having attained it, to seek to perpetuate it. On the basis of that psychological assumption, Michels generates his theory that democracy requires organization which in turn leads necessarily to oligarchy. His "iron law of oligarchy" is, he says, "like every other socio-logical law, beyond good and evil" (p. 12); this so-called "sociological law" rests on what he took to be a constant, his conception of human nature.

In Marx's view, social conditions typically elicit a subjective response from men; how they define those conditions, whether good or evil, can make a difference for the perpetuation or abolition of those conditions. There are, to be sure, certain periods when social conditions appear to impose insuperable limits on the actions of men, but there are other periods when opportunities for change emerge. Given the consciousness of such opportunities on the part of a sufficient number of individuals who are willing to act in concert, the opportunities may be seized. Michels himself acknowledged that the "democratic currents of history," though they "break ever on the same shoal" are "ever renewed." It would seem undeniable that at least part of the reason for the renewal is that the oligarchies are felt by the people to be oppressive and are thus overthrown. What Michels insists upon, however, is that the democratic currents will inevitably break again and again upon the same shoal. That is his "universally applicable iron law."

There can be no doubt that the facts *qua* facts that Michels described were true. His study is a sound sociological description of what is—which is not to say that the pessimistic conclusions often drawn from his analysis are valid. Moreover, a brief review of that analysis will show that he himself had his more optimistic moments and that in the end he allowed for the interpretation that his "iron law" must not be regarded as anything more than a metaphor—a metaphor that he employed to dramatize certain conspicuous tendencies of men in organizations under specific sociohistorical circumstances.

The people are incapable of governing themselves! Michel's support of that assertion is based first on the theory of crowds and crowd psychology: "It is easier to dominate a large crowd than a small audience" (p. 25). A crowd is easily given to suggestion and irrational outbursts; both serious discussion and thoughtful deliberation are impossible in its midst. Second, and more important, however, is the technical and practical problem involving the huge multitudes in democratic decision making. If democracy is taken to mean that the multitude adopts resolutions and makes decisions *directly*, then democracy is indeed impossible. Rousseau understood that and so did most of the other, later democratic theorists. Michels quotes Louis Blanc who in his polemic against Proudhon asked, "whether it is possible for thirty-four millions of human beings (the population of France at the time) to carry on their affairs without … the intermediation of representatives" (p. 25). What is true of nation-states is also true of modern organizations. The staggering demographic proportions of the socialist parties Michels studied made both direct discussion and direct action impossible. The party in Berlin alone, for example, had a membership "of more than ninety thousand."

The enormity of the populations in modern party organizations renders it technically impossible for all members to govern or administer directly their common affairs. Unavoidably, then, once a collectivity is formed for any specific purpose and attains a certain demographic size, a division of labour becomes necessary. As the organization grows larger, its growth is accompanied by an increasing complexity. New functions emerge and are distributed, and along with the differentiation of functions comes the delegation of authority. Men are chosen to "represent the mass and carry out its will."

In the early stages of this development—speaking more particularly about organizations based upon democratic and socialistic ideals—the various functions stand in a *coordinate* relationship to one another: No hierarchy is implied in the various functions and positions. They are all equal in the sense that differential amounts of wealth and power are not associated with the various positions. The social honour accorded the "chief" does not enable him to transform that honour into special perquisites and privileges. In Michels's words: "Originally the chief is merely the servant of the mass" (p. 27).

At first the democratic and equalitarian character of the organization is assured by the strong commitment on the part of its members to the principles of democracy and equality. Functions are rotated, delegates and representatives are totally subject to the will of the collectivity, and in general a high degree of camaraderie prevails. That was true of the early English labour movement, for example. But that state of affairs is possible only when the organization in question is relatively small in scale. The growing scale of the organization makes this form of democracy increasingly inapplicable. In addition to size, however, there is still another important variable involved, which is at least in part a function of the organization's growth. Within the division of labour, certain tasks and duties become more complicated and require ability, training, and "a considerable amount of objective knowledge" (p. 28). Differentiation of functions now implies specialization and specialization, in turn, expertise. Party schools are established to train functionaries and officials, and what results is "a class of professional politicians, of approved and registered experts in political life." Michels notes that "Ferdinand Tönnies advocates that the party should institute regular examinations for the nomination of socialist parliamentary candidates, and for the appointment of party secretaries" (p. 29).

Expertise becomes a "foot in the door." The experts increasingly resemble not servants but masters, and the organization becomes increasingly hierarchical and bureaucratic. Acquiring to an ever greater degree the attributes of leaders, the experts withdraw from the masses and concentrate in their hands a variety of prerogatives. In Michels's words,

> It is undeniable that all these educational institutions for the officials of the party and of the labor organizations tend, above all, toward the artificial creation of an élite of the working class, of a caste of cadets composed of persons who aspire to the command of the proletarian rank and file. Without wishing it, there is thus effected a continuous enlargement of the guild which divides the leaders from the masses. (p. 31)

Thus results the familiar process by which men originally appointed to serve the interests of the collectivity soon develop interests of their own often opposed to that collectivity. What began as a democratic and equalitarian situation culminated in leaders and led, in rulers and ruled. It is organization *qua* organization which is the efficient cause of that transformation. Democracy implies organization, and organization, in turn, "implies the tendency to oligarchy.… As a result of organization, every party or professional union becomes divided into a minority of directors and a majority of directed" (p. 32). Michels expresses that general proposition in a variety of ways: "With the advance of organization, democracy tends to decline. Democratic evolution has a parabolic course.… It may be enunciated as a general rule that the increase in the power of the leaders is directly proportional with the extension of the organization" (p. 33).

According to Michels, then, every organization, however democratic in its inception, given a growth in its membership and complexity, increasingly exhibits oligarchic and bureaucratic tendencies. What began as a technical and practical necessity is transformed into a virtue: Democracy and equality within the party are now no longer regarded as essential and a new ideology emerges to justify the changes wrought by the "inexorable" processes of organization.

> Not even the most radical wing of the various socialist parties [writes Michels] raises any objection to this retrogressive evolution, the contention being that democracy is only a form of organization and that where it ceases to be possible to harmonize democracy with organization, it is better to abandon the former than the latter. Organization, since it is only the means of attaining the ends of socialism, is considered to comprise within itself the revolutionary content of the party, and this essential content must never be sacrificed for the sake of form. (p. 35)

In that way, and by insisting in addition "that true democracy cannot be installed until the fight is over," the members are persuaded that it is the highest revolutionary virtue to be disciplined and to follow faithfully a few individuals at the top. The organization as an instrument of class struggle now adopts rather easily the vocabulary of military science: "There is hardly one expression of military tactics and strategy, hardly even a phrase of barrack slang, which does not recur again and again in the leading articles of the socialist press" (p. 43).

"Experience" and "expertise" are among the main words the leaders use to legitimize their positions of power. The impression is created among the rank and file that their leaders are indeed indispensable. Indispensability, whether apparent or real, becomes an efficient tool in the leader's hands. Whenever his decisions or judgment are challenged, he threatens to resign—which appears as a fine democratic gesture, but which in reality is intended to remind his followers of his indispensability and hence to force their submission to his will.

Generally, it is Michels's view that the masses have a need for leadership and are actually quite content to have others attend to their affairs. Of course, that serves to strengthen the aristocratic and bureaucratic character of the party or union.

The masses are apathetic. None of the reasons, however, which Michels adduces need lead to the conclusion that that must be their permanent attribute—what he later calls the "perennial incompetence of the masses." That they are indifferent is evident, Michels writes, from the "slackness of attendance at ordinary meetings." And, since the various political and ideological issues "are not merely beyond the understanding of the rank and file, but leave them altogether cold," they are incompetent. Some of the reasons for slackness of attendance, Michels himself notes, are really quite simple and prosaic: "When his work is finished, the proletarian can think only of rest and getting to bed in good time" (p. 52). There is, then, "an immense need for direction and guidance [which] is accompanied by a genuine cult for the leaders, who are regarded as heroes" (p. 53). Add to that the great differences in culture and education between the leaders and the rank and file (the former more often than not being of bourgeois origin, as we shall see), and one understands the submissiveness of the ordinary members.

Although such tendencies are "manifest in the political parties of all countries," Michels notes that Germany is a special case. His observations in this connection must be considered important, because his own earlier experiences and impressions were in the German movement—where the submission of the masses and adulation of the leaders were greater than elsewhere. Michels writes,

> The German people in especial exhibits to an extreme degree the need for someone to point out the way and to issue orders. This peculiarity, common to all classes not excepting the proletariat, furnishes a psychological soil upon which a powerful directive hegemony can flourish luxuriantly. There exist among the Germans all the preconditions necessary for such a development: a psychical predisposition to subordination, a profound

instinct for discipline, in a word, the whole still-persistent inheritance of the influence of the Prussian drill sergeant, with all its advantages and disadvantages; in addition, a trust in authority which verges on the complete absence of a critical faculty. (p. 53)

Michels notes further that Marx was quite aware of the "risks to the democratic spirit" of this national character and that "he thought it necessary to warn the German workers against entertaining too rigid a conception of organization." Marx insisted that in Germany, "where the workers are bureaucratically controlled from birth upward, and for this reason have a blind faith in constituted authority, it is above all necessary to teach them to walk by themselves" (p. 55).

As for the German leaders, on the other hand, "Engels," writes Michels, "regarded it as deplorable that [they] could not accustom themselves to the idea that the mere fact of being installed in office did not give them the right to be treated with more respect than any other comrade" (p. 222). The leaders of the German socialist party thought and acted in a manner reminiscent of the Sun King; each was inclined to think of himself, in Michels's phrase, "*Le Parti c'est moi.*"

Michels cites the remarkable stability of both the German and the Italian socialist parties. The latter, he says, "for the same reasons as in Germany, has exhibited a similar stability" (p. 93). It is interesting that those were the parties with which he had firsthand experience and the two main cases on which he based his generalizations.

The masses, then, are politically indifferent and incompetent (in need of guidance), and those factors together with the gratitude and veneration they show toward those "who speak and write in their behalf" strengthen the position of the leaders. Their need for a religion is evident from the idolatrous manner in which they venerate the party's secular books, symbols, and leaders; that "is not peculiar to backward countries or remote periods; it is an atavistic survival of primitive psychology" (p. 66). Moreover, they are easily hoodwinked and deceived, more inclined to follow mediocre men with a flair for showmanship than men of talent and cultivation. That explains why Eduard Bernstein and Paul Lafargue, for instance, remained relatively unknown to the rank and file of their respective parties: Both were men of outstanding intelligence and scientific sophistication, but they were also lacking in oratorical talent.

There are still other "peculiarities of the masses" that contribute to both their incompetence and indifference and to the superiority of the leaders. Those peculiarities are reflected in the age composition of the general membership of the socialist parties and unions. "The great majority of the membership ranges in age from 25 to 39 years." The young have other things to do with their leisure; "they are heedless, their thoughts run in erotic channels, they are always hoping that some miracle will deliver them from the need of passing their whole lives as simple wage earners, and for these reasons they are slow to join a trade union" (p. 78). The older men, on the other hand, who have become "weary and disillusioned, commonly resign their membership.… In other words, the leaders have to do with a mass of numbers to whom they are superior in respect of age and experience of life, whilst they have nothing to fear from the relentless criticism which is so peculiarly characteristic of men who have just attained to virility" (p. 78).

Many factors contribute to the widening distance between the masses and leaders. In many countries, party leaders are of a predominantly middle-class origin and therefore possess from the beginning a cultural or intellectual superiority. But even in those countries where there are few intellectuals in the leadership, as was the case in Germany in Michel's time, a similar *distance* develops between leaders of working-class origin and the general membership. That Michels explains in the following ways:

> Whilst their occupation and the needs of daily life render it impossible for the masses to attain to a profound knowledge of the social machinery, and above all of the working of the political machine, the leader of working-class origin is enabled, thanks to his new situation, to make himself intimately familiar with all the technical details of public life, and thus to increase his superiority over the rank and file. (pp. 81–82)

And, again,

> The questions which they [leaders of working-class origin] have to decide, and whose effective decision demands on their part a serious work of preparation, involve an increase in their own technical competence, and a consequent increase in the distance between themselves and their comrades of the rank and file. Thus the leaders, if they are not "cultured"

already, soon become so. But culture exercises a suggestive influence over the masses. (p. 83)

Finally,

> This special competence, this expert knowledge, which the leader acquires in matters inaccessible, or almost inaccessible, to the mass, gives him a security of tenure which conflicts with the essential principles of democracy. (p. 84)

Again and again we are told that "the incompetence of the masses is almost universal throughout the domains of political life, and this constitutes the most solid foundation of the power of the leaders" (p. 86). The expertise of the leaders also leads to oligarchy, since the incompetent masses submit to them and give them "an authority which is in the long run destructive of democracy" (p. 86). However, a careful reading of Michels's work shows that his analysis is "one-sided," as he himself admits in the end.

If he was asserting something more than the thesis that there will always be a need for some kind of leadership—in the sense that a symphony orchestra will always require a conductor—then he did not distinguish carefully the difference between leaders and oligarchs. As an objective scientific proposition, one could perhaps "demonstrate" the *technical* impossibility on the part of the masses of governing themselves *directly*. In that case, one would be demonstrating the need for leadership, not for oligarchy.

To pursue the example of the symphony orchestra, many orchestras have tried, but have failed, *to conduct themselves*. It is generally agreed among musicians that a conductor is a technical necessity for the functioning of a symphony orchestra. If that is the case, one can say that so-and-so is a good or bad conductor, depending on the aesthetic results achieved, but it makes no sense to say that the conductor is an autocrat because he or she has remained in "office" for a long time.

Insofar as there may be objective criteria of oligarchy, Michels does not define them precisely—that is, he does not indicate at what point the elected representatives cease to be mere leaders and become oligarchs. At times, Michels uses the term "oligarchy" simply to describe remarkable stability or longevity of leadership, for example, for more than thirty years. At other times, however, he uses the term to refer to the "aristocracy" of talent and expertise that inevitably emerges and separates itself from the mass. Specialization creates authority: "Just as the patient obeys the doctor," writes Michels, "because the doctor knows better than the patient, having made a special study of the human body in health and disease, so must the political patient submit to the guidance of his party leaders, who possess a political competence impossible of attainment by the rank and file" (p. 89).

But the analogy does not seem really appropriate for Michels's purposes. Was the purpose of his study merely to demonstrate that specialization leads to authority, in the sense conveyed by the just-quoted passage? Surely he was after something more than that. Otherwise why call it oligarchy? What he really wanted to demonstrate was the inevitability of the abuse of power and authority—to the extent of undermining democracy: That those who are placed in positions of authority to serve the interests of the collectivity soon develop interests of their own which are antagonistic to those of the collectivity. It would seem that whether or not that in fact occurs is the best criterion by which to determine whether those in authority have become oligarchs. Yet, that is not the way Michels proceeds: Too often he employs the concepts of leadership and oligarchy as if they were necessarily synonymous and interchangeable.

As compared with the leaders of other political parties, Michels acknowledges, the abuse of power was drastically reduced among the leaders of the social-democratic parties; party work was more often based on idealism and the leaders were enthusiastic volunteers. A few individuals carried on the party's work, for which they were "unpaid or almost wholly unpaid." In Germany, on the other hand, although many party functionaries were unpaid volunteers, certain positions, party journals, and newspapers, had "a paid editorial staff and paid contributors." But paying the leaders does not necessarily lessen either their idealism or their relative immunity to "temptations." Michels pays a high tribute to the socialist leaders: "It would … be quite wrong," he insists, "To suppose that socialist propagandists and socialist officials are paid on a scale which enables them with the hard-earned pence of the workers to lead the luxurious existence which, with an ignorance bordering on impudence, is often ascribed to them by the 'respectable' press and the loungers of the clubs." A leader's labours "demand an abundance of self-denial and sacrifice and are nervously exhausting; whilst the remuneration he receives is a modest one when compared with the gravity of his task." Finally, Michels notes, "Men of the ability and education of Karl Kautsky, Max Quarck, Adam Müller, and a hundred others, would have been able, had they chosen to devote themselves to some other service than that of the workers, to obtain a material reward much greater than that which they secure in their present positions" (p. 115).

Nevertheless, idealism alone, at a number of levels at least, does not suffice to sustain the party, and paying for services does bring with it some negative results. It impairs somewhat the initiative of members and their socialist values and at the same time contributes both to the growing bureaucratization of the party and to the centralization of power. Ironically, however, paying and not paying, or paying poorly, all tend to lead, Michels observes, to the same result—that is, they conduce to oligarchy. For example, "In France, where it is still the rule to pay the trade union leaders very small salaries, there is lacking a new generation of leaders ready to take the place of the old, and for this reason at the trade union congresses the same members continually appear as delegates" (p. 127). That results in a concentration of power that inevitably perverts the original aims of the party. The men at the top abuse their power by gaining control of the party press so as to diffuse their fame and popularize their names, and the parliamentary leaders often become "a closed corporation, cut off from the rest of the party."

The controls the masses have over the process are merely theoretical. In the constant struggle between the leaders and the masses, the former are destined always to win out. "It cannot be denied," Michels writes, "that the masses revolt from time to time, but their revolts are always suppressed" (p. 162).

The so-called masses never revolt spontaneously—that is, without leadership. The process of revolt presupposes that the masses are being led by certain leading elements of their own who, once having achieved power in the name of the people, transform themselves into a relatively closed caste apart from and opposed to the people. Moreover, in "normal," nonrevolutionary situations, the most "talented elements," the potential revolutionary leaders, are always subject to a variety of seductive influences; they are smitten by the ambition to enter the privileged positions of the labour movement. That is a particular manifestation of the general process of cooptation described by Pareto whom Michels quotes: "*Si les B [nouvelle élite] prennent peu à peu la place des A [ancienne élite] par une lente infiltration, et si le mouvement de circulation sociale n'est pas interrompu, les C [la masse] sont privés des chefs qui pourraient les pousser à la révolte*" (pp. 161–62 n.).

Thus it would appear unavoidable that "the rank and file become continually more impotent to provide new and intelligent forces capable of leading the opposition which may be latent among the masses" (p. 161). The *real* struggle is not between masses and leaders but between the existing leaders and the new, challenging, ascending ones. Even when appearances are to the contrary and the existing leaders seem to be guided by the good will and pleasures of the mass, that is not actually the case: "The submission of the old leaders is ostensibly an act of homage to the crowd, but in intention it is a means of prophylaxis against the peril by which they are threatened—the formation of a new élite" (p. 165). The struggle between the old and the new elites very rarely culminates "in the complete defeat of the former." Slightly modifying Pareto's doctrine, Michels states that "The result of the process is not so much a *circulation des élites* as a *réunion des élites,* an amalgam, that is to say, of the two elements" (p. 177).

For Michels, the benefits which accrue to the majority of the party members as a result of that process are "practically nil." His description, in a brilliant passage, of the impact of bureaucracy on socialist values probably is as valid today as it was in his time:

> As the party bureaucracy increases, two elements which constitute the essential pillars of every socialist conception undergo an inevitable weakening: an understanding of the wider and more ideal cultural aims of socialism, and an understanding of the international multiplicity of its manifestations. Mechanism becomes an end in itself. (p. 187)

Furthermore, *decentralization* in itself cannot prevent such a development from taking place. It does not lead to greater individual liberty nor does it enhance the power of the rank and file. More often than not, it is a mechanism by which the weaker leaders seek to escape the dominion of the stronger, but that, of course, does not prevent the weaker from establishing a centralized authority within their own domains. The party is "saved" from one gigantic oligarchy only to fall into the hands "of a number of smaller oligarchies, each of which is no less powerful within its own sphere. The dominance of oligarchy in party life remains unchallenged" (p. 201). And the causes of that, for Michels, are not only sociological—need for organization, mass apathy, and so on—but psychological, that is, due to the leaders' "natural greed for power" and "the general characteristics of human nature" (p. 205).

Earlier it was asserted that Michels, despite his criticism of Marxism, retained certain elements of the Marxian method of analysis. That is true, but he employed the reconstructed method to expose the apparent errors—primarily of omission—of the "master."

Classes, class conflict, and class consciousness are all essential categories in Michels's thinking. He agrees, for instance, that it is not oppressive conditions in themselves but the *recognition* of those conditions that has been "the prime factor of class struggles" (p. 236). Historically, it has been the bourgeoisie that has played a central role in generating proletarian class consciousness. The bourgeoisie, having to defend its existence on a number of fronts at once—against the aristocracy and against those sections of its own class whose interests are opposed to industrial development—and unable to carry on the struggle alone, is compelled to mobilize the proletariat and thus places in its hand a weapon (political consciousness and experience) which it can employ against the bourgeoisie itself. In addition, there have always been those bourgeois intellectuals who for a variety of reasons have detached themselves from their original class and have joined the ranks of the workers to give them direction. As a matter of fact, Michels regards it as a

> psychologico-historical law that any class which has been enervated and led to despair in itself through prolonged lack of education and through deprivation of political rights, cannot attain to the possibility of energetic action until it has received instruction concerning its ethical rights and politico-economical powers, not alone from members of its own class, but also from those who belong to what in vulgar parlance are termed a "higher" class. (p. 237)

What better example of that is needed than the founders of modern socialism themselves? They "were with a few exceptions men of science primarily, and in the second place only were they politicians in the strict sense of the term" (p. 238). Moreover, Michels continues, it "was only when science placed itself at the service of the working class that the proletarian movement became transformed into a socialist movement, and that instinctive, unconscious, and aimless rebelling was replaced by conscious aspiration, comparatively clear, and strictly directed towards a well-defined end" (p. 238). Finally, Michels concurs that "The proletariat is … perfectly logical in constituting itself into a class party, and in considering that the struggle against the bourgeoisie in all its gradations, viewed as a single class, is the only possible means of realizing a social order in which knowledge, health, and property shall not be, as they are today, the monopolies of a minority" (p. 247).

But Marx had not anticipated the extent to which the entry of the bourgeois intellectuals into the socialist movement, and their occupation of leadership positions, would bring about basic changes in that movement that "may be summed up in the comprehensive customary term of the *embour- geoisement* of working-class parties." Also, although Marx had been quite aware of strata within the working class, on balance he tended to underes- timate the conflicts that could arise among them; instead he viewed it as a much more unitary category than it turned out to be in practice. Ironically, moreover, the socialist movement itself, Michels argues, has created new petty-bourgeois strata. A variety of leadership and other functions are given over to workers—or more precisely to *former* workers—who now inevitably undergo a profound psychological transformation that creates as great a social distance between them and the rank and file as between the bourgeois and proletarian. In that way, "Certain groups of individuals, numerically insignificant but qualitatively of great importance, are withdrawn from the proletarian class and raised to bourgeois dignity" (p. 271). The socialist party and other organizations, in providing opportunities for social ascent to former manual labourers, generate the very same tendencies one sees in originally bourgeois leadership.[10]

None of the traditional democratic mechanisms, either within socialist parties and other working-class organizations or in large national political systems, has been effective in countering the oligarchic abuse of power. The *referendum*, for instance, has not only proved to be for the most part impractical due to the incompetence of the masses and the lack of time to submit every question to popular vote; it has also yielded *less*, not more, democracy—for example, the well-known phenomenon of plebiscitarian "democracy," in reality, a dictatorship. Michels notes that George Sand had regarded "the plebiscite, if not counterpoised by the intelligence of the masses, as an attack upon the liberty of the people." Michels himself cites Bonapartism whose power was "based on the referendum" (p. 337).

As for the syndicalists and anarchists, they are merely deluding them- selves when they "reason as if they were immunized against the action of sociological laws of universal validity" (p. 347). They have not avoided the situation in which "the masses do not represent themselves but are represented by others" (p. 348). Often their "direct action," for example, "the strike, instead of being a field of activity for the uniform and compact masses, tends rather to facilitate the process of differentiation and to favor the formation of an élite of leaders" (pp. 349–50).

None of the various proposed "prophylaxes," then, has proved effective in preventing what elite theorists have deemed an inexorable process. Those prophylaxes include Marxism, too—Michels' primary target, of course; at first Marxism seems the "only scientific doctrine which can boast of ability to make an effective reply to all theories, old or new, affirming the immanent necessity for the perennial existence of the 'political class'" (pp. 381–82). But Marxism also fails because the members of the new society in their very efforts to abolish class distinctions will create new ones. That is inevitable because the delegation of authority will be necessary to administer and to allocate material resources. The administrators would thus acquire enormous "influence at least equal to that possessed by the private owner of capital" (p. 383). And, Michels continues, there is no basis for assuming that administrators "will not utilize their immense influence in order to secure for their children the succession to the offices which they themselves hold" (p. 383). Once a group of men, elected or not, gains control of the existing instruments of power, they will do everything they can to retain it.

Thus, the weakest link in the Marxian view of the new society is the whole gamut of problems relating to administration—that is, the concentration of power in the hands of administrators and the means those individuals might utilize to retain their privileges. It seems inescapable, concludes Michels, that conflicts of interest will emerge between leaders and led, not unlike the class conflicts of the old society. That process appears to be subsumed under an absolute social law.

> By a universally applicable social law, every organ of the collectivity, brought into existence through the need for the division of labor, creates for itself, as soon as it becomes consolidated, interests peculiar to itself. The existence of these special interests involves a necessary conflict with the interests of the collectivity. Nay, more, social strata fulfilling peculiar functions tend to become isolated, to produce organs fitted for the defense of their own peculiar interests. In the long run they tend to undergo transformation into distinct classes. (p. 389)

This Michels intends not as a refutation of Marx's theory of class struggle but of his utopia, the classless society (pp. 390–91). "The socialists might conquer," he writes, "but not socialism, which would perish in the moment of its adherents' triumph" (p. 391).

Michels had written those lines before a single socialist regime had taken power anywhere. However, the victory of the bureaucratic organization over the socialist soul had already become evident in the violation of a fundamental socialist principle: international solidarity. The working-class masses were fated to suffer most from the violation of that principle. Yet, as Michels notes of the German workers during World War I, "throughout the proletarian mass there has not been reported a single instance of moral rebellion against the struggle which enlists the socialists to fight on behalf of German imperialism and to contend with the comrades of other lands" (p. 394). Ultimately, that must be viewed as a consequence of *organization* itself "which gives birth to the domination of the elected over the electors, of the mandatories over the mandators, of the delegates over the delegators. Who *says organization, says oligarchy*" (p. 401). That is predicated, for Michels, on the inherent nature of the masses, which, however much they may advance educationally, culturally, or morally, will remain *perennially* incompetent. The mass "*per se* is amorphous, and therefore needs division of labor, specialization, and guidance" (p. 404)—the very processes that lead inevitability to its manipulation and subordination.

However, nothing could be farther from Michels's intentions than to provide a rationale for resignation to those processes. He emphatically states that in this work he "desired to throw light upon certain sociological tendencies which oppose the reign of democracy, and to a still greater extent oppose the reign of socialism" (p. 405). He quite deliberately adopted a one-sided view and laid "considerable stress upon the pessimistic aspect of democracy which is forced upon us by historical study" (p. 405). He employed the term "iron law" to dramatize the difficult and formidable obstacles that lay before the realization of democracy, but not in order to deny altogether the possibility of its realization. From his analysis, "it would be erroneous to conclude," Michels maintains, "that we should renounce all endeavors to ascertain the limits which may be imposed upon the power exercised over the individual by oligarchies (state, dominant class, party, etc.). It would be an error to abandon the desperate enterprise of endeavoring to discover the social order which will render possible the complete realization of the idea of popular sovereignty" (pp. 404–5). Moreover, the writer does not wish to deny that every revolutionary working-class movement, and every movement sincerely inspired by the democratic spirit, may have a certain value as contributing to the enfeeblement of oligarchic tendencies. (p. 405)

In the end, furthermore, he emphasized that free inquiry, and criticism and control of the leaders, so essential for the strengthening of democracy, can be developed increasingly among the masses themselves: "A wider education involves an increasing capacity for exercising control" (p. 406). As Michels develops that point it becomes clear that although there are in his view at any given time certain limits on the degree of perfection democracy can attain (here as elsewhere, the actual falls short of the ideal), still, the ideal can be more and more approximated. "It is," he insists, "the great task of social education to raise the intellectual level of the masses, so that they may be enabled, within the limits of what is possible, to counteract the oligarchical tendencies of the working-class movement" (p. 407).

In the concluding paragraphs of his work, Michels goes on record, unequivocally, in favour of democracy: "The defects inherent in democracy are obvious. It is none the less true that as a form of social life we must choose democracy as the least of evils" (p. 407). Finally he writes, "It may be said, therefore, that the more humanity comes to recognize the advantages which democracy, however imperfect, presents over aristocracy, even at its best, the less likely it is that a recognition of the defects of democracy will provoke a return to aristocracy" (p. 407).

It is in that spirit, therefore, that Michels's classic study should be read—namely, as "a serene and frank examination of the oligarchical dangers of democracy [which] will enable us to minimize these dangers, even though they can never be entirely avoided." (p. 408).

NOTES

1. Roberto Michels, *First Lectures in Political Sociology*, trans. Alfred de Grazia (New York: Harper & Row, 1965), p. 10.
2. Ibid., p. 16.
3. Ibid., p.18.
4. Quoted by Michels in ibid., p. 19.
5. Ibid., p. 21.

6. Ibid.
7. Ibid.
8. Ibid., p. 54.
9. Robert Michels, *Political Parties* (New York: Dover Publications, 1959), p. viii. (Hereafter all page references to this work will be indicated in parentheses immediately following the quoted passage.)
10. In some cases, Michels argues, former proletarians as leaders may be worse. See ibid., p. 302.

CHAPTER 12

Émile Durkheim (1858–1917)

To understand the sociology of Émile Durkheim, one must, in his case as in the case of so many of his contemporaries, examine his relation to socialist thought and to the socialist movement of his time. Apparently, Durkheim had begun to concern himself with the problems of socialism as early as 1883, about the same time that he had drawn up the first plan of his *Division of Labor*. As he progressed in his work on the *Division of Labor, Suicide, The Family*, and *Religion*, all eventually to become full-scale studies, his interests shifted from socialism to sociology and then mainly to social problems. As Marcel Mauss observed, however, Durkheim never lost sight of his point of departure.[1] When, in 1895, he again took up the study of socialism and delivered a series of lectures on the subject at the University of Bordeaux, he sought to treat it both objectively and sociologically: How does one explain the various forms of socialist ideology? What were the social conditions and pressures that prompted Saint-Simon, Fourier, Owen, and Marx to advance their respective theories? Thus Durkheim's studies of socialism were to be an "analysis of the causes of an idea."[2]

Durkheim had an intimate knowledge of socialist literature, including the works of Karl Marx, "whom a Finnish friend, Neiglick, had advised him to study during his stay in Leipzig" (p. 3). Nevertheless, throughout his life, he remained opposed to socialism though his closest friends and students were committed to it in its Marxian, Guesdist, and other forms. The features of socialism which, according to Mauss, he disliked were "its violent nature, its class character—more or less purely workingmen's—and therefore its political and even politician-like tone" (p. 3).

Thus, in opposition to a conception of society and social change based on classes and class conflict, Durkheim put forward a theory based on "organic solidarity."

Durkheim's concern with "solidarity" was related to his fear of the social and political conflicts of his time. The strength and prominence of the socialist movement, as well as the analyses and solutions it proposed, pressed him to seek some kind of intellectual mediation between two prominent theoretical systems: the Comtean and the Marxian. That he attempted to do by exploring the work of their common intellectual ancestor, Saint-Simon; it is in Durkheim's study, *Socialism and Saint-Simon*, that much of his later thinking is anticipated.

DURKHEIM AND SAINT-SIMON

Although class conflict, for Saint-Simon, played an important role in the transition from the feudal to the bourgeois order, it lost virtually all significance once the new scientific-industrial order was established. Though he clearly recognized the existence of classes and strata in the new society, he believed that the new conditions could lead to a hierarchical but nonetheless organic order of social peace and stability. Integration was to be achieved primarily by instituting the appropriate moral ideas. That becomes the leading idea of Durkheim's system as well. The new division of labour—that is, science and industry—need not lead, as Comte had feared it would, to "disorganization" and "anarchy." Everything depended, for Saint-Simon as for Durkheim, on whether the *appropriate* moral order could be developed to suit the new social and technical conditions.

By reviewing the basic principles of Saint-Simon's philosophy, the degree to which Durkheim was indebted to him will become clearer, for it is quite evident that it was Saint-Simon and *not* Comte whom Durkheim regarded as his intellectual master. The "idea, the word, and even the outline of positivist philosophy," wrote Durkheim, "are all found in Saint-Simon.... Therefore, it is to him that one must, in full justice, award the honor currently given to Comte" (p. 104). In these essays, Durkheim vehemently defends and proves that proposition. It was important for him to establish that fact, since the Saint-Simonian principles (which Durkheim summarizes rather well) all reappear in his own works; in fact, those principles form the bases of his own sociology.

Moral ideas for Saint-Simon as for Durkheim are the real cement of a society. For both thinkers a society is above all a community of ideas: "The similarity of positive moral ideas is the single bond which can unite men into society" (p. 91). If Saint-Simon saw as his major task to determine what kind of moral system post-Revolutionary European society required, Durkheim viewed his own work in a similar light: to provide a secular, moral system that would bind together into a unified social order the classes, strata, and occupational groups of contemporary France. Like Saint-Simon, he viewed the role of theory as essentially positive and constructive and shared with the founder of positive philosophy a certain disdain for the negative-critical outlook of the *Philosophes* and the Revolutionaries. Durkheim wholeheartedly agreed that contemporary philosophy must be constructive and organizational, not critical and revolutionary. His emphasis on the constructive and organizational, however, was to serve as an antidote to the critical and revolutionary ideas of the socialists.

It was Saint-Simon's conception of society as enunciated in his *Physiologie Sociale* and elsewhere that led Durkheim to his own positivistic and functional view and that inspired the organismic analogies and metaphors we find throughout his work. Durkheim's fundamental premise, that "society" is not a simple aggregate of individuals but a reality sui generis, had already been explicitly defined by Saint-Simon:

> Society is not at all a simple conglomeration of living beings whose actions have no other cause but the arbitrariness of individual wills, nor other result than ephemeral or unimportant accidents. On the contrary, society is above all a veritable organized machine, all of whose parts contribute in a different way to the movement of the whole. The gathering of men constitutes a veritable being whose existence is more or less certain or precarious according to whether its organs acquit themselves more or less regularly of the functions entrusted to them. (p. 99)

Likewise, Durkheim's evolutionary conception of society is anticipated in Saint-Simon's "law of progress." The Saint-Simonian emphasis—that men are the instruments rather than the authors of that law—remains a dominant theme in Durkheim's treatment of the individual and in his reification (and sometimes even deification) of society and social processes. For both thinkers, social laws dominated men; the best they could hope for was to discover the direction of those laws—the task of positive science—so as to adjust to them with the least pain.

Saint-Simon had described, in essentially a dialectical way, the origins of the scientific-industrial order within the womb of the feudal-theological system. The two contradictory systems could not coexist indefinitely, and the tensions and conflicts ultimately resulted in the French Revolution. The conflict and anarchy of the post-Revolutionary epoch could be eliminated by imposing a religious-moral order *appropriate* to the new scientific-industrial conditions. Eventually, that led to his call for a "new Christianity."

That Durkheim took over Saint-Simon's view in its essentials is quite clear, notably in his *Division of Labor* in which *mechanical* solidarity was giving way to a "higher" solidarity he called *organic*. Although both thinkers viewed the older social order as based on conflicting principles, classes, and class interests, they both read conflict out of their respective higher, organic societies. There was nothing normal about conflict in the new society; the existence of classes did not preclude the moral unity and solidarity of the society as a whole. Durkheim believed that the mission Saint-Simon had set himself—to elaborate a new and appropriate body of universally acceptable moral and rational beliefs—still remained unaccomplished in his time. He agreed that the old order could not be restored; therefore, the new one had to be "integrated." That was essential to avoid the recurring economic and political crises, the chronic mood of exasperation and discontent, and, finally, the "disintegration" of society. The "revolution" Saint-Simon had envisioned was still incomplete in his own time, Durkheim believed, because the new integrative institutions appropriate to the modern division of labour had yet to be established. A new law and morality had to be developed to mediate among the diverse interest groups of industrial society and thus serve to integrate all its parts and functions.

That appeared feasible to Durkheim because he accepted the Saint-Simonian view of industry as a unifying and pacific force. Describing Saint-Simon's view, Durkheim writes: "From military—which it was formerly—the human spirit became pacific. Industry was offering nations a means—as fruitful as war—of becoming rich and powerful" (pp. 130–31). Once the old feudal, military, and theological functions had lost their significance, there was no apparent reason for social conflict in the new "organic" society. The main source of conflict in the older system had been the conflicting interests and principles of the feudal and industrial classes—ergo, to achieve an "organic" quality, the new society had to be based on only *one* of those principles. Modern societies, writes Durkheim, following Saint-Simon's formula, "will be definitely in equilibrium only when organized on a purely industrial basis" (p. 131). Like his master, Durkheim saw a harmony of interests not only among the many and varied occupational groups ("functions") but between the industrial capitalists and workers as well. He adopts Saint-Simon's formula that "the producers of useful things—being the only useful people in society—are the only ones who should cooperate to regulate" (p. 134) the course of the new industrial society. That formed the basis for the role Durkheim assigned to "occupational guilds." Only those who live on unearned income, Saint-Simon argued, should be placed beyond the pale of regular society. "As for those who themselves make their wealth productive, who enrich it with their toil—they are industrials. Consequently, industrial society comprises all those who actively participate in the economic life, whether they are owners or not" (p. 134).

Durkheim's theory of the integrative consequences of the growing division of labour is likewise derived from Saint-Simon. That Durkheim elaborated in his *Division of Labor* ideas that had already appeared in all their essentials in Saint-Simon's scheme may be seen from the following excerpts from *Système Industriel*. In that work and others, Saint-Simon held that the growing division of labour would lead to greater interdependence and mutual responsibility among individuals, and to a greater dependence upon society as a whole.

> In the measure that civilization makes progress, the division of labor—considered from the spiritual as from the secular side, grows in the same proportion. Thus men depend less on others as individuals, but more on the mass.… [The] organization of a well-ordered system required that the parts be strongly tied to a whole and subordinated. (p. 138)

Even Durkheim's frequently reiterated idea of the integrative role of occupational guilds and corporations was first expressed by Saint-Simon. In order that the division of labour should result in a unified industrial society, it was necessary "that in the large majority of the nation, individuals be joined in industrial associations, more or less numerous and connected … to permit their formation into a generalized system by being directed toward a great common industrial goal" (p. 139). Like Saint-Simon, Durkheim sees the industrial system as possessing an inherent unity. His summary of Saint-Simon's conception describes his own equally well. The growing division of labour was, in his view, leading to a solidarity of interests among all classes ("parts") of society. Classes are termed "functions" and are regarded as coordinative, cooperative, and unifying—never as conflictive. "Each people today," he writes, "forms a homogenous whole, not because it acquired the habit of identifying itself with such and such a function or class, but because it is a system of functions inseparable from one another and mutually complementing each other" (p. 148).

If the industrial system was only a system of "functions," all that was necessary to assure their harmonious operation was proper regulation. Here, too, the rudiments of his theory appear first in Saint-Simon. In the new society, "it is not the strongest who control but those most capable in science or industry. They are not summoned to office because they have the power to exercise their will but because they know more than others, and consequently their functions do not consist in saying what they want, but what they know. They do not dictate orders, they only declare what conforms to the nature of things" (p 150). And again, "Those who direct are not above those who are directed; they are not their superiors. They fulfill a different function—that is all" (p. 151).

Throughout Durkheim's work, one encounters the injunction, "Fight egoism!" for egoism left unbridled "would of necessity finally result in the dissolution of society." But those words are Saint-Simon's and first appear in his *Système Industriel*. What Durkheim regarded as the best antidote for egoism—namely, an altruistic moral commitment to "Society"—was derived from Saint-Simon's *New Christianity*. "Love one another" was Saint-Simon's motto. "The fundamental principle established by the divine author of Christianity commands all men to regard themselves as brothers and to cooperate as completely as possible for their well-being. This principle is the most general of all social principles" (p. 165). The real task was to organize "temporal power in conformity with this divine axiom." A new charity and a new philanthropy were required, Saint-Simon emphasized, "to improve as much as possible the fate of the class which has no other means of existence but the labor of its hands" (p. 166). That is important not only for its own sake but for the sake of social peace. Durkheim correctly observed about that aspect of Saint-Simon's doctrine (and his own as well) that it was inspired by "compassion for the unfortunate, along with a fear of their dangers to the social order" (p. 168).

Durkheim follows Saint-Simon in still another point: the integrative role of moral sentiments. When he argues that the division of labour conduces to a higher solidarity, he does so only in the sense that men are increasingly dependent on one another; but he recognizes at the same time that interdependence is not sufficient to bring about real solidarity—which can only be effected through a moral education and commitment to "society as a whole."

In his discussion of Saint-Simon, Durkheim's moral values clearly emerge. He despised and feared restlessness, social conflict, and "anarchy"; the insatiable appetites of modern man were a sign of his morbidity. Along with Bonald, Maistre, and Saint-Simon, Durkheim believed that the decline of religious forces had left a moral vacuum. A morality of contentment was required because social peace could never be achieved so long as men were not content with their lot. "What is needed if social order is to reign," writes Durkheim, "is that the mass of men be content with their lot. But what is needed for them to be content, is not that they have more or less but that they be convinced they have no right to more. And for this, it is absolutely essential that there be an authority whose superiority they acknowledge and which tells them what is right" (p. 200). What is necessary above all is a strong moral force capable of moderating and regulating the various "functions" and of curbing "egoism" and special interests.

Durkheim thus wanted to pose the social question in a manner entirely different from the way the socialists did. His way of posing the question, he believed,

> no longer stirs questions of classes, it no longer opposes rich to poor, employers to workers—as if the only possible solution consisted of diminishing the portion of one in order to augment that of the other. But it declares, in the interest of both, the necessity of a curb from above which checks appetites and so sets a limit on the state of disarrangement, excitement, frenzied agitation, which do not spring from social activity and which even make it suffer. Put differently, the social question, posed this way, is not a question of money or force; it is a question of moral agents. What dominates it is not the state of our economy but, much more, the state of our morality. (p. 204)

THE PROBLEM OF ORDER

Durkheim's central concern, therefore, was with the "problem of order"—that is, with the question of how the society of his time might establish and maintain social stability and cohesiveness. Thomas Hobbes explained social order as a result of the fear of a Leviathan, a central power. For Hobbes, that was the single most important condition which made society possible. In France of Durkheim's time, it was the Saint-Simonians and Comteans who advocated a Hobbesian solution to the problem of order. They recognized that industrial developments and the conflicts of interest accompanying them were tearing the fabric of existing society and undermining the social peace. Their solution was a state-imposed social peace.

At the other extreme were the *utilitarians*. If Hobbes rested his theory of order on the fear of a central authority, the utilitarians dispensed with a central authority altogether. For the utilitarians, social order and harmony resulted from the division of labour. Order was viewed as an *automatic* consequence of an economic system in which every individual pursued his own interests. That theory expressed itself in laissez faire—the doctrine that the economy works best when left alone. No central regulatory agency is required for the smooth operation of the economy. Indeed, the intrusion of such an agency can only serve to disrupt what is essentially a self-regulating system. All economic affairs take place through the medium of free exchange, and if each individual dedicates himself to the pursuit of his own interests, that will lead to the "greatest good of the greatest number."

It is doubtful whether the market system ever worked in the automatic, self-regulating way in which the classical economists and other utilitarians conceived of it. It is even more doubtful that it worked for the general good. As early as the second decade of the nineteenth century, the economist Sismondi in his *Nouveaux Principes d'Economie Politique* (1819) demonstrated that the poor suffer most from economic crises, and that the utilitarians were therefore simply wrong. Those matters aside, however, the important socio-logical question is whether free exchange and other contractual relationships must lead to social order.

In a most telling critique, Durkheim observed that if we look carefully into the so-called total harmony of interests of the utilitarians, we can see that it conceals a latent conflict. It is clear that if an individual's own interests are the sole regulator of his conduct, there is nothing to prevent everyone's relentless pursuit of self-interest from degenerating into a Hobbesian war of all against all. "There is nothing less constant than interest," writes Durkheim in his *Division of Labor in Society*. "Today it unites me to you; tomorrow it will make me your enemy."[3] It is true, argues Durkheim, that interests can bind people together, but they can do so only temporarily and partially. When the mutual interest in exchange of two or more parties ceases, they will either turn away from each other or even turn against each other. It follows that *contractual interests* alone, no more than *fear of the Leviathan* alone, can account for social order. Each of those may constitute one element of order, but neither element in and of itself can serve as a sufficient condition of order. In developing his critique, Durkheim provides the third element that any adequate theory of order must include.

What the utilitarians have overlooked, Durkheim notes, is that not everything in a contract is contractual. Every contract contains *noncontractual* or *sociomoral* elements that exercise some regulative control over the parties concerned. In fact, a contract has no validity if it fails to fulfill the conditions required by law. The contracting parties acquire obligations of a moral or legal kind that are not specified in the terms of the contract. Thus, contract law, rooted in custom, tradition, and precedent, provides the sociomoral context of every exchange relationship. We may exchange and cooperate because it is in our mutual interest, but the relationship we thereby form is necessarily hedged in by duties and obligations not of our own making. "The agreement of parties," writes Durkheim, "cannot render a clause just which by itself is unjust, and there are rules of justice whose violation social justice prevents, even if it has been consented to by the interested parties" (p. 216).

But Durkheim also rejected a third approach to the problem of order, that of the socialists. In his first major work, Durkheim set himself the task of demonstrating that the expanding industrial division of labour brings with it a higher form of solidarity than existed before. That idea, borrowed from Saint-Simon, was not only a positive thesis but a polemical one as well. Contemporary socialists, and particularly the Marxists, had also regarded the growth of science and industry as inevitable, but for them, in order that humanity in general should reap the benefits of modern technical developments, a fundamental restructuring of social relations was necessary. In the Marxian view, the modern industrial division of labour was not merely a system of coordinate functions; quite to the contrary, it was a system of structural inequalities based on socioeconomic classes with antagonistic interests.

What Durkheim sought to provide, then, was a cogent rebuttal to both the Comtean and Marxian positions, while exposing at the same time the erroneousness of the utilitarian view. In the main, however, Durkheim's theory is a form of mediation between Comte and Marx. To Comte, Durkheim conceded that moral consensus was a precondition of social order, but against him, he argued that the division of labour need not lead to a dispersion and conflict of interests. There were other, *nonmoral* conditions that were at least equally important for the establishment of social solidarity. The development of science and industry, promoting an increasing interdependence among individuals and groups within society as a whole, could serve as the objective basis of a new and higher solidarity.

To the Marxian and other socialists, Durkheim conceded the need for significant socioeconomic reforms, without which there could be neither true solidarity nor true justice. But against them he argued that no fundamental restructuring of socioeconomic relations was necessary. Thus, Durkheim proceeded to mediate between the Comteans and the socialists; he did so by adapting the ideas of their common ancestor, Saint-Simon, to the society of his time.

Durkheim begins by proposing that the modern, industrial divisions of labour be viewed in a new light. The "economic services that it can render are picayune compared to the moral effect that it produces, and its true function is to create in two or more persons a feeling of solidarity. In whatever manner the result is obtained, its aim is to cause coherence among friends and to stamp them with its seal." (p. 56). Once upon a time, society was unified because it was homogenous; everyone was alike. With the growing differentiation of occupations, however, and the increasing complexity of society, the original solidarity was undermined and lost. But that does not mean that solidarity is forever destroyed. A new and higher type of social solidarity is being generated by the industrial division of labour. That is the central thesis which Durkheim developed in his first major work.

Constructing his model on the basis of what was known about "primitive" societies, Durkheim posits an original unity which he calls "mechanical solidarity." Such solidarity rested on common collective sentiments, on a *conscience collective*, which in French carries the connotation of both a common consciousness and a common conscience. The collective sentiments are engraved, rather strongly, on all the individual consciences. The best empirical indication of the existence of a "totality of social similitudes" is the social reaction to crime. In fact, an act is "criminal," for Durkheim, precisely because it is carried out in opposition to the collective sentiments. We "must not say," he writes, "that an action shocks the common conscience because it is criminal, but rather that it is criminal because it shocks the common conscience" (p. 81). Crime is "an offense against an authority in some way transcendent" (p. 85). Anything that offends or violates the common conscience threatens the solidarity—the very existence—of society. An offense left unpunished weakens to that same degree the social unity. Punishment therefore serves the important function of restoring and reconstituting social unity. In the "primitive" context, it is expiatory and retaliatory; it is a passionate reaction by society against those who dared violate its basic rules. Restitution is not enough; the social body "must have a more violent satisfaction. The force against which the crime comes is too intense to react with very much moderation. Moreover, it cannot do so without enfeebling itself; for it is thanks to the intensity of the reaction that it keeps alive and maintains itself with the same degree of energy" (p. 85). Thus Durkheim describes a social state based on a uniform conscience present in all members of society.

If repressive and expiatory law is characteristic of mechanical solidarity, it is *restitutive* law which is most typical of organic solidarity. Here the point is not punishment but restoring damaged interests; law becomes "a means of reviewing the past in order to reinstate it, as far as possible, to its normal form." And now, since society is a complex of many and diverse groups and interests, law acts through specialized organs. Nevertheless, it is society that empowers those organs and acts through them. Even contractual relations, which are ostensibly private and individual, are binding precisely because society gives power to such relations; society sanctions "the obligations contracted for.… Every contract thus supposes that behind the parties implicated in it there is society very ready to intervene in order to gain respect for the engagements which have been made" (p. 114).

Not all the relationships in the complex society, Durkheim acknowledges, conduce to solidarity. Some are negative. For instance, the rights of some persons are different from those of others. "I cannot enjoy my right without harming someone else; such is the case with certain servitudes" (p. 118). Law is then necessary to repair wrong and to prevent it. But such rules do not demand real cooperation; "they simply restore or maintain, in the new conditions which are produced, this negative solidarity whose circumstances have troubled its functioning" (p. 118). Rules governing those relationships do not lead to "positive social links"; they lead to the separation of spheres but not to cooperation. The other rules of restitutive law, the residue, Durkheim writes, "express a positive union, a cooperation which derives, in essentials, from the division of labor" (p. 122).

Durkheim begins now to develop his thesis on the positive consequences of the division of labour: It leads to exchange of services, reciprocity of obligations, interdependence, and so on. Contracts and other formal-legal relationships governing exchange lead to what he defined as *organic solidarity*: "Spencer has not without justice qualified as a physiological contract the exchange of material which is made at every instant between the different organs of the living body" (p. 125). In that way, Durkheim conceives of the complex social system as a multiplicity of distinct functions which need to be coordinated.

Durkheim thus maintains that the division of labour, in its *normal* condition, engenders cooperation and solidarity. In opposition to those who thought otherwise, Durkheim held that modern economic developments need not lead to social conflict and disorder. A higher, organic solidarity could be achieved, for it "is the division of labor which, more and more, fills the role that was formerly filled by the Common Conscience. It [the division of labor] is the principal bond of social aggregates of higher types" (p. 173). Yet, Durkheim felt a certain uneasiness with that proposition, because, after all, it was quite evident that the division of labour had so far failed to bring forth the results he was predicting. How did he deal with that fact?

If the increasingly complex division of labour had yet to produce social solidarity, that was a result of the *abnormal* or pathological forms that the division of labour presently assumed. "Though *normally*," writes Durkheim, "the division of labor produces social solidarity, it sometimes happens that it has different, and even contrary results. Now, it is important to find out what makes it deviate from its natural course, for if we did not prove that these cases are exceptional, the division of labor might be accused of logically implying them" (p. 353).

In Durkheim's treatment of the so-called pathological forms of the division of labour, one sees clearly an attempt on his part to deal with the issues raised by the socialists. There were, for example, the recurrent industrial and commercial crises which Marx had regarded as inherent in capitalist relations of production. For Durkheim, such crises were explained by the lack of adjustment among the various "functions" of the social organism. He acknowledges that "insofar as labor is divided more, these phenomena [crises] seem to be more frequent, at least in certain cases. From 1845 to 1869, failures increased 70%" (p. 354). "The conflict between capital and labor," he continues, "is another example, more striking, of the same phenomenon. Insofar as industrial functions become more specialized, the conflict becomes more lively, instead of solidarity increasing" (p. 354). So, Durkheim observed those salient facts and even agreed that class conflicts assume the greatest intensity with "the birth of large-scale industry" (p. 355). With the growth in the division of labour, class warfare has become more violent. For Durkheim, however, all that is a consequence of the division of labour not in its normal form, but in its *abnormal* forms.

The first of the abnormal or pathological forms he calls the *anomic* division of labour. That word comes from the Greek *anomia*, referring to a state of society in which normative standards of conduct are weak or absent. Durkheim employed that term to convey that what was lacking or poorly developed in modern industrial society was a moral-legal code appropriate to the new conditions. Such a code was essential in order to mediate among the many and diverse interest groups in society and thus to regulate and moderate social conflicts.

But Durkheim realized that rules and regulations cannot be the whole solution and that often the rules themselves serve to perpetuate certain social ills. That is particularly evident in class conflicts. Socioeconomic classes, an integral aspect of the industrial division of labour, are a source of dissension and conflict. The "lower classes not being … satisfied with the role which has devolved upon them from custom or law aspire to functions which are closed to them and seek to dispossess those who are exercising these functions. Thus civil conflicts arise which are due to the manner in which labor is distributed" (p. 394). Thus Durkheim introduces a second major pathological form—the *forced division of labour.*

Under the heading "forced division of labor," Durkheim examines the relationship between order and justice. The higher organic solidarity requires new rules, but if those rules are inherently unjust, the solidarity will never materialize. Justice, for Durkheim, implied a basic social equality:

If one class of society is obliged in order to live, to take any price for its
services, while another can abstain from such action thanks to resources
at his disposal …, the second has an unjust advantage over the first at
law. In other words, there cannot be rich and poor at birth without there
being unjust contracts. (p. 384)

Durkheim therefore considers the task of modern society as a "work of
justice."

At the same time, another theme emerged and became a leading idea in
Durkheim's proposal for reform. If the prevailing anarchy and anomy are to
decline and ultimately to disappear, what is required is the resurrection of an
old social institution and its reintroduction, in a modified and appropriate
form, into modern social life. Comte was wrong in assigning the regulative
function exclusively to the State; modern economic life is much too complex
for its regulation to be given over to that institution. Instead, that tried and
tested institution, the *occupational corporation or guild*, which was already
known in antiquity and which flourished during the Middle Ages, can be
readapted to modern conditions and can again serve the regulatory function
it had served so well in the past. The men of the French Revolution acted
rashly when they destroyed that institution instead of only modifying it.
The occupational group should become the basis of an occupational ethic,
for "[a]n occupational activity can be efficaciously regulated only by a group
intimate enough with it to know its functioning, feel all its needs, and able
to follow all their variations" (p. 5).

The occupational guilds must again become a public institution. They
are to be based on the existing class structure and their function would
be to lay down general moral and legal principles according to which
relations among the various occupations and classes would be regulated.
Representatives of both the employers and employees would be elected to
the corporation assembly "in proportions corresponding to the respective
importance attributed by opinion to these factors in production" (p. 25 n.).
And Durkheim adds,

But if it is necessary that both meet in the directing councils of the
corporations, it is no less important that at the base of the corpora-
tive organization they form distinct and independent groups, for their

interests are too often rival and antagonistic. To be able to go about their ways freely, they must go about their ways separately. The two groups thus constituted would then be able to appoint their representatives to the common assemblies. (p. 25 n.)

ORDER AND JUSTICE

Just as Saint-Simon had called for a new secular religion, Durkheim now called for a new secular morality. A theme that would become stronger as he grew older—the need for altruism, and the individual as well as social hazards of egoism—already finds expression here.

> We are not naturally inclined [he writes] to put ourselves out or to use self-restraint; if we are not encouraged at every step to exercise the restraints upon which all morals depend, how should we get the habit of it? If we follow no rule except that of a clear self-interest, in the occupations that take up nearly the whole of our time, how should we acquire a taste for any disinterestedness, or selflessness, or sacrifice?[4]

The employer as well as the worker "is aware of no influence set above him to check his egotism; he is subject to no moral discipline whatever and so he scouts any discipline at all of this kind." Moral standards have to be raised "so that the conflicts which disturb [economic life] have an end.... There should be rules telling each of the workers his rights and his duties, not vaguely in general terms but in precise detail, having in view the most ordinary day-to-day occurrences" (p. 12). Employers and workers must, in their respective groups, impose restraint upon their special and selfish interests; they must see the interests of the whole, and then conflict will diminish and become moderate while the solidarity of society is correspondingly enhanced.

In his concluding discussion of property, property rights, and contracts, Durkheim returns to the problem of justice. Inheritance and exchange by contracts are the two main ways of acquiring property; he tries to show by means of historical analysis that the former is "bound up with archaic concepts and practices that have no part in our present-day ethics" (p. 174). Of "the two main processes by which property is acquired, inheritance is the one that is going to lose its importance more and more" (p. 175). What remains then is the contract, and whether the conditions under which it is made can be just.

The contract is a juridical-moral bond between two subjects that specifies their mutual rights and obligations. Generally, says Durkheim, "a right exists on both sides" (p. 176). He is quick to add, however, that "these mutual rights are not inevitable. The slave is bound in law to his master and yet has no right over him" (p. 176). Thus, Durkheim returns to a fundamental issue: Some contracts are made between social unequals where one dominates and the other serves and where the latter has no choice but to serve or to suffer worse consequences. Can such a contract, though sanctioned by "a moral authority that stands higher," be just? To that question Durkheim replies with an unequivocal no.

In tracing its development as an institution, Durkheim shows that a bona fide consensual contract "could not be one of good faith except on condition of its being one by mutual consent" (p. 203). But consent "binds truly and absolutely the one who consents only on the condition that it has been *freely* given. Anything that lessens the liberty of the contracting party, lessens the binding force of the contract." As Durkheim proceeds to develop his argument, one sees just how close he moved in that instance to the socialist point of view:

> This rule should not be confused with the one that requires the contract to be made with deliberate intent. For I may very well have had the will to contract as I have done, and yet have contracted only under coercion. In this case, I will the obligations I subscribe to, but I will them by reason of pressure being put upon me. The consent in such instances is said to be invalidated and thus the contract is null and void. (p. 204)

Thus, a contract cannot be viewed as just simply because a person has subjectively willed it. What is crucial is how much freedom and power one has to resist entering into certain contractual relationships. Whether a contract is binding or not depends, therefore, not merely on subjective will but on the *objective* conditions under which it is made. If

> contracts imposed by constraint, direct or indirect, are not binding, this does not arise from the state of the will when it gave consent. It arises

from the consequences that an obligation thus formed inevitably brings upon the contracting party. It may be, in fact, that he took the step that has bound him only under external pressure, that his consent has been extracted from him. If this is so, it means that the consent was against his own interests and the justifiable needs he might have under the general principles of equity. The use of coercion could have had no other aim or consequence but that of forcing him to yield up something which he did not wish to, to do something he did not wish to do, or indeed of forcing him to the one action or the other on conditions he did not will. Penalty and distress have thus been undeservedly laid on him. (p. 206)

Such a contract, Durkheim observes, is increasingly regarded as invalid and that is not merely because "the determining cause of the obligation is exterior to the individual who binds himself. It is because he has suffered some unjustified injury, because, in a word, such a contract is unjust." Increasingly, a contract is regarded as moral and just only if it is not a "means of exploiting one of the contracting parties" (p. 213). The *objective consequences* for the parties concerned, and not their formal, subjective consent, must constitute the real criterion of a just contract.

Here, in the final pages of *Professional Ethics and Civic Morals*, Durkheim draws certain far-reaching conclusions from the class structure of society. The institution of inheritance is again singled out by Durkheim as a "supreme obstacle" to just relations in society:

Now inheritance as an institution [writes Durkheim] results in men being born either rich or poor; that is to say, there are two main classes in society, linked by all sorts of intermediate classes: the one which in order to live has to make its services acceptable to the other at whatever the cost; the other class which can do without these services, because it can call on certain resources.... Therefore as long as such sharp class differences exist in society, fairly effective palliatives may lessen the injustice of contracts; but in principle, the system operates in conditions which do not allow of justice. (p. 213)

Durkheim conceived of social change not as a function of class and other social conflicts, but as a result of the slow evolution of the collective moral conscience. One important change, however, was immediately possible, which would at one stroke eradicate a fundamental source of inequality and thus make for a qualitatively new stage of justice: "One primary reform is possible at once and almost without any transition. This is the discontinuance of inheritance *ab intestat* or by next of kin" (p. 216). Who, then, will inherit the wealth? Durkheim regarded the occupational corporations as best suited to fulfill that function. Like the socialists, he thus saw the need to socialize property and wealth, but it is the professional groups that, in his opinion, "would satisfy all the conditions for becoming in a sense, in the economic sphere, the heirs of the family" (p. 218).

But Durkheim is prepared to go even farther. Even after the abolition of inheritance, inequalities will remain—differences of talents and intelligence. Can it not be said that such inequalities of merit are also fortuitous?

> To us it does not seem equitable that a man should be better treated as a social being because he was born of parentage that is rich or of high rank. But is it any more equitable that he should be better treated because he was born of a father of higher intelligence or in a more favorable moral milieu? It is here that the domain of charity begins. Charity is the feeling of human sympathy that we see becoming clear even of these last remaining traces of inequality. It ignores and denies any special merit in gifts or mental capacity acquired by heredity. This, then, is the very acme of justice. (p. 220)

That is the note on which Durkheim concludes *Professional Ethics and Civic Morals*.

DURKHEIM'S SOCIOLOGY OF DEVIANT BEHAVIOUR

Durkheim was a pioneer in the sociological analysis of deviant behaviour. He was the first to set forth the proposition that deviance is no less firmly rooted in social conditions than conformity. Deviance, he maintained, is neither morbid nor pathological but rather normal. In any society there exists an inevitable diversity of human conduct as well as a variation in moral values. How, then, does one distinguish "normal" from "deviant" behaviour?

For Durkheim, a scientific reply to that question rests on a statistical criterion. The "normal," he writes, refers to "those social conditions that are most generally distributed."[5] The social norm consists of the most frequent forms of behaviour. Other, less frequent forms which depart from the norm are deviant. Yet, paradoxically, perhaps, although crime is a form of deviance, it is nonetheless normal.

Most criminologists in Durkheim's time looked upon crime as a pathology rooted in an individual's physiological or psychological makeup. Durkheim, in contrast, insisted that crime is a normal phenomenon. It is normal because it is present

> in all societies of all types. There is no society that is not confronted with the problem of criminality. Its form changes; the acts thus characterized are not the same everywhere; but, everywhere and always there have been men who have behaved in such a way as to draw upon themselves penal repression.[6]

If a society utterly devoid of crime is unknown, then crime must be a normal and integral facet of every social order.

That conception of things should not be misunderstood. When Durkheim asserts that crime is necessary, he does not mean that *specific types* of crime are inevitable or that crime *rates* cannot be decreased by appropriate social measures. No, what Durkheim intends to argue instead is, first, that wherever human beings congregate, they display diverse forms of behaviour; and, second, that some of those forms will be seen as departing from established norms, and will be punished accordingly. "Crime" thus ranges all the way from minor infractions of decorum at one end of the scale to major felonies on the other.

> Imagine a society of saints [writes Durkheim], a perfect cloister of exemplary individuals. Crimes, properly so called, will there be unknown; but faults which appear venial to the layman will create there the same scandal that the ordinary offense does in ordinary consciousness. If, then, this society has the power to judge and punish, it will define these acts as criminal and will treat them as such. For the same reason, the perfect and upright man judges his smallest failings with a severity that the majority reserves for acts more truly in the nature of an offense.[7]

Individuals in every society differ in respect to the social and cultural milieux in which they find themselves. No society, therefore, is capable of achieving perfect moral uniformity. The diversification of behaviour is a social process which results in both extraordinary and ordinary deviants. It produces individuals who may be geniuses and "criminals" at one and the same time. Thus Durkheim observes,

> according to Athenian law, Socrates was a criminal, and his condemnation was no more than just. However, his crime, namely, the independence of his thought, rendered a service not only to humanity but to his country. It served to prepare a new morality and faith which the Athenians needed, since the traditions by which they had lived until then were no longer in harmony with the current conditions of life. Nor is the case of Socrates unique; it is reproduced periodically in history. It would never have been possible to establish the freedom of thought we now enjoy if the regulations prohibiting it had not been violated before being solemnly abrogated. At that time, however, the violation was a crime, since it was an offense against sentiments still very keen in the average conscience.[8]

It is the process of social diversification that yields the higher order of deviant such as Socrates; it is the same process that brings forth ordinary deviants and common criminals. Among all the divergent actions that one finds in any given society, some will inevitably acquire a criminal character. It is not the intrinsic quality of the actions themselves that confers a criminal character upon them. It is rather the definition that is placed on those acts by the dominant consensus.

For Durkheim, then, crime is fundamentally bound up with the conditions of social life. Crime, far from being a pathology, is a normal phenomenon. Indeed, crime is not an unmitigated evil since it is indispensable for the development of morality and law.

CRIME AND PUNISHMENT

If the criminal character of an act does not reside in the act itself, where, then, does it reside? What makes an act criminal? Durkheim believed that the small, "primitive" society, characterized by "mechanical solidarity," presents the clearest and most direct reply to that question. In such a society, he noted, there are numerous acts which are considered crimes—for example, touching a tabooed object, failing to make a traditional sacrifice, departing from a precise ritual-formula, and so forth. Upon reflection it is clear that such diverse acts have only one thing in common: They are universally disapproved of by the members of the society in question. Those acts are crimes because they shock the collective conscience. In order for an act to qualify as a crime, it must offend strong and intense sentiments and break precise rules. A crime, therefore, is an act which antagonizes the powerful and well-defined sentiments of a collectivity. In Durkheim's words, "we must not say that an action shocks the common conscience because it is criminal, but rather that it is criminal because it shocks the common conscience. We do not reprove it because it is a crime, but it is a crime because we reprove it."[9] An act is a crime because it offends the transcendent authority of society.

If that conception of crime is sound, Durkheim reasoned, it ought to account for the nature of punishment. Punishment is first and foremost a passionate social reaction against the offender. That is especially evident in a primitive setting. Punishment is a form of vengeance, which may appear socially useless and unnecessarily cruel. But, actually, it enables the community to do something vital for itself. By means of punishment society heals the wounds inflicted upon it by the offender; through punishment, society restores its moral integrity and reaffirms its most fundamental values.

In modern society, the essence of punishment remains much the same. It is still "at least in part, a work of vengeance."[10] We may attempt to rationalize our treatment of the offender in terms of rehabilitation and the like, but we find it just that he should expiate his outrage through suffering. For us as for our ancestors, Durkheim convincingly argues, punishment remains a passionate reaction by means of which we reaffirm the validity of our rules and laws. That the reaction is passionate is evident from the conduct of both the prosecutor and the defence attorney in the modern courtroom. The former strives to awaken in the jury the sentiments that have been violated by the defendant, while the latter tries to rouse sympathy for him. Today punishment is carried out not by the collectivity as a whole but by the institutions of the State. But the essence of punishment continues to be a more or less zealous reaction against those who have violated our basic rules of conduct.

Crime therefore wounds the common conscience while punishment heals and restores it. Crime furnishes the community with an opportunity to revitalize itself by reacting intensely against the criminal order. "Crime," writes Durkheim,

> brings together upright consciences and concentrates them. We have only to notice what happens, particularly in a small town, when some moral scandal has just been committed. They stop each other on the street, they visit each other, they seem to come together to talk of the event and to wax indignant in common. From all the similar impressions which are exchanged, from all the temper that gets itself expressed, there emerges a unique temper … which is everybody's without being anybody's in particular.[11]

The offended sentiments derive their peculiar force from the fact that they are common to everybody. They are unanimous, uncontested, and commonly respected. An act is a crime precisely because it damages the unanimity. To do nothing in the face of a crime, to let it go unpunished, would therefore result in the enfeeblement of the collective sentiments. It is only by acting in common against the offender that the community can reinforce itself and its basic values.

Hence, the main object of punishment, for Durkheim, is certainly not to chasten or correct the offender, nor even to deter others from following in his path. Its true object is to maintain the vitality of the community's fundamental values and to safeguard its social cohesion. Punishment enables society to repair the "evil" which the crime has inflicted upon it. There is thus a continuity between crime and punishment. The criminal violates the cherished standards of the community and the upright retaliate "to heal the wounds made upon collective sentiments.…"[12] In that way Durkheim laid the foundation for a sociological understanding of crime and punishment.

Durkheim's sociological theory was an implicit repudiation of the theories of crime that were rampant in his day. Crime, it was widely believed, is the result of original sin or of innate depravity. It is caused by certain instinctual or racial predispositions; it is rooted in one's personality makeup or physiological structure. Clearly, Durkheim's conception of the *normality* of crime not only has nothing in common with such theories but is also a repudiation of them. One example will suffice to show just how far apart he was from some of his contemporaries.

One of the most famous nineteenth-century criminologists was a physician and psychiatrist named Cesare Lombroso (1836-1909). While serving as an army doctor, Lombroso thought he noticed that recalcitrant offender-soldiers differed from the disciplined troops by the greater prevalence and indecency of their tattoos. Later he employed experimental methods in studying insane patients. Comparing the insane patients with convicted criminals and those two in turn with normal persons, he measured their skulls and their sensitivity to touch. Once, while performing a postmortem examination of a notorious bandit, Lombroso found a distinct depression at the rear of his skull, in the opening in which the spine and skull are connected. Earlier he had found a similar depression in animals. From that, Lombroso concluded that a criminal is an atavistic being, a kind of throwback to an earlier evolutionary stage, possessing the ferocious instincts of early humans. The physical stigmata of atavism, Lombroso believed, were a low forehead, a receding chin, ears standing out from the head, too many fingers, unusual wrinkling of the skin, atypical head size or shape, and eye peculiarities.

In response to criticism, Lombroso eventually revised his "atavistic" theory. In his last book he conceded that there were environmental factors at work and listed a host of them from climate to religion. Retaining his original view that the "born criminal" and "insane criminal" are major types, he added a third category, the "criminaloid," who engages in vicious criminal behaviour though he is born with neither physical stigmata nor mental aberrations. The "born criminal," he believed, comprised about a third of all criminals. Those he explained as a reversion to an earlier evolutionary stage. As for the "insane criminal," that was a mixed category of offenders suffering from paralysis, dementia, pellagra, alcoholism, epilepsy, idiocy, and hysteria—all of which Lombroso regarded as causes of crime.[13]

Today there is scarcely a criminologist who continues to subscribe to Lombrosian views. Indeed, few criminologists take seriously any theory that attempts to explain crime in terms of the alleged "organic inferiority" or "degeneracy" of criminals. Even the most sophisticated studies purporting to demonstrate the physiological basis of criminality are methodologically defective and lacking in scientific validity.[14] It is now increasingly recognized that early criminologists were deceived. They took the unattractive appearance of prisoners as a sign of their mental deficiency. "Abnormality" was reflected in their shaved heads, ungainly uniforms, and bitter facial expressions in reaction to harsh discipline. Durkheim, however, was not fooled by appearances. He recognized the normality of criminals. He rested his theory solidly upon *social*, and not upon physiological or psychological, foundations.

DURKHEIM'S SOCIOLOGY OF RELIGION

Durkheim's major study of religion is called *The Elementary Forms of Religious Life*. The main aim of that work was to lay bare the fundamental elements of religion. Such elements, Durkheim assumed, could not be easily discovered in the religions of advanced civilizations. Those religions are the product of long, complex historical developments in which the fundamental elements have been obscured. If, however, one may assume that small, simple, and economically less complex societies possess correspondingly simple religious forms, then perhaps the basic elements of religious life will be more readily accessible. That was in fact Durkheim's assumption. He attacked the problem by employing data on the most "primitive" contemporary societies known to anthropologists: the Australian aborigines.

The first task was to define the subject matter. What do we mean by religion and what does it comprise? The definitions prevalent at the time all stressed a belief in supernatural and spiritual beings. That was the view, for example, of the great British anthropologist E. B. Tylor. He suggested that the best minimal definition of religion is "the belief in Spiritual Beings."[15] That definition is inadequate, Durkheim argues, since it fails to embrace those religions in which the idea of spirits or gods is absent. Buddhism is a case in point. In none of its basic principles does it concern itself with the notion of divinity.

After reviewing several other definitions and finding them deficient, Durkheim offers his own. All known religious beliefs divide the world into two domains: the *sacred* and the *profane*. For Durkheim, it is the totality of beliefs and practices concerned with the sacred that constitutes what we call "religion." When members of a society think and act in the same way with respect to the sacred, they share a common religion. They are members of a common "Church"—a moral community formed by all the believers in a single faith. Thus "a religion," writes Durkheim, "is a unified system of beliefs and practices relative to sacred things, that is to say, things set apart and forbidden—beliefs and practices which unite into one single moral community called a Church, all those who adhere to them."[16]

Armed with that definition, Durkheim confronted the leading theories of his day, which could be divided into two schools. The first put forth the theory of *animism*. Tylor, a leading representative of that school, held that early religion is a form of animism, a belief in souls, spirits, and a future state. Where did early man get the idea of a soul or spirit? He got it, wrote Tylor, by reflecting on two questions: "what is it that makes the difference between a living body and a dead one …? [And] what are those human shapes which appear in dreams and visions?"

> Looking at these two groups of phenomena [Tylor continues], the ancient savage philosophers probably made their first step by the obvious inference that early man has two things belonging to him, namely, a life and a phantom…. As both belong to the body, why should they not also belong to one another, and be manifestations of one and the same soul? Let them then be considered as united and the result is that well-known conception which may be described as an apparition-soul, a ghost-soul.[17]

For Tylor, then, the idea of the soul originated in the experience of dreams and fantasies.

But for Durkheim, that theory was quite unsatisfactory, for even if one admitted the plausibility of the dream origin of the soul-idea, the theory had one crucial defect: It failed to explain why a phantom—"a simple reproduction of the individual"—should have been elevated to the rank of a *sacred* being, as in the ancestor cult, for instance. Animistic theory, Durkheim argues, fails to provide a convincing answer to this all-important question: "If it [the phantom-soul] was only a profane thing, a wandering vital principle, during life, how does it become a sacred thing all at once, and the object of religious sentiments?" (p. 61).

The other school with which Durkheim quarrels may be called naturism. Animistic theories had claimed that the divine was derived from internal, mental experiences. Naturistic theories, in contrast, held that the first objects of religious sentiment were external natural phenomena. The things and forces of nature were the first to be deified. Nature presumably presents to early man numerous awesome spectacles which suffice to inspire religious ideas in him. He personifies and spiritualizes those spectacles by means of metaphors and images.

For Durkheim, however, that theory suffers from the same defect as the first. Natural forces are, after all, natural forces, however intense and spectacular they might be. Missing from the theory, therefore, is an explanation of how they acquired a sacred character. It is doubtful, argues Durkheim, that the sense of sacredness can be directly derived from natural phenomena. Thus rejecting the conclusions of both schools, Durkheim has prepared the way for his own distinctive sociological theory.

Totemism: An Elementary Religion

The small aboriginal societies of Australia afforded the best opportunity for the study of totemic beliefs. Such beliefs, it was widely agreed, formed an "elementary religion," the most elementary known to scholars. Totemism was first discovered among the natives of North America. Evidence for totemic beliefs also existed for ancient Egypt, Arabia, Greece, and the southern Slavs. But in none of those societies did totemism appear in as pure a form as it did among the Australian groups. That is why Durkheim largely limits his attention to the Australian data.

The typical Australian grouping was a clan, an exogamous unit, the members of which presumed themselves to be descended from a common ancestor. Each clan had its "totem"—that is, an *emblem* designating a particular species of animal or plant, which, in turn, represented the clan. The emblems of the Kangaroo and Crow, for instance, represented two distinct clan groups, and every clan member identified himself by the name of the respective species. The totem, it should be stressed, was not a pictorial representation of a species but rather a sign or "coat-of-arms." Totemic images were placed on the walls of huts, on the sides of canoes, and on the bodies of men. In fact, one of the principal initiation rites by which a young man entered into the religious life of the group consisted of painting the totemic sign on his body.

That suggests that the totem is more than just a name and emblem. It is employed in religious ceremonies and is a part of the liturgy. It has a religious character. "It is the very type of sacred thing," says Durkheim (p. 132). That becomes evident from the role of the *churinga*, a ritual instrument that anthropologists have called a "bull-roarer." Oblong pieces of wood or polished stone, suspended by a string, are rapidly whirled in the air so as to produce a loud humming sound. The churinga is employed in all important rituals. However, ritually profane persons, such as women and boys yet to be initiated into religious life, are prohibited from touching the instrument. The churinga is also believed to possess extraordinary properties. By contact it heals wounds and sickness; it gives clan members strength and courage, and it ensures an adequate reproduction of the totemic species.

The churinga is distinguished not only by its use in a ritual context, but also by the totemic mark engraved upon it. Typically, such instruments are constructed each time anew, and then, once the rite is over, stripped of the sign, dismantled, and scattered. It is the totemic emblem that is sacred.

The next step in Durkheim's inquiry was to examine the clan's attitude toward the totemic species. As an animal or plant, its profane use would have been to serve as food. But its sacredness was demonstrated by the fact that all clan members were forbidden to eat it. And yet, surprisingly, although the churinga and other objects bearing the clan emblem were never to be touched or seen by ritually profane persons, the totemic animal or plant could be touched or seen. If, therefore, the degree of sacredness of an object may be measured by the pains taken to isolate it from the profane, "we arrive at the remarkable conclusion that the *images of totemic beings are more sacred than the beings themselves*" (p. 133).

To Durkheim, that was a highly significant fact. If the totemic sign is more sacred than the totemic species, that suggests that the sign is so highly sacred not because it represents a species of plant or animal, but because it represents something else. Furthermore, since the totemic species and the clan members are also regarded as sacred, that must mean that the sign, the species, and the clan all share some common "principle." It is the common partaking of that principle that makes them all sacred. What is that principle? *It is an anonymous impersonal force.* It is independent of all subjects in whom it incarnates itself; it precedes them and survives them. That force is the *divine*. In a sense, says Durkheim, "it is the god adored by each totemic cult. Yet it is an impersonal god, without name or history, immanent in the world and diffused in an innumerable multitude of things" (p. 189).

The divine principle is a "force" in both the physical and the moral sense. An individual failing to take proper ritual precautions receives a shock comparable to the effect of an electric charge. On the other hand, an individual observes his rites not merely out of fear of such physical effects.

Rather, he observes them because his ancestors have always done so and because he feels a strong moral obligation to behave likewise. Thus, the totemic cult, though it may appear to be addressed to plants, animals, or other objects, is actually directed to the "power" that permeates them. If a species of plant or animal, or even the sun, moon, or stars, are adored, it is not due to their intrinsic nature, but to the fact that they partake of that sacred power. The believers themselves have only a vague notion of the force. But an awareness of its existence is evident in more advanced polytheistic cultures. The Greeks, for example, called it *Moira* or Fate, and even the most powerful gods were powerless before it. Yet the gods partake of that force when they produce rain or wind or crops. Zeus, Poseidon, Hades, and the other Greek gods all retain marks of their original impersonality.

Moreover, the impersonal power lying behind the later personified gods is the chief cause of all the movements occurring in the universe. Hence, what we find in Australian religion is the first form of the idea of "force" as it was later conceived in Western philosophy and science. Students of ancient Greek culture have shown that Greek philosophical ideas such as Necessity, Cause, Substance, Nature, Matter, and so on, are all rooted in the much more ancient religious conceptions of a sacred, all-powerful, impersonal, cosmic Force.

But the most important question remains: What is the ultimate origin of the idea of a divine cosmic force or god?

We have said that the totemic emblem was so highly sacred because it was, above all, a symbol of something else. If we can discover what that "something else" actually is, reasoned Durkheim, then we will have found the real basis for the idea of the Divine.

If we have followed Durkheim's analysis thus far, we can see that the totem symbolized two things: (1) the impersonal divine force, or "god," and (2) a specific society called the clan. The totem is the clan's "flag," it is the sign by which one clan distinguishes itself from another. "So," writes Durkheim,

> if it is at once the symbol of the god and of the society, is that not because the god and the society are only one? How could the emblem of the group have been able to become the figure of this quasi-divinity, if the group and the divinity were distinct realities? The god of the clan, the

totemic principle, can therefore be nothing else than the clan itself, personified and represented to the imagination under the visible form of the animal or vegetable which serves as totem. (p. 206)

Upon reflection, argues Durkheim, it seems quite evident that Society has all the attributes necessary to inspire a sense of the divine. Society is, after all, experienced as a superior force on which everyone depends. Members submit to its authority even when it is felt to be repressive. They yield to its rules not only because it is strong enough to overcome them, but also because it is an object of respect. The social pressure brought to bear on individuals by "Society" is largely of a spiritual kind. Ultimately it is social reality that gives men the idea that there exists a superhuman principle, all-powerful and moral, on which they all depend. It is the experience of Society, therefore, that gives rise to what Durkheim calls a "collective representation"—a collective intuiting of the Divine.

But it is not the profane, everyday experiences that achieve that effect. It is rather those special, sacred ritual occasions in which men find themselves dominated and carried away by an external power. Often lasting days on end, such ceremonial occasions transport the participants from the gray world of everyday life into the extraordinary and effervescent world of the sacred. It "is out of this effervescence itself," writes Durkheim, "that the religious idea seems to be born. The theory that this is really its origin is confirmed by the fact that in Australia the really religious activity is almost entirely confined to the moments when these assemblies are held." Durkheim continues: "Since religious force is nothing other than the collective and anonymous force of the clan, and since this can be represented in the mind only in the form of the totem, the totemic emblem is like the visible body of god" (pp. 218–19, 221).

Hence, when men believe in a moral power on which they depend, that is no illusion. For that power exists; it is Society. Sacred assemblies serve the apparent function of strengthening men's bonds with the Divine, but at the same time they serve the real function of strengthening the bonds of an "individual to the society of which he is a member, since the god is only a figurative expression of the society." "Religious force," concludes Durkheim, "is only the sentiment inspired by the group in its members, but projected outside of the consciousness that experience them, and objectified" (pp. 226, 229).

From that perspective, the nature and origin of the soul are also illuminated. It follows from Durkheim's analysis that the "soul" is no mere phantom, dream-image, or mental reproduction of the individual. Rather, it is the experience each clan member has of the totemic principle incarnate in him. Or, in sociological terms, the soul is what Society implants in every individual. The individual soul is a particle of the great collective soul of the group.

Similarly, the idea of immortality also originates in the reality of the group or society. Though individuals die, early man observed, the clan survives. There must therefore exist some principle or force that enables the clan-group to possess eternal life. Finally, the idea of spirits and deities, far from being directly aroused by natural spectacles, is awakened in us by the sociomoral processes of the social world.

In sum, the ultimate source of the religious experience, for Durkheim, is Society. Religion accordingly reflects both the good and bad sides of society, its just ideals and practices as well as its moral ugliness.

> There are gods of theft and trickery, of lust and war, of sickness and death. Christianity itself, howsoever high the idea which it has made of the divinity may be, has been obliged to give the spirit of evil a place in its mythology. Satan is an essential piece of the Christian system; even if he is an impure being, he is not a profane one.... Thus religion, far from ignoring the real society and making abstractions of it, is in its image; it reflects all its aspects, even the most vulgar and the most repulsive. (p. 421)

Criticisms of Durkheim's Theory

For Durkheim and his followers, Society and God are therefore one. Society, unconsciously divinized, is the Stuff all religions are made of. Since Durkheim rested his theory on evidence from "primitive" cultures, it will be instructive to hear the critical comments of Bronislaw Malinowski, one of the outstanding anthropologists of all time.

It is evident, Malinowski observes, that Durkheim rests his entire case on the behaviour of the collectivity, not the individual. Yet anyone who has experienced religion profoundly will agree that some of the strongest and most meaningful religious moments come in solitude, not in the group or crowd. That is no less true of "primitive" than of "modern" man.

Among "primitives," the novice is often secluded at initiation, and he undergoes a personal ordeal including a communion with spirits and deities. It is hard to see the social basis of those sacred powers in such lonely spots. It is equally difficult to see how the belief in immortality can be explained without considering the state of mind of the *individual* facing his inevitable death in fear and sorrow. That is not all. Though Durkheim's theory virtually ignores the role of the individual, evidence is plentiful that prophets, seers, interpreters, and other practitioners play a key role. Those facts strongly indicate that the stuff of religion cannot be regarded as purely social.

Also questionable is Durkheim's central argument that the idea of the Divine is somehow derived from ceremonies and festivities. The religious idea, he maintains, "is born out of their effervescence" (pp. 218–19, 221). Durkheim thus tends to place the entire weight of his argument on the emotional excitement one feels while participating in such gatherings. To that Malinowski replies that just

> a little reflection is sufficient to show that even in primitive societies the heightening of emotions and the lifting of the individual outside of himself are by no means restricted to gatherings and to crowd phenomena. The lover near his sweetheart, the daring adventurer conquering his fears in the face of real danger, the hunter at grips with a wild animal, the craftsman achieving a masterpiece, whether he be savage or civilized, will under such conditions feel altered, uplifted, endowed with higher forces. And there can be no doubt that from many of these solitary experiences where man feels the forebodings of death, the pangs of anxiety, the exaltation of bliss, there flows a great deal of religious inspiration. Though most ceremonies are carried out in public, much of religious revelation takes place in solitude.[18]

As for the presumed connection between the religious idea and collective *effervescent* festivities, that too seems dubious. There are numerous existing and effervescent occasions of a collective sort in "primitive" societies, which are nevertheless lacking in the faintest religious colouring. Malinowski cites the collective work in the gardens of Melanesia:

when men become carried away with emulation and zest for work, singing rhythmic songs, uttering shouts of joy and slogans of competitive challenge, [and which] is full of this "collective effervescence." But it is entirely profane, and society which "reveals itself" in this as in any other public performance assumes no divine grandeur or godlike appearance.[19]

Collective effervescence is also evident in battle, in sailing expeditions, in tribal gatherings for trading purposes, and in numerous other occasions, all of which generate no religious experience. It seems clear, then, that religious inspiration must take account of the solitary experiences of an individual, and that social effervescence may have no religious meaning at all.

There is still another objection raised by Malinowski. How can Society be the prototype of the Divine when so large a portion of what we inherit socially—traditions, knowledge, customs, norms, skills, and so on—are profane, not sacred? Society as keeper of both the sacred and profane traditions cannot be the basis of Divinity, for it is in the sacred domain only.

In sum, though there may be an element of truth in Durkheim's view; it is going too far to say, as he does, that society is the author of religious truth and that at bottom, the concepts of society and divinity are different aspects of the same notion. In expanding the role of the group to an extreme, as Durkheim does, he effectively eliminates the role of the individual. As Malinowski rightly insists, "without the analysis of the individual mind, we cannot take one step in the understanding of religion."[20]

For Durkheim, God and society are one because what people call "God" is actually the symbolic manifestation of the powers of Society. Each man is right, says Durkheim, in believing that there exists a power greater than himself, for that is the "moral power upon which he depends and from which he receives all that is best in himself: this power exists, it is society" (p. 225). The divine and the sacred are thus reduced to the social. Implying that there is no essential difference between one religion and another, and between religious and national assemblies, Durkheim asks,

What essential difference is there between an assembly of Christians celebrating the principal dates of the life of Christ, or of Jews remembering the exodus from Egypt or the promulgation of the decalogue, and a reunion of citizens commemorating the promulgation of a new moral or legal system or some great event in the national life? (p. 427)

The answer is, of course, that there exists a world of difference in the minds of the participants.

Hence, the inevitable result of Durkheim's approach is that it entirely ignores the *subjective meaning* that religious beliefs and acts have for the actors concerned. But one cannot grasp the authentic meaning of religious acts without recognizing that they are directed to the divine, not society. Grasped authentically, religious acts must be understood in their own right, and not reduced to the social. Thus, Durkheim's approach was quite antithetical to that of Max Weber, for whom the meaning and motives of actions were of paramount importance.

Durkheim's sociology of religion is therefore defective in that it effectively ignores the role of the individual. It also overlooks the fact that "personal religion" is

> more fundamental than either theology or ecclesiasticism. Churches, when once established, live at second-hand upon tradition; but the founders of every church owed their power originally to the fact of their direct personal communication with the divine. Not only the superhuman founders, the Christ, the Buddha, Mahomet, but all the originators of Christian sects have been in this case;—so personal religion should still seem the primordial thing, even to those who continue to esteem it incomplete.[21]

Durkheim's expansion of the determining power of "Society" to an extreme, and his corresponding neglect of the individual, are characteristic of his other writings. Throughout his work, he exhibits a conspicuous tendency toward the reification of society, a tendency that appears to be rooted in his social values and methodological principles.

METHODOLOGICAL RULES AND VALUES

Earlier we saw that in his sociology of deviance, Durkheim used a statistical criterion to distinguish the "normal" from the "deviant." "We shall call 'normal' those social conditions that are most generally distributed, and the others 'morbid' or 'pathological.'"[22] That definition may be useful, as we have seen, for the study of socially deviant behaviour. But Durkheim goes beyond the statistical criterion. His analogy between "Society" and a living organism led him to conclude that what is most widespread is also best: "It would be incomprehensible," he asserts, "if the most widespread forms of organization would not at the same time be, at least in their aggregate, the most advantageous" (p. 58). Advantageous for whom? For the "social organism" as a whole, of course. But how does one determine what is advantageous for society as a whole? Cannot widespread forms of organization be advantageous for some individuals and groups and not for others? Is it not true that certain widespread social forms prevail because some individuals and groups have the power to perpetuate them? Are there not in every society social relations and social forms that are positively disadvantageous to some groups and individuals? Such questions are never brought to the fore by Durkheim, and the issues of power and domination are virtually ignored. Though he understands, of course, that every real society consists of a plurality of groups with different, competing, and conflicting interests, and though he understands, too, that the power and advantages of some groups work to the detriment of others, he continues to speak of the good of the social organism as a whole.

If Durkheim is not saying that existing society is the best of all possible worlds, he is saying that at the present stage of evolution, the prevailing conditions are necessary for the adaptation of the social organism and are therefore useful and good. He is not, however, altogether happy with that conception of things. There are transition periods, he writes, when a

> phenomenon can ... persist throughout the entire range of a species although no longer adapted to the requirements of the situation. It is then normal only in appearance. Its universality is now an illusion, since its persistence, due only to the blind force of habit, can no longer be accepted as an index of a close connection with the general conditions of its collective existence. This difficulty is especially peculiar to sociology. (p. 61)

How shall sociology determine whether a given condition is "normal"? In "order to determine," he writes, "whether the present economic state of Europe ... is normal or not, we shall investigate the causes that brought it about. If these conditions still exist in our present-day society, this situation is normal in spite of the dissent it arouses" (p. 62). The system under those conditions still has "utility." Here we must observe that Durkheim's method for determining whether the "normal" is real or illusory is not unambiguous; we must also observe that his not-unambiguous method is directed against socialists and other critics of the economic system. It is as if Durkheim is trying to persuade them that since the conditions that brought about the present economic system still exist, their dissent is pointless.

Durkheim apparently believed that by means of positivist-scientific methods one could determine whether a particular stage in a society's evolution is in fact "adaptive," whether it has "utility," whether it is "advantageous." When practices not adapted to any vital end persist, they are treated by Durkheim as "survivals"; they continue "to exist by the inertia of habit alone." On the other hand, "if the usefulness of a fact is not the cause of its existence, it is generally necessary that it be useful in order that it may maintain itself" (p. 97). Thus Durkheim insists upon talking about whether social facts are "useful," "harmful," "advantageous," and so on, without asking for whom. In effect, he solves deductively and tautologically the problem of "society's" survival: "If … the majority of social phenomena had a parasitic character, the budget of the organism would have a deficit and social life would be impossible" (p. 97). The fact that a given society does survive shows that somehow "the phenomena comprising it combine in such a way to put society in harmony with itself and with the environment external to it" (p. 97).

In his *The Rules of the Sociological Method,* Durkheim is supposed to be setting forth the principles of a scientific, sociological method based on logic and facts. Yet, we see that Durkheim provides no facts to substantiate his claim that certain conditions are adaptive, useful, and advantageous for the society as a whole. Instead, his "proof" is strictly deductive. That problem aside, however, it is not difficult to discern Durkheim's apparent motivation for arguing as he does. Evidently, he wants to assure the critics of the existing economic system that the conditions arousing their indignation are "normal" and "necessary." If society represses and constrains, that "is not derived from a conventional arrangement which human will had added … to natural reality; it issues from the innermost reality; it is the necessary product of given causes" (p. 123). There is no doubt, therefore, that even Durkheim's "scientific" rules were designed to "create a sociology which sees in the *spirit of discipline* the essential condition of all human life" (p. 124, italics added).

THE STUDY OF SUICIDE

Durkheim's use of sociocultural variables to explain variations in suicide rates must be regarded as ingenious and brilliant. Here, however, we shall not concern ourselves with the empirical aspects of his study, discussions of which are widely available in the sociological literature. Instead, we shall continue to explore the values underlying Durkheim's study.

Durkheim chose to study suicide because he had hoped that from his study would emerge "some suggestions concerning the causes of the general contemporary *maladjustments* being undergone by European societies and concerning remedies which may relieve it."[23] If in his earliest works Durkheim gave attention to *both* the anomic and the forced division of labour, he now focused almost exclusively on the first. The problems of modern man were a matter of "maladjustment." The most pressing task, therefore, was to develop for modern man an appropriate morality that would give him a sense of satiety, that would help him overcome his restlessness and discontent, and that would enable him to adjust happily to modern society.

Modern man kills himself, Durkheim argues, primarily as a result of two conditions: the loss of cohesion in modern society and the absence of suitable moral norms by which to orient himself. Modern man is egoistic and anomic. Both conditions can be remedied by creating a new moral code and resurrecting and reorganizing the occupational guild so that it may serve an integrative and regulatory function under modern conditions. The most urgent task is to bring about a high degree of social integration—moral, domestic, political, and economic—because the data tend to support the proposition that "*Suicide varies inversely with the degree of integration of … society*" (p. 208).

A third type of suicide Durkheim called "altruistic"; this occurred when social integration was too strong. That, however, was endemic to "lower societies," and therefore no cause for concern to higher ones. A definite cause for concern, however, was the "excessive individualism" characteristic of modern civilization. So again, the remedy is cohesion, consensus, and solidarity. Noting the rise in the rate of self-destruction *after* the war of 1870, Durkheim writes,

> On the morrow of the war in 1879 a new accession of good fortune took place. Germany was unified and placed entirely under Prussian

hegemony. An enormous war indemnity added to the public wealth; commerce and industry made great strides. The development of suicide was never so rapid. From 1875 to 1886 it increased 90 percent. (p. 244)

The juxtaposition of suicide and war, both of which result in the destruction of human life, is revealing. Given Durkheim's values and focal concerns, suicide loomed as a bigger problem than war. A rising suicide rate indicated diminishing integration. War, on the other hand, brought with it greater solidarity. Durkheim's attitude reached its logical conclusion in the patriotic articles he wrote during the great carnage that began in 1914. The translation into practice of his doctrine that the individual must subordinate himself to Society (which, in practice, could only mean to the State) mortally wounded him. He lost his son in the war and, brokenhearted, died himself soon afterward. Durkheim had apparently failed to perceive the dangers inherent in a "social integration" that was the product of nationalist chauvinism and that compelled men to kill one another en masse as their patriotic duty. Furthermore, it is ironic that for all his concern with social integration, he never anticipated the extreme disorganizing consequences of World War I—social convulsions and revolutions throughout Europe and, in the end, far-reaching structural changes.

What Durkheim called "anomic" suicide is especially interesting since it was associated with both rising prosperity and economic crises. If the suicide rate increased under both circumstances, Durkheim reasoned, that must mean that the rate has nothing to do with either prosperity or economic crises per se. Rather, it is associated with the fact that both types of events are "disturbances of the collective order. Every disturbance of equilibrium, even though it achieves greater comfort and a heightening of general vitality, is an impulse to voluntary death" (p. 246). In explaining that phenomenon, Durkheim elaborates his philosophy for modern man.

The needs of all other animal creatures are strictly organic in nature; they are driven instinctively to replenish the energy exhausted in their metabolic interaction with nature; once having done so, they are satisfied and crave nothing more. Natural limits are set on their craving and striving. In contrast, "[n]othing appears in man's organic nor in his psychological constitution which sets" limits on his desires. Man has needs which transcend the strictly vital requirements of his organism; those needs are "unlimited so far as they depend on the individual alone." In the absence of an "external regulatory force, our capacity for feeling is in itself an insatiable and bottomless abyss" (p. 247). That can be only a "source of torment" to man. "Unlimited desires are insatiable by definition and insatiability," writes Durkheim, "is rightly considered a sign of morbidity" (p. 247). The infinity of man's desires and goals is what really causes him pain and suffering; the only solution, therefore, is to limit his passions. Some regulative force must be imposed upon him that will "play the same role for moral needs which the organism plays for physical needs. This means that the force can only be moral" (p. 248). Since the imposed limits will be effective only so long as men recognize them as just, they must receive the sense of what is just "from an authority which they respect, to which they yield spontaneously" (p. 249). And, of course, as we have come to expect, it is "Society" which is the ultimate authority in this regard: "society alone can play this moderating role; for it is the only moral power superior to the individual, the authority of which he accepts. It alone has the power necessary to stipulate law and to set the point beyond which the passions must not go. Finally, it alone can estimate the reward to be prospectively offered to every class of human functionary, in the name of the common interest" (p. 249). "Society" can and should determine the rewards to be assigned to each "function"—to the men in each occupation. "A genuine regimen exists therefore, … which fixes with relative precision the maximum degree of ease of living to which each social class may legitimately aspire" (p. 249).

Durkheim perceived that the living standards of all classes, including the workers, continued to improve; nevertheless, there was no contentment. Restlessness, social conflict, and "anarchy" prevailed despite the betterment of material conditions for all. But there still remained the "relative deprivation" of those in the lower and disadvantaged strata. Therefore, society must exert moral pressure so that "each in his sphere vaguely realizes the extreme limit set to his ambitions and aspires to nothing beyond. At least if he respects regulations and is docile to collective authority, that is, has a wholesome moral constitution, he feels that it is not well to ask more" (p. 250). The only real solution to man's malaise is to curb and bridle aspirations; only then will he be contented with his lot and strive "moderately to improve it, and this average contentment causes the feeling of calm, active happiness, the pleasure in existing and living which characterizes health for societies as well as for individuals" (p. 250).

Durkheim understood, however, that "society's" moral authority would be accepted by men only if they regard the existing "distribution of functions" as just. "The workman is not in harmony with his social position if he is not convinced that he has his deserts" (p. 250). And now there is a definite shift of emphasis in Durkheim's argument as compared with *Professional Ethics and Civil Morals*. There he argued that at least one structural change required immediate institution: the abolition of the private inheritance of wealth. That was necessary because without it, the relations among men were inherently unjust. Now, in *Suicide*, he retreats from that position or, at the very least, is highly ambivalent. It is true, he writes, that "the nearer this ideal equality were approached, the less social restraint will be necessary. *But it is only a matter of degree.* One sort of heredity will always exist, that of natural talent" (p. 251, italics added). To demand of those "naturally superior" that they function without greater rewards would require a discipline even stronger than the existing one. If earlier he argued that "natural inequalities" need not be accompanied by material inequalities, now Durkheim changed his view. Since *all* social systems regulate and repress, since man can never escape altogether from social restraint, the abolition of institutionalized economic inequalities, he now tells us, would only result in a diminution in the degree of restraint. That being the case, there is no point in agitating oneself about existing inequalities and injustices; their abolition will make only a minor difference for man's existence. The main task for Durkheim, therefore, is not to change social conditions so that constraint and repression are constantly reduced, but to bring about a collective order that is obeyed and respected. Man must be given a moral education that will teach him, above all, to be content with his condition and to improve it moderately. "All classes contend among themselves," he painfully observed, "because no established classification any longer exists" (p. 253). The task, then, was to arrive at a new "classification" that all would accept.

Durkheim was impressed with the greater immunity to suicide of the poor; but his discussion of that fact becomes a celebration of poverty:

> [T]he less one has the less he is tempted to extend the range of his needs indefinitely. Lack of power, compelling moderation, accustoms men to it.... [Poverty] is actually the best school for teaching self-restraint. Forcing us to constant self-discipline, it prepares us to accept collective discipline with equanimity, while wealth, exalting the individual, may

always arouse the spirit of rebellion which is the very source of immorality. (p. 254)

Regulation, moderation, discipline, duty—those are the highest virtues. Durkheim wanted a "highly socialized" man, "for if one were highly socialized one would not rebel at every social restraint" (p. 288).

It was only the egoistic and anomic types of suicide that Durkheim regarded as morbid. The former, for example, "results from the fact that society is not sufficiently integrated at all points to keep all its members under its control.… Thus, the only remedy for the ill," writes Durkheim, "is to restore enough consistency to social groups for them to obtain a firmer grip on the individual, and for him to feel himself bound to them" (p. 373). Durkheim therefore calls once again for the restoration of occupational groups. The individual would be firmly integrated in his group, and the groups subordinated to the state, thus yielding an "organic" solidarity. The conflictive character of the previous system would thus be eliminated.

Durkheim, of course, understood that a higher form of social solidarity presupposed the elimination of basic social inequalities. But in the context of his intellectual work as a whole, the concern with justice, so effectively articulated in his *The Division of Labor in Society* and *Professional Ethics and Civic Morals*, figures far less prominently than his concern for anomie. Anomie could only be reduced and done away with by raising "Society" to the status of the divine.

Durkheim felt the need to hypostatize and deify "Society" because he feared the moral vacuum that might result from the decline of traditional religion. In an earlier era, God was the supreme guarantor of the moral order; in giving God his due, people were in effect assuring that their relations would rest on a firm moral basis. But in his own day, Durkheim, like several other social thinkers, believed that God was dead in the moral sense. The gods are growing old or are already dead, he believed, and "others are not yet born."[24] Religion had declined as a consequence of both the dissolution of traditional society and the growth of industry and science. If religion has become a moribund institution, reasons Durkheim, and no longer fulfills its central moral function, then present-day society is faced with a great danger: the denial of morality altogether. If no secular substitute is found for religion, then public morality will be threatened at its roots. To forestall that condition and thus to overcome anomie, it was necessary to find new gods suited to the new conditions. To discover what the nature of the new gods (that is, the new moral norms and values) must be was the task of social science. Durkheim's positivist conception of social science led him to conclude that "Society" was the appropriate new god, for it "is the highest form of the psychic life," "the consciousness of the consciousness." Society "sees from above" and "sees farther."[25] When one reads such descriptions by Durkheim of Society as the "Supreme God," one also understands why duty, devotion, discipline, and abnegation were his most cherished values.

NOTES

1.   See Marcel Mauss's introduction to the first edition of Durkheim's *Socialism and Saint-Simon,* ed. and with an Introduction by Alvin W. Gouldner (London: Routledge and Kegan Paul, 1959).

2.   Ibid., p. 2. (Hereafter all page references to this work will be indicated in parentheses immediately following the quoted passage.)

3.   Émile Durkheim, *The Division of Labor in Society* (New York: The Free Press, 1965), p. 204. (Hereafter all page references to this work will be indicated in parentheses immediately following the quoted passage.)

4.   Émile Durkheim, *Professional Ethics and Civic Morals* (London: Routledge and Kegan Paul, 1957), p. 12. (Hereafter all page references to this work will be indicated in parentheses immediately following the quoted passage.)

5.   Émile Durkheim, *The Rules of the Sociological Method,* trans. Sarah A. Solovay and John H. Mueller, ed. George E. G. Catlin (New York: The Free Press, 1964), p. 55.

6.   Ibid., p. 66.

7.   Ibid., p. 69.

8.   Ibid., pp. 71–72.

9.   Durkheim, *Division of Labor*, p. 81.

10.   Ibid., p. 81.

11.   Ibid., p. 102.

12.   Ibid., p. 108.

13.   For details about Lombroso and other key figures in the history of criminology, see Bernaldo de Quiros, *Modern Theories of Criminality* (Boston: Little, Brown, 1911), and Hermann Mannheim, ed., *Pioneers of Criminology* (Chicago: Quadrangle/The New York Times Book Co., 1960).

14.   For a detailed critique of the methods employed in such studies, see George B. Vold, *Theoretical Criminology* (New York: Oxford University Press, 1958).

15. E. B. Tylor, *Religion in Primitive Culture* (New York: Harper Torchbooks, 1958), p. 8. (First published in 1871.)

16. Émile Durkheim, *The Elementary Forms of Religious Life*, trans. and ed. J. W. Swain (London: George Allen and Unwin, 1964), p. 47. (Hereafter all page references to this work will be indicated in parentheses immediately following the quoted passage.)

17. Tylor, *Religion*, pp. 12–13.

18. Bronislaw Malinowski, *Magic, Science and Religion* (Garden City, N.Y.: Doubleday/ Anchor Books, 1954), p. 58.

19. Ibid., p. 58.

20. Ibid., p. 69.

21. William James, *The Varieties of Religious Experience* (New York: Collier Books, 1976), p. 42. (Originally published in 1902).

22. Émile Durkheim, *The Rules of Sociological Method* (New York: The Free Press, 1964), p. 55. (Hereafter all page references to this work will be indicated in parentheses immediately following the quoted passage.)

23. Émile Durkheim, *Suicide*, trans. John A. Spaulding and George Simpson (London: Routledge and Kegan Paul, 1963), p. 37. (Hereafter all page references to this work will be indicated in parentheses immediately following the quoted passage.)

24. Émile Durkheim, *The Elementary Forms of Religious Life* (London: George Allen and Unwin, 1964), p. 427.

25. Ibid., p. 444.

CHAPTER 13

Karl Mannheim (1893–1947)

Like Max Weber before him, and in a sense following his example, Mannheim accepted the suggestion that the value of Marx's method lay in the "hint that there is a correlation between the economic structure of a society and its legal and political organization, *and that even the world of our thought is affected by these relationships.*"[1] Most conspicuously in his sociology of knowledge, Mannheim considered political, legal, philosophical, religious, and other ideas in their relationship with economic and social changes. That the ideas people hold vary with changing economic circumstances and that they are "somehow connected with the social context in which they live,"[2] remained a central guiding principle throughout his work.

Mannheim's life's work may be divided into two distinct but interrelated phases and projects. The first, for which he is more famous, is his contribution to the sociology of knowledge. It began with his doctoral dissertation entitled "The Structural Analysis of Epistemology" and culminated in his classic work *Ideology and Utopia* and in his later essays published in one volume under the title *Essays on the Sociology of Culture.* The second phase, the fruit of his reflections on the crisis of his time and on life in England during World War II, included such works as *Man and Society in an Age of Reconstruction; Diagnosis of Our Time;* and *Freedom, Power, and Democratic Planning.* It was in the latter phase that one sees most clearly the ethical commitment underlying all of Mannheim's work—namely, that sociological studies must be regarded "as a response to the challenging present." Bramsted and Gerth have observed that for Mannheim, "sociology was a specifically modern way of thought which contributes to the rational self-orientation of man in industrial society. By raising us to a new level of self-awareness, the intellectual tools that the sociologist forges open up for us an insight into the dangerous processes of the modern world with its drift toward social upheavals and world wars."[3] There was, then, a first, or German, phase in which Mannheim directed his main efforts toward a sociological analysis of knowledge and a second, or English, phase in which he attempted to use his sociology to sketch the guidelines for a rational and democratic reconstruction of society.

IDEOLOGY AND UTOPIA

Although the principles enunciated in these essays can apply to the general problem of "how men actually think" and to the relationship of thinking to other aspects of human action, in practice Mannheim confines his attention to the narrower question of how thinking functions in the public and political spheres of social life. Now, as earlier, his major working hypothesis is derived from Marx's celebrated idea that is it the conditions of men's social existence which tend to determine their social consciousness. Mannheim adopts that principle in its full conflictive and dialectical sense: Men "act with and against one another in diversely organized groups, and while doing so they think with and against one another."[4]

Depending on the position men occupy in the social structure and their consciousness of that position, they join together in groups and strive collectively either to change or to preserve the conditions of their existence. Like Marx, Mannheim protests the separation of thought from action. The unity of theory and action must be recognized and restored in practice so that men may gain a fuller consciousness of the consequences of their acts. For Marx, the function of theory was to guide men in changing the world; for Mannheim, similarly, the raison d'être of his sociological theory of knowledge was to provide scientific guidance for action directed toward social change—for what he eventually called *planning for freedom*.

At the very outset he points quite clearly to both the advantages and limitations of his sociology of knowledge; "the ultimate criterion of truth or falsity is to be found in the investigation of the object, and the sociology of knowledge is no substitute for this" (p. 4). Relating men's ideas to the particular location they occupy in the social structure is a process quite different from assessing their truth and validity. The sociological theory of knowledge can tell us how those ideas emerged but not whether they are true or false.

For Mannheim, the sociological theory of knowledge is a peculiarly modern instrument of analysis and reflection. It accompanied the greater tempo of social change of the capitalist-industrial era, including vertical and horizontal mobility, and the more intense and overt class conflicts of that era. Such a theory never could have arisen in medieval Europe, for example, which was a relatively static society characterized by closed castes or ranks. Nobles, clerics, peasants, artisans, and merchants had their own respective views of the world which merely coexisted as isolated *Weltanschauungen*—a reflection of the relative social isolation of those strata from one another. Only with the great social mobility and communication of the capitalist era did a decisive change take place. That becomes evident "when the forms of thought and experience, which had hitherto developed independently, enter into one and the same consciousness impelling the mind to discover the irreconcilability of the conflicting conceptions of the world" (p. 7). In addition, the greater mobility, communication, and conflict which accompanied capitalist-industrial developments brought in their wake greater democratization. That gave the thinking of the lower strata a greater public significance; one example in philosophy of the attempt to formalize such thinking is pragmatism. Social changes have resulted in a social system fundamentally different from the *Gemeinschaft* of the Middle Ages and are reflected in the thought of the "free intelligentsia"—also a characteristically modern product. They are "recruited from constantly varying social strata and life situations and [their] mode of thought is no longer subject [as it was in the Middle Ages] to regulation by a caste-like organization" (p. 10).

The greater understanding which the sociological approach to knowledge facilitates becomes evident by comparing it with others. Historically, one may distinguish at least three distinct approaches to problems of knowledge: (1) the *epistemological*, (2) the *psychological*, and (3) the *sociological*. An example of the first may be seen in the various philosophical controversies between the idealists and materialists, the realists and the nominalists, the empiricists and the rationalists, and so on. To take the last dispute, there can be no doubt that the participants raised an important question. Is knowledge a result of immediate sensory experience as Locke, for example, had held? Or is it the outcome of experience mediated by a priori categories as Kant had postulated? Mannheim sided with the latter school—but with the important qualification that the categories are not a priori. The mind and all its logical categories are a social product, and without that insight the epistemological question could never be adequately resolved. Though epistemology has enriched our understanding by posing certain problems, it needs sociology to solve them.

The psychological approach has also yielded the greater understanding of the form and content of certain thoughts. Biographical data, for instance, are often very illuminating since they suggest why a given thinker thought the way he did. Yet, that approach, too, has definite limitations. Studying the life of Jesus or the Apostles, for example, can never adequately convey the full meaning of the biblical saying: "The last shall be the first." A full and adequate understanding of that utterance, Mannheim strives to show, could only be gained by going beyond the strictly psychological approach to consider not only biography but social structure and history as well. Combining the ideas of Marx, Nietzsche, and Scheler, Mannheim suggests that the phrase, "The last shall be first," can only be understood if one becomes aware of "the significance of resentment in the formation of moral judgments" (p. 22). An analysis of the sociohistorical context in which the sentence was first uttered suggests "that it has a real appeal only for those who, like the [early] Christians, are in some manner oppressed and who, at the same time, under the impulse of resentment, wish to free themselves from prevailing injustices" (p. 23). The merit of the sociological approach, then, is that it sets "alongside the individual genesis of meaning the genesis from the context of group life" (p. 25).

The conditions of existence and conflict of interests between oppressors and oppressed engender antithetical movements of thought. Mannheim employs what he calls "two slogan-like concepts 'ideology and utopia'" to describe these antithetical thought forms. Early Christian thought, for instance, was "utopian" in that it expressed the resentment of the oppressed. Their weakness led them to deprecate power and to glorify passivity—for example, "turn the other cheek." The early Christians constituted a "stratum which had as yet no real aspirations to rule" (p. 12), thus the saying, "Render unto Caesar the things that are Caesar's." Their resentment was therefore sublimated into a mere psychic rebellion: "The last shall be the first." All the values of the Roman oppressors ("ideology") were repudiated in the countervalues ("Utopia") of the oppressed Christians. Both ideological thought and utopian thought are thus "situationally determined," not only in the sense that each reflects the different conditions of existence of rulers and ruled, oppressors and oppressed, or upper and lower strata, but also in the sense that each reflects the interests of its "carriers."

Two distinct meanings may be discerned in the development of the concept ideology, and Mannheim calls them the *particular* and *total* conceptions. The first refers to the "more or less conscious disguises of the real nature of the situation, the true recognition of which would not be in accord with [one's] interests. These distortions range all the way from conscious lies to half-conscious and unwitting disguises; from calculated attempts to dupe others to self-deception" (p. 49). The *total* conception of ideology, on the other hand, refers, for example, to the *Weltanschauung* of a class or epoch, or to the ideas and categories of thought which are bound up with the existential conditions of that class or epoch. In the *particular*, or psychological, conception, one deals with an individual and attempts to "unmask" him by discovering the true personal interests he deceitfully hides or denies; in that case one designates "only a part of the opponent's assertions" as ideology while continuing to share with him a common universe of discourse and common standards of validity. The total conception, in contrast, "calls into question the opponent's entire *Weltanschauung* (including his conceptual apparatus) and attempts to understand these concepts as an outgrowth of the collective life of which he partakes" (p. 50). Examples of the *total* conception might be "conservative thought," "bourgeois-liberal" ideology, and so on. When men express such ideas, it is not a matter of deceit or even "interests" in any narrow sense but rather an expression of the outlook of a whole social group or stratum whose existential circumstances they share. Marxism fused both conceptions into one and thus became a formidable ideological weapon in the hands of the proletariat and its spokesmen. "It was this theory which first gave due emphasis to the role of class position and class interests in thought" (p. 66). Soon afterward, however, the opponents of Marxism learned to use the weapon of ideological analysis and to turn it against Marxism itself. It was that process that made possible the "transition from the theory of ideology to the sociology of knowledge" (p. 67).

For Mannheim, then, the *total* conception of ideology requires *sociological* analysis, and here two formulations may be distinguished: the *special* and the *general*. At first a group discovers the *Seinverbundenheit* or "situational determination" of its opponents' ideas while remaining unaware that its own thought is also influenced by the social situation in which it finds itself.

When that is the case, Mannheim calls it the special formulation of the total conception of ideology. The *general* formulation, on the other hand, is employed when one "has the courage to subject not just the adversary's point of view but all points of view, including his own, to the ideological analysis" (p. 69). If the *general form of the total conception* is used in an investigation in a nonevaluative manner—that is, judgments are temporarily suspended as to the truth or falsity of the ideas in question—then one has a *sociology of knowledge.*

Does not the sociology of knowledge imply that truth is "relative"—that is, "dependent upon the subjective standpoint and the social situation of the knower"? To that Mannheim replies in the negative, for while the study of history from the standpoint of the sociology of knowledge does not reveal any absolute truths, that implies not "relativism" but "relationism." The probability is great that the perspective of an observer or knower will vary with his social standpoint, but the question "[W]hich social standpoint offers the best chance for reaching an optimum of truth?" still remains (p. 71). For Mannheim, then, the social basis of an idea and its validity are two separate questions.[5]

The student of a given social or historical question, even one who has a truly objective intention, is made aware by the sociology of knowledge that all points of view, including his own, are partial and one-sided. His objective posture leads him to consider carefully the many contending viewpoints, which he relates to their respective social situations. "Through this effort the one-sidedness of our own point of view is counteracted, and conflicting intellectual positions may actually come to supplement one another."[6] Our knowledge and ability to get at the truth are presumably enhanced by the very fact that one can employ a variety of perspectives through which to study a given phenomenon, and are enhanced, too, by discovering the social bases of the various perspectives.

This may be illustrated by recalling Max Weber's view. There can be no doubt that he regarded Marx's perspective as strategically important for an understanding of historical change, and his own perspective as supplementary to that of Marx. For Weber, it was not a matter of one perspective being true and the other false. Rather, by adding his own to Marx's, a richer and more adequate understanding of the origins of capitalism was made possible. One partial truth supplemented and enriched another. That was also Mannheim's attitude toward historical questions. Under no circumstances were the postulates of the sociology of knowledge to be regarded as a substitute for empirical research. "We, too, appeal to 'facts' for our proof, but the question of the nature of facts is in itself a considerable problem."[7] In the end, Mannheim believed that, however objective an analysis may be, there still remains "an irreducible residue of evaluation inherent in the structure of all thought," but that there was perhaps one stratum in society which was more capable than any other of becoming conscious of its evaluations (p. 15). That was the intelligentsia.

THE INTELLIGENTSIA

It is not quite accurate to say that Mannheim found "a structural warranty of the validity of social thought in the 'classless position' of the 'socially unattached intellectuals' [*sozialfreischwebende Intelligenz*]."[8] If the impression of such a "warranty" might occasionally be inferred from Mannheim's remarks in *Ideology and Utopia* and other early essays, he makes quite clear in a later essay, devoted entirely to the subject of intellectuals, that such an impression is not the one he had intended to convey and, in fact, that it is a misinterpretation of his thesis. Mannheim's point about the intelligentsia was that they are not a class; they have no common interests, they cannot form a separate party, and, finally, they are incapable of common and concerted action. They are, in fact, *ideologues* of this or that class but never speak for "themselves."

For Mannheim, the intelligentsia was essentially a "classless aggregation," or an "interstitial stratum" which willy-nilly became "a satellite of one or another of the existing classes and parties."[9] It was "between, but not above, the classes." He is quite explicit on this score: The intellectuals are not a "superior" stratum, nor does their peculiar social position assure any greater validity for their perspectives. Their position does, however, enable them to do something which members of other strata are less able to do. It is true that most intellectuals do in fact share the orientations of one or another of the existing classes and parties. "But," writes Mannheim,

> over and above these affiliations he [an intellectual] is motivated by the fact that his training has equipped him to face the problems of the day in several perspectives and not only in one, as most participants in the controversies of their time do. We said he is equipped to envisage the

problems of his time in more than a single perspective, although from case
to case he may act as a partisan and align himself with a class. (p. 105)

The emphasis here is on the *potential* ability of the educated individual to adopt a variety of perspectives toward any given social issue or phenomenon. Intellectuals are *not*, Mannheim reemphasizes, "an exalted stratum above the classes and are in no way better endowed with a capacity to overcome their own class attachments than other groups" (p. 105). In his earlier essays, he explains, the term "relatively" in the phrase "relatively unattached intelligentsia," which he borrowed from Alfred Weber, "was no empty word. The expression simply alluded to the well-established fact that intellectuals do not react to given issues as cohesively as for example … workers do" (p. 106). Being a member of the so-called intelligentsia, then, provides no structural warranty of validity nor does it make one "privy to revelations." Apparently, all that Mannheim wanted to convey in his thesis about the intelligentsia "was merely that certain types of intellectuals have a maximum opportunity to test and employ the socially available vistas and to experience their inconsistencies" (p. 106). Right or wrong, that is a considerably more modest thesis than his critics have attributed to him.

One of the main points Mannheim wanted to make with the phrase "relatively unattached" was that after the Middle Ages the intellectuals, to an increasing degree, were emancipated from the upper classes and unaligned as yet with the lower. The institutions in which the intellectuals could first be discerned as relatively free and detached were the *salons* and the coffee-houses. While the salons enabled individuals of different social backgrounds, views, stations, and allegiances to mingle, entry to the salon required social acceptability and was in that sense restricted. The coffee-houses, on the other hand, were open to all and thus "became the first centers of opinion in a partially democratized society" (p. 138). Membership and participation were now determined not by rank and family ties but by intellectual interests and shared opinions; the latter being especially true when the houses became political clubs. "Not the common style of living and not common friends, but like opinion constituted now the basis of amalgamation" (p. 139).

In the modern era, *some* intellectuals at least were able to escape a relationship of dependence on local habitat, institution, class, and party. To be sure, they "may have their political preferences, but they are not committed to any party or denomination. This detachment, however, is not absolute" (p. 157). *Some* journalists, *some* writers, *some* scholars, and *some* scientists "enjoy" a relatively uncommitted position which, however, has for Mannheim negative as well as positive consequences; for although it is true that the "free" intellectual has a potentially wider view and is potentially less blinded by particular interests and commitments, he lacks at the same time the restraints of real life. He is more inclined to generate ideas without testing them in practice—that is, in the actions and consequences of everyday life. He may lose touch with reality and forget that a main purpose of thought is the orientation of action. Such observations helped illuminate the changing historical role of the intellectual.

More important for Mannheim, however, was the fate of the relatively free intellectuals in the face of the tendency so well described by Max Weber: the growing bureaucratization of all aspects of social life including scholarship and science. Increasingly, Weber had pointed out, not only the workers but the scientists and scholars were being "separated" from the means of "production" (research). That, together with specialization, which narrows the compass of thought and activity, discourages the "will to dissent and innovate" (p. 168). More and more, research, thinking, and scholarship were now carried out in the context of large organizations, private and governmental, and the increasing dependence of the mental labourer led to an increasing "intellectual dessication" (p. 168). There were now few professions that were "free" in the sense that they could be practiced independently, outside a bureaucratic context.

No matter how small the intellectual stratum may be, still it retains an important role at once diagnostic, constructive, and critical. There is nothing automatic about those functions—they do not follow "naturally" from a social position. In effect, it is only by conscious and deliberate commitment that the intellectual can prevent his affiliation with parties and organizations from resulting in self-abnegation. His conscious posture must at all times be critical—of himself as well as of others. Mannheim recognized that the intellectuals were powerless, but he believed, nevertheless, that they could play an influential role in the preservation of freedom and in the reconstruction of society.

NOTES

1. Karl Mannheim, *Systematic Sociology* (New York: Grove Press, 1957), p. 137, italics added. For a brief discussion of Marxian and other theoretical influences on Mannheim, see Robert Merton's essay "Karl Mannheim and the Sociology of Knowledge," in *Social Theory and Social Structure* (Glencoe, Ill.: The Free Press, 1968), p. 544.

2. Mannheim, *Systematic Sociology*, p. 137.

3. See "A Note on the Work of Karl Mannheim," by Ernest K. Bramsted and Hans Gerth in Karl Mannheim, *Freedom, Power, and Democratic Planning* (London: Routledge and Kegan Paul, 1950), pp. vii–xv.

4. Karl Mannheim, *Ideology and Utopia* (London: Routledge and Kegan Paul, 1960), p. 3. (Hereafter all page references to this work will be indicated in parenthesis immediately following the quoted passage.)

5. An excellent critical discussion of this and other problems may be found in Merton, "Karl Mannheim and the Sociology of Knowledge" (see note 1, this chapter), pp. 543–62.

6. Mannheim, *Ideology and Utopia,* p. 76.

7. Ibid., p. 91.

8. Merton, "Karl Mannheim and the Sociology of Knowledge" (see note 1, this chapter), p. 561.

9. Karl Mannheim, *Essays on the Sociology of Culture* (London: Routledge and Kegan Paul, 1956), p. 104. (Hereafter all page references to this work will be indicated in parenthesis immediately following the quoted passage.)

CHAPTER 14

George Herbert Mead (1863–1931)

Among sociologists, Mead is probably the best known of the extraordinary thinkers associated with the American pragmatic philosophical tradition. Mead's work is, of course, informed by the basic insights of Peirce and James; and early in Mead's career, John Dewey had hired him as his assistant, and the two scholars became the closest of friends until Mead's death in 1931. Mead's work on the social self, and the "I" and the "Me" in particular, laid the foundations of modern American social psychology in the field of role-theory and symbolic interaction. Mead's approach was so original and persuasive that Dewey adopted it in its entirety whenever he found it relevant to the specific issues he addressed.[1] To understand why Mead's theory is original and sound, we have to grasp its *dialectical* character, the meaning of which will become clear in due course.

For Mead, the traditional bifurcation of nature into "mind" on the one hand and physical nature on the other was fallacious. The philosophical result of such a bifurcation was either that nature was divested of all independence and devoured by mind, as with the various Idealists, or mind was effectively extinguished by reducing it to material particles, as with the Materialists. Mead recognized that such extreme and defective views could not be fruitfully applied in the study of human nature and action. In *Mind, Self and Society*, and throughout his other works, Mead undertook a single philosophical task: to overcome the traditional dualism by means of a dialectical conception of the relation of human beings to one another, and of human beings to nature. In Mead's dialectical view, the individual as a sensitive, active social being contributes to the constitution of his effective environment as truly as the environment (natural and social) influences his sensitivity and action. Throughout, Mead stresses that "the individual is no thrall of society. He constitutes society as genuinely as society constitutes the individual."[2] In these terms, Mead's philosophical critique of the traditional dualism, and his repudiation of both Idealism and Mechanistic Materialism are reminiscent of Marx's efforts in that regard.

MIND, SELF, AND SOCIETY

There are aspects of human interaction that are immediate, that is, mediated by little or no thought, and which therefore resemble the interaction of animals. In Mead's famous illustration of a dog fight, each dog's gesture is a stimulus for the other's response, which in turn becomes a new stimulus.[3] They are engaged in a *conversation of gestures*, though these gestures are not significant ones, for they carry no meaning. The dogs interact with each other, each anticipating the action of the other *reflexively*.

Similarly, two boxers or fencers, Mead proposes, respond to each other's gestures reflexively, without deliberation. Although we shall want to qualify this statement, it appears that animals remain at this level of interaction: *conversation of nonsignificant gestures.* In human beings, in contrast, this constitutes a relatively small proportion of our total interactions. A man can strike another without intending to do so, or recoil from something before he knows why. But he can also shake his fist in anger, displaying a deliberately hostile attitude. In that case, there is an *idea* behind his gesture. Indeed, when a gesture carries with it a specific meaning and arouses in the other individual the same idea it arouses in the first, Mead says "we have a significant symbol" (p. 45). That is what we commonly mean by "language," or communication by means of symbols. Among meaningful gestures the *vocal* ones are the most important for daily communication.

Gestures and significant gestures are therefore phases and aspects of actions that facilitate cooperation and the carrying out of tasks. However, a significant gesture offers a much greater facility for cooperation because it evokes the same attitude in the other participating actors that it does in the individual making it. A gesture, as a significant symbol, arouses in the individual making it the same response (meaning) he intends to arouse in the other. A conversation of significant gestures thus requires that *one take the attitude of the other toward one's own gestures* (p. 47).

It is precisely by means of such significant gestures, or symbols, that *thinking* takes place. What is "thinking," if not an internal conversation like the conversations we carry on externally with others! "Mind" may therefore be defined as *the presence in conduct of significant symbols.*

For Mead, then, mind presupposes a social process. In opposition to certain schools of "Idealist" psychology that posited minds and selves as antecedent to social process, Mead demonstrated logically that "selves must be accounted for in terms of the social process, and in terms of communication" (p. 49). It is only within that process that minds and selves can emerge. If one begins with mind and derives social process from it, "then the origin of minds and the interaction of minds become mysteries" (p. 50). If, on the other hand, one assumes the priority of social process and communication—priority in the sense that they are antecedent to any individual mind or self, and in the further sense that neither mind nor self can emerge except in the context of a social process—then the mystery ceases. For Mead there can be no equivocation here: mind first arises through communication by means of a conversation of significant gestures in a social process.

The origin of distinctively human communication—*language*—cannot be derived from imitation. In humans and in higher animals, imitation plays a minimal role. Monkeys, dogs, and foxes, for instance, do not purely imitate; they learn, and even learn quickly. The young fox runs away from man not merely because that is what the older fox does; he rather comes to link the response of flight to the stimulus of man—the fox hunter's scent. That is learning, not imitation.

Animals do, of course, learn much. Their behaviour is neither strictly instinctive nor imitative. They acquire adaptive "habits" in a given environment by responding adequately to specific stimuli. Among such stimuli is the gesture. In the conversation of (nonsignificant) gestures common to both animals and humans, the stimulus and the response *differ*: One animal's threat leads to another's flight; the baby's cry leads to the mother's care; a boxer's jab leads to the other's block. In all such cases the response differs from the stimulus. In a conversation of *significant gestures*, in contrast, stimulus and response are identical for all participants. "What language seems to carry," says Mead, "is a set of symbols answering to certain content which is measurably identical in the experience of the different individuals. If there is to be communication as such, the symbol has to mean the same thing to all individuals involved" (p. 54).

Although most animals learn to act appropriately and even to cooperate in their specific, natural environments, Mead asserts that the stimulus-gesture of one can never evoke the identical response-gesture in another. Animals do not possess the ability to produce significant symbols or language. There is no way of getting from the animal condition, in which stimulus and response differ, to the human condition, in which stimulus and response can be identical. The latter requires that uniquely human capacity for creating and transmitting symbols, meanings, ideas, and content. As a generalization, Mead's view is no doubt valid. When we consider that the Oxford unabridged dictionary of the English language contains over a half-million words, and that Shakespeare employed some 300,000 different words, and if we further consider that every man and woman employs many hundreds of words in their everyday lives, we can appreciate the cogency of Mead's proposition. If it required any qualification at all, it would be that some animals, notably certain insects and birds, do seem to possess a small repertory of significant gestures. Bees, for example, according to Karl von Frisch, appear capable of communicating "messages," such as the availability of flowers and nectar in another locale, and sparrows appear to convey the availability of seeds or grain in another locale. However, even if such "meaningful" communication is possible among animals, their total repertory of significant gestures could be counted on the fingers of one hand, and in that light Mead's generalization holds true.

The vocal gesture, and the human physiological ability to form a great variety of complex sounds, may involve a small element of imitation: We imitate when we learn to pronounce certain words. But by no means can vocal, symbolic communication be accounted for by a theory of imitation. No amount of vocal imitation will ever produce *meaning*—it never has among canaries or parrots.

Mead is not placing human beings on a pedestal; he is merely exploring as objectively as possible a basic difference between animal and human communication. It is a uniquely human capacity to symbolize and to interact with others and oneself by means of abstractions, generic concepts, and, in a word, universals of discourse. This has been understood since antiquity. Yet the various currents of behaviourism have fostered a conception of human beings in which they differ hardly at all from other animals. Psychologists like J. B. Watson denied mind and consciousness altogether, while Idealist psychologists like Wundt simply posited mind as if it were a metaphysical entity given at birth or at conception. Mead's arguments must be viewed in context, as polemically directed against the Behaviourists and the Idealists. Mead insists on the ontological validity of the concepts "mind" and "consciousness," rejecting, however, a metaphysical interpretation of them.

MEANING

Meaning, for Mead, is generated *in* the social process. Meaning can be objectively present even in the absence of awareness. "Meaning is … a development of something objectively there as a relation between certain phases of the social act; it is not a physical addition to that act and it is not an 'idea' as traditionally conceived" (p. 76). The adjustive response of one organism to another is its "meaning." When, however, one becomes *conscious* of one's own and the other's gestures and responses, and the context, gestures become significant symbols. But what we call "interpretation" is not exclusively in the mind; it is in the "actual field of social experience":

> meaning can be described, accounted for, or stated in terms of symbols or language at its highest and most complex stage of development (the stage it reaches in human experience), but language simply lifts out of the social process a situation which is logically and implicitly there already. (p. 79)

Mead's point here is that "meaning" resides in a total social process, and not in "mind" as if it were a separate province. Take a violinist who has memorized an entire concerto. The virtuoso violinist has so often and thoroughly practiced the concerto that the technique has become flawless. Strictly speaking, then, "memorization" of the concerto resides also in the body and not merely in the mind. There is such a thing as "muscle-memory," after all. Furthermore, in the violinist's performance of the music with a symphony orchestra, the habitual experience has given the performer a sensitivity to pitch, nuances of interpretation, and so forth, which enable him or her to adjust and blend spontaneously and automatically. Adjusting and blending have become "second nature"—or as William James had observed, "tenth nature." In these terms the "meaning" of the situation resides in a "field," consisting of the violinist, the orchestra, its conductor, and the audience. Meaning resides in the total social process. Similarly, in the everyday interaction of every man and every woman, meaning resides in the total social process, not merely in the individuals' minds.

Mead employs the term "constitute" to describe how we select specific sensory objects from a mass of events and objects. We select from what William James called the "blooming, buzzing confusion" only such objects as are relevant and of interest to us. Not all the objects or stimuli out there exist for us; only such objects exist as are relevant to our everyday social life. In that sense we constitute or "create" the objects and stimuli of our experience by abstracting them from a totality of objects and stimuli. Animals also constitute their objects and stimuli. Animals, however, can only relate to *specific* others, objects, and gestures. Humans, in contrast, can relate to abstract objects, to concepts, and to categories of things and organisms. "Dog" as a *universal* simply has no meaning or existence for dogs. Whenever I say "dog" in the presence of my dog, his ears prick up and his whole body becomes alert because he has the impression that I am talking about him. But "dog" and "human" in *general,* are the very kinds of universals that humans communicate with and about. This human ability enables us to break out of narrowly and inevitably specific responses. When we say "dog," "tree," or "hammer," we think not of a particular dog, tree, or hammer, but of a *universal,* which means we are thinking about something "not given in the particular occurrence which is the occasion of the thought. The thought transcends all occurrences" (p. 88).

Human perspectives also acquire universality. If one individual indicates to himself the same thing he indicates to others, they share a meaning. One individual indicates to the other from his own perspective and to himself from the other's perspective. And since that which is indicated is identical to all observers or participants, regardless of their different perspectives, it must be a universal. Indeed, the tendency to generalize or universalize is developed in the process of socialization, whereby any given individual goes beyond all particular attitudes toward himself and soon crystallizes

> all those particular attitudes into a single attitude or standpoint which may be called that of the "generalized other." (p. 90)

This ability to generalize, to grasp universals and to communicate them, gives humans their unique capacity for thinking and reflecting. *Reflection* takes place when one has stopped acting, if only for a moment. By means of reflection, humans can explore alternative courses of action without taking actual steps in any of the apparently available directions. Humans can assess the consequences of their actions before actually engaging in them. Humans can also convey the character of that future state to their fellow humans without the latter engaging in actual acts. A dog can pick out specific odour, but he cannot indicate that odour to another dog. A man can identify another man to a detective; a dog, however, can only follow a scent himself. This, says Mead, absolutely distinguishes man from beast, or a detective from a bloodhound.

Human beings can draw attention, their own and that of others, to specific analytical aspects of a situation or field, and thus guide and control their actions. An animal has no such ability to focus on an analyzed element. Animals can only guide their actions in actual trials and errors in the here and now. It is this complex human ability to construct and deconstruct mentally, and to explore alternate possibilities of future response, which contrasts fundamentally with behaviour that is either reflexive, habitual, or impulsive. There are, therefore, significant degrees of freedom in human conduct, not found in animal behaviour.

What this means, Mead stressed throughout, is that human actions are never strictly determined by past events, and cannot, therefore, be precisely predicted in advance. Because of the elements of creativity, spontaneity, and contingency, and because a human's ideas of the future and its alternatives enter his or her present conduct as determinants, human conduct is inherently unpredictable. For humans, their expectations concerning the future are an active determinant of their actions, though they never know precisely the nature of that future. Humans thus possess a unique capacity: the ability to solve present problems or cope with present adversity in the light of past experience and in terms of possible future consequences. Humans are able to act "in the light of or by reference to, both the past and the future … both memory and foresight" (p. 100).

All of this is made possible, as Mead demonstrates, by the fact that a human being can become an object to himself by taking the role of another toward himself. That is how an individual's "self" emerges, and with it the ability to project the self into reflective situations in which he is now subject, now object. Self, like mind, emerges and develops as an aspect of the social process of interaction.

THE SELF

Mead, as we have seen, defines "mind" as the presence in conduct of significant symbols, and he defines "self" as the process of taking the attitude of the other toward oneself. The self is a social entity distinct from the physical organism, although, of course, it cannot emerge except as a quality of that organism. The self emerges only in the context of social experience and interaction, and continues to develop in such contexts. Eventually the self becomes an object to itself and, hence, the centre about which all bodily experiences are organized. I can experience this hand, foot, or spine as my own because I am aware of my self and all that belongs to it. The hand, foot, and spine belong to the self in a way that the dog never can experience the tail as his own—which is why dogs tend to chase their tails as if they do not belong to them.

The self is both subject and object; it is an object to itself. This is what fundamentally differentiates humans from animals. The ability to become an object to oneself means that one can achieve *self*-consciousness, not just consciousness. And self-consciousness means that one can adopt an objective and impersonal attitude toward oneself and the situation in which one acts. The human capacity for intelligent and rational action rests squarely on this uniquely human ability to look upon oneself *objectively*. Indeed, in the development of the self, it is the objective side that appears first. The self is an object before it is a subject because one's first experiences of oneself are from the standpoint of others—mother, father, siblings. An individual's first experience and awareness of self are objective because he first becomes an object to himself by taking toward himself the attitudes of the significant others about him. It is symbolic communication that makes this phenomenon possible. The very young child begins to relate to himself as others do, by means of words: He addresses himself and responds to himself, so that soon the *subjective* side emerges ("I," "me," "mine," and so forth), and he becomes both subject and object.

The self, then, is a "social structure" (Mead's term) and once formed achieves a certain autonomy—that is, it "provides for itself its social experiences" (p. 140). We can therefore conceive of an adult hermit who has only himself as a human companion and who talks to himself as he would with others, but what is absolutely inconceivable is a "self arising outside of social experience" (p. 140).

Conversation with oneself is an essential aspect of communication with others. When one speaks to another, one, in effect, speaks to oneself. One affects oneself while one affects the other, so that in the very process of speaking, one checks, controls, and guides one's speech by assessing its effect on others according to its effects on oneself. One also takes account of the specific other to whom one is relating, and one speaks and acts accordingly. In that way, one becomes many selves, exhibiting one self here and another there.

Each of us, then, has multiple and different selves, depending on our relationships and associates. "A multiple personality is in a sense normal" (p. 142). But each of us is also a unified self, exhibiting a degree of consistency in our personality characteristics, a relatively stable configuration. It is not the conversation of gestures, but the conversation of *significant* gestures that makes the emergence and development of self possible. In the absence of language or communication by symbols, or universals, neither mind nor self is conceivable. All symbols are universal, Mead reminds us. "You cannot say anything that is absolutely particular; anything you say that has any meaning at all is universal" (p. 146). The term "universal" conveys the fact that thinking and talking involve symbols which, in any given society, evoke in others the same response they evoke in oneself. Symbols enable one to say to oneself what one says to others. Hence, "such a symbol is a universal of discourse" (p. 147). Helen Keller had become blind, deaf, and mute due to a severe illness that afflicted her while still in the crib; but prior to the illness she had, of course, already experienced language. And it was only after she had, as a young girl, rediscovered the symbol or word "water" that she regained the ability to communicate symbolically. It was only then that she could arouse in her self the response she aroused in others.

THE "I" AND THE "ME"

The "I" is the actual process of thinking and acting; the "me" is the reflective process. By taking the attitudes of others, one introduces the "me," to which one reacts as an "I." One can never catch oneself as "I," because one cannot literally observe oneself at the same time that one thinks, speaks, or acts.

> The "I" therefore appears only in memory and by that time it has become a "me." The "I" of this moment is present in the "me" of the next moment.

The "I" in memory is there as the spokesman of the self of the second, or minute, or day ago. As given, it is a "me," but is a "me" which was the "I" at the earlier time. If you ask, then, where directly in your own experience the "I" comes in, the answer is that it comes in as a historical figure. (p. 174)

If the "me" is the organized attitudes of others that one assumes toward oneself, the "I" responds to the "me" and the "me" reflects the "I" in an ongoing dialectical process. The "I" is inherently unpredictable. What one does as "I," one does not precisely know in advance. The "I" exists in the specious, knife-edge present, which means one can become aware of the "I" only as a memory image, as a part of the "me." The "I" is the actual steps one takes into the future with all the uncertainty that this necessarily entails. The "I" is therefore associated with spontaneity, novelty, freedom, and initiative. An important implication of the "I" is that humans can never be wholly passive or totally socialized so as to become "mes" exclusively, as it were. In opposition to the Behaviourists, Mead thus insists that the "I" changes the world, however infinitesimally.

THE "BIOLOGIC I"

The "I" involves a paradox: on the one hand, it represents freedom, creativity, spontaneity, novelty, and initiative; on the other hand, because the "I" is essentially biologic and impulsive, it is blind. The "I" is a process we become aware of only after it has become an accomplished fact. It is the "biologic I" that is involved in our enjoyment and excitement in the present. It is the realization in some sense of this pleasurable self that we are continually seeking (p. 204). But it is also the "biologic I" that tends to laugh when an individual falls. If he hurts himself, we sympathize, but it was funny, after all, to see him sprawling out. Mead's "biologic I" thus shares some parallels with Freud's *id* or *libido*. In a formulation not too remote from Freud's, Mead says that the sophisticated "me" soon gains control of the naive "I":

> one behaves perfectly proper, suppresses his laughter, is very prompt to get the fallen person on his feet again. There is the social attitude of the "me" over against the "I" that does enjoy the situation. (p. 207)

The "biologic I" is the source of our creativity, our passions, our vital energy. In the artist's attitude, therefore, the "me," the *conventional* side of the self, is reduced to a minimum, while the "I," the novel element, is "carried to the limit" (p. 209). Explicitly employing Freud's concepts, Mead further elucidates the relation between the "I" and the "me":

> Impulsive conduct is uncontrolled conduct. The structure of the "me" does not there determine the expression of the "I." If we use a Freudian expression, the "me" is in a certain sense a censor. (p. 210)

The "me," in a word, is the conventional side of the self that regulates the relation of the "biologic I" to the outside world, in much the same sense in which the *ego*, in Freudian psychology, regulates the *id*'s relation to the outside world.

For Mead as for Freud, there exists a definite tension between the "biologic or impulsive I" and the conventional "me." The "biologic I"—think of children at play—seeks fun, enjoyment, pleasure, and exciting and gratifying experiences. The "me" represents the values and norms of the society. In some circumstances the "me" loosens its control and enables the "I" to carry out its actions. Hence, the "I" is rooted in our biological nature. It is active, impulsive, and blind. But if it is blind, how can it be the source of freedom? What good is spontaneity if one does not know what one is actually doing, and one becomes aware of one's actions only after they are accomplished facts?

Mead's reply rests on the nature of the self as a dialectical, processual unity, enabling humans to *reflect* on acts, modifying them accordingly. In Mead's homely example, it is strictly *impulsive* to tug harder and harder on the handle of a wooden drawer that refuses to open. The process of *reflection* enters when we think intelligently and analytically about the drawer: It is a wooden thing; it may be swollen here and there; it has contents that might account for the drawer's resistance, and so on.

When we act under impulse, the drawer is strictly something to be tugged at, and once the handle comes off, all we can say is, "What have I done?" With reflection, in contrast, the "drawer has ceased for the time being to be a mere something to be pulled" (p. 356). Reflection and analysis now accompany and guide action, so we can say, "What am I doing?" or "What is to be done?" Here action and theory are more nearly a unity. But reflection never takes us totally out of the field of impulses, for we continue to use our hands, feeling for resistance and trying to overcome it. Thus, applying Peirce's proposition that thwarted action leads to *doubt*, which in turn prompts inquiry, Mead defines *reflection* as the unique human capacity for analyzing and recombining our impulses "in the presence of obstacles and inhibitions" (p. 362). That is the way the otherwise impulsive "I" receives guidance from the reflective self and acquires the possibility of conscious and rational action.

THE PHILOSOPHY OF THE ACT

In his brilliant essays in *The Philosophy of the Act*, we find a further enrichment of Mead's theory. For Mead, "sociality"—the tendency to associate in or form social groups—characterizes, in varying degrees, the relationship of all organisms to their environments. Building on William James's "insurgent character" of the organism, and on John Dewey's essay, "The Reflex Arc Concept in Psychology," Mead assigns due weight to the *active* side of all organisms and the reciprocal determination of organism and environment. The main trend in Mead's time was to portray the organism as passively adapting to an environment that actively determined and controlled it. This one-sided, defective view, Mead recognized, must be replaced by another: *That an organism actively seeks to express its impulses, and it is only in terms of such impulses that it attends to, or takes an "interest" in a given stimulus. A stimulus becomes such only insofar as it corresponds to the organism's sensitivity and impulsive needs. The organism thus actively constitutes the objects of its environment.* And, of course, what is true of the "lower" organisms is all the more true of human beings.

Behaviourism, as we have seen, *begins* an organism's act with a response to an external stimulus, thus implying that an organism possesses no inner principle, with which to initiate an act. Mead, in contrast, fully recognized the inner principle, which—like James and Dewey—he called "impulse" or "impulsive need." Mead thus makes a momentous contribution to our understanding of organisms, *by designating impulse as the first stage of the act.* The stages of the act in animals, therefore, are: *impulse, perception*, and *consummation.* A hungry animal feels an impulse to find food. The impulse impels it to act—to seek food. The impulse determines what will stand out in the environment as a stimulus to guide the developing action. A carnivorous animal, for example, approaches the stimulus-object, clawing, biting, and downing it; finally, it eats, consummating the act with the satisfaction of the original impulse. In humans, however, there is an additional stage in the social act—*manipulation*—which involves *reflection*. Impulse is illuminated by reason, and action takes place in a world of meaning. Thus, in humans the stages of the social act are: *impulse, perception, manipulation,* and *consummation*. The significance of the additional stage, manipulation, will soon become clearer.

Mead follows Peirce in defining thinking and reflection as instrumental, problem-solving acts. Thought and action are moments in a dialectical, processual unity. It is precisely when action is blocked that reflective thinking arises to test the hypothetical, alternative ways of resuming the action. The exploration of alternative options, which animals can engage in only directly by trial and error, humans can engage in reflectively. Like Peirce, Mead draws no sharp distinction between the thinking of the scientist and that of every person in everyday life. In both cases, the point is to get back to some useful or worthwhile process. And for Mead, a real process cannot be grasped with either the mechanistic thinking of the Behaviourists and the Instinctualists or the metaphysical categories of the Idealists.

Theory and knowledge, then, from Mead's pragmatic standpoint, is the process of active discovery that enables us to solve the problems and overcome the obstacles thwarting our action. If we are able to resume acting, more or less realizing our purposes, our knowledge has proved itself adequate and practicable. This kind of knowledge, Mead maintains, is the only kind that justifies our confidence in it. We search in the past in order to better understand the present problematic world. And the only test we have of whether we understand it or not is our ability to change the condition that has stymied us. The goal of theory or reflective thinking, whether in science, everyday life, or historiography, is therefore practical. That is the heart, then, of the pragmatic epistemology.

MORE ON MEAD'S PRAGMATIC EPISTEMOLOGY

Following Peirce, Mead proposes that it is the inhibited or interrupted act that gives rise to reflective thinking, a process in which the individual represents to himself his relational experiences in the world through images and symbols. The interruption of the act and the resulting reflection make abstraction possible. Human beings can analytically separate objects from themselves, separate one sensory experience from another, separate sensory experience from contact experience, and separate contact experience from distance experience. We can also separate spatial from temporal experiences and the experience of the specious present from the experiences of the past and future. (Mead always calls the knife-edge present "specious" because of the Heraclitean flux of reality in which there is no real present.) Human beings can thus grasp aspects of process and represent them to themselves symbolically. Only human beings become "metaphysical" in that sense when their actions are thwarted.

A good illustration of Mead's pragmatic epistemology pertains to the stage of *manipulation* in the human social act. The traditional philosophical dichotomy (for example, Locke's) between "secondary qualities," such as colour, sound, odour, and the like, as "subjective" and "primary qualities," such as extension, occupation of space, motion, and so forth, as "objective" is a false one for Mead. What the philosophers have called "secondary qualities" are simply the character objects have in distance experience while the "primary qualities" are the character they have in contact experience. Both depend on the relation of the individual to the objects concerned.

Mead therefore regards as uncritical the distinction between the so-called primary and secondary qualities, rightly insisting that neither is more objective than the other since neither is independent of the active, sentient, observing, knowing individual. For Mead, however, it is pragmatically understandable why the distinction has been made: The association of subjectivity with distance experience and objectivity with contact experience is "natural" because we test "the reality of what affects us from a distance … by coming into contact with it."[4] As we touch and feel the object, it retains its colour, sound, odour, and the like. With further handling it "crumbles," analytically speaking, until we reach its ultimate elements, particles of energy "so minute that they could not subtend a light vibration" (p. 286). In that way, science creates the hypothetically ultimate elements of material reality, translating into abstract mathematical models an assumed contact experience in which distance experience disappears or becomes impossible. Hence, this scientific theory of nature and material reality has its experiential basis in everyday life—

> in the fact that the *hand* naturally breaks things up into parts which can be rolled between the thumb and the finger. (p. 296, italics added)

But while the crumbled object in the hand retains both its distance and contact qualities, the scientifically analyzed object substitutes contact quality for distance quality—but a contact quality of an assumed or hypothetical character.

In these terms, the emergence of the "physical or material thing" and its accompanying concept, must be seen, Mead avers, in the context of the *social act*—or more precisely in relation to its interruption at the *manipulatory stage* by the human hand. It is in the context of this stage that "matter" appears, and

> which under the crumbling analysis of the hand suggests the hypothetical atom. (p. 326)

Mead stresses the uniquely human mode of practical action in which the *hand* mediates human interaction with nature and with other humans. With regard to the evolution of the human species, Mead underscores the interdependence of practical experience, mediated by the hand, and the emergence and development of speech, consciousness, and self-consciousness:

> Speech and the hand go along together in the development of the social human being.[5]

Mead's recognition of the role of the hand was anticipated in an essay by Frederick Engels titled, "The Part Played by Labour in the Transition from Ape to Man." Engels had recognized that the human being's faculties evolved "only side by side with the development of the human hand itself through the medium of labor."[6] The concept of "labour" here refers to the practical activities of the protohumans who became humans in the course of interacting with nature and cooperating with one another. Engels and Mead are in basic agreement that the *practical*, cooperative experiences of the protohumans antedate speech and self-consciousness. Engels wrote:

> First labor, after it and then with it speech—these were the two most essential conditions under the influence of which the brain of the ape gradually changed into that of a man.[7]

And Mead:

> It is true that some sort of cooperative activity antedates the self. There must be some loose organization in which the different organisms work together, and the sort of cooperation in which the gesture of the individual may become a stimulus to himself of the same type as the stimulus to the other ..., so that the conversations can pass over into the conduct of the individual. Such conditions are presupposed in the development of the self.[8]

Earlier, we observed that Mead consistently places the accent on the "dialectical" or interactive character of human relations with the environment. Far from being passively conditioned as in the behaviourist doctrine, humans determine the conditions of their existence, and are not merely determined by such conditions. Marx had defended and qualified this proposition by saying that humans make history, but "not just as they please, not in circumstances wholly chosen by themselves." Conditions created before we ever came into the world continue, like a nightmare, to weigh heavily upon us. It seems clear that just as Hegel's philosophy contributed to Marx's dialectical approach, Hegel's philosophy also contributed to Mead's conception of the "self-other" dialectic. Hegel's philosophy, Mead averred,

> marks the first time that the self had been definitely given a function in the experience of reaching the truth.[9]

Moreover, Mead acknowledges a more general applicability of the Hegelian dialectic to social development:

> If we take the starting point of the appearance of the reflective attitude in society, we can locate a Hegelian moment in the social development; the self realizing itself over and against the individuals of the community so that it finds itself in opposition to the other as essentially a social being. That is, when a man finds himself in opposition to some social order, as in labor conflicts, then the attitude between the laborer and employer is one of hostility, which we call class war. It appears,

of course, in the conflict with the employer over such control as is expressed in wages and labor conditions, but the laborer as such under those conditions has to realize himself in relation to the employer. This character, as we know, appears in class war. *Individuals do realize themselves definitely in their oppositions to one another. Those oppositions are the starting point for the development of the new social order. This is characteristic of social development as such*, not simply of such modern problems as labor troubles.[10]

Given this Hegelian influence on Mead, we can say that for him, as for Marx, the external world is a humanly shaped world that humans mould and change by means of their theoretical-practical activity. For both thinkers, nature is no mere object independent of the human will, and humanity is no *tabula rasa* passively receiving impressions from the outside world, or merely responding to external stimuli. On the contrary, human beings are active, creative, cognizing subjects who come to know the world as they act upon it, thereby changing themselves in the process.

We said in our introduction to this chapter on Mead that in order to grasp why his theory is original and sound, we have to recognize its *dialectical* character. And we have in fact discerned a prominent dialectical element in his pragmatic approach. Let us therefore try to give a more definite meaning to the concept "dialectical" and explain how a dialectical approach would help us avoid errors. A dialectical approach would keep us alert to the following: That an adequate comprehension of the human condition entails a twofold task, giving due attention to the processes that constrain and highly influence human actions, but also due attention to the active and creative efforts humans make to diminish and remove constraints by changing practices that are unnecessarily repressive.

There are two types of errors that often result from the failure to think dialectically. The first is to minimize or ignore altogether the constraining influences of social relationships and institutions. This error looks upon human beings as if they were superhuman and thus able to transform their existential conditions at will. The opposite error is to exaggerate the staying power of existing institutions, objectifying them and thereby underestimating the ability of humans to modify their circumstances. This error leads to a pronounced diminution of the human potential. By avoiding these errors, we may more effectively learn of real human possibilities.

NOTES

1. Alan Ryan, *John Dewey and the High Tide of American Liberalism* (New York and London: W.W. Norton & Company, 1997), p. 79.

2. George H. Mead, *Mind, Self and Society*, ed. and with Introduction by Charles W. Morris (Chicago and London: The University of Chicago Press, 1962: orig. 1934) p. xxv. (Hereafter, all references to this work will be cited in parentheses immediately following the quoted passage.)

3. Although Mead, like James and Dewey, rejects the one-sided premises of Behaviourism and the mechanistic way in which Behaviourists conceived of the terms "stimulus" and "response," he deliberately employs these terms heuristically to make his point.

4. George H. Mead, *The Philosophy of the Act* (Chicago and London: The University of Chicago Press, 1938), p. 285. (Hereafter all references to this work will be cited in parentheses immediately following the quoted passage.)

5. Mead, *Mind, Self and Society*, p. 237.

6. F. Engels, "The Part Played by Labor in the Transition from Ape to Man," in Marx and Engels, *Selected Works* (Moscow: Foreign Languages Publishing House, 1951), vol. II, pp. 74–85.

7. Ibid.

8. Mead, *Mind, Self and Society*, p. 240.

9. Mead, *Philosophy of the Act*, p. 634.

10. Ibid., p. 655, italics added.

Epilogue

We have now completed our survey of the contributions of the pioneers of sociological theory and analysis. Although the contributions of these thinkers vary in their quality, many of them have stood the test of time in this sense: We refer to their writings again and again; we rely on their theoretical ideas; we employ their concepts; we continue to investigate questions they raised; and we strive to emulate their intellectual craftsmanship.

To understand any thinker, it is often not enough to know what he or she is affirming. To grasp the full meaning of a thinker's affirmations, we need to grasp that thinker's negations—what he or she is arguing against. That is why I employed the framework of a "debate" for the exposition of the theories discussed in this book. The Romantic-Conservative Reaction to the Enlightenment and the critical response to the Marxian legacy were, of course, definite historical events, but they also aid us in understanding the respective theories more adequately. Furthermore, the organizational device of a debate or critical encounter enriches our understanding by alerting us to the strengths and weaknesses of both sides.

We have seen that knowing what one is arguing against is also essential for an understanding of the great Pragmatist philosophers and social psychologists. It is certainly true of Mead that his affirmations can only be adequately understood by recognizing the reasons for his rejection of the Instinctualist, Behaviourist, and Idealist positions.

In conclusion, it is noteworthy that Mead's epistemology and social psychology are the most fitting complement to the method of social and historical analysis we derive from the two giants, Marx and Weber.

Index

a prioris, 18–19, 150, 164, 266. *See also* Kant, Immanuel
Advice to a Young Tradesman (Franklin), 100
agriculture, 65, 66, 70, 75, 77–78, 81, 107–108, 130
Akkad, 111
Alcibiades, 171–172
Alexander the Great, 70
alienation, xii, 24, 26, 43–48, 51–52, 81–82, 112, 117, 187
Amalek, 130
American Revolution, 8, 20, 117
Amos, 131–132
Anabaptism, 102
Analytical Review (Wollstonecraft), 10
anarchy, 25, 29–30, 32–33, 36, 174, 187, 196, 217, 223, 228, 235, 259
Ancient Society (Morgan), 86
animism, 119–120, 125, 246
anomia, 234
anthropology, 85, 245, 247, 251
Anti-Dühring (Engels), 77
Aquinas, Thomas, 102
Arabia, 75, 247
Archiv für Sozialwissenschaft und Sozialpolitik, 97
Arendt, Hannah, 56n4
aristocracy
    Marx on, 83
    Michels on, 204, 209, 212, 216, 220
    Mosca on, 181, 184–188, 193, 196, 198
    Pareto on, 155, 162, 167, 170
    Weber on, 106, 125
    Wollstonecraft on, 12
Aristotle, 24, 51, 56n4, 185–189, 193, 196–197
asceticism, 48, 98, 100, 102–104, 119, 120, 122, 125, 135, 137
Asiatic despotism. *See* Oriental despotism
Asiatic mode of production. *See* Marx, Karl
Assyria, 111
astronomy, 31, 35
atheism, 1, 44
Athens, 171–172, 241

Australia, 245, 247, 249–250
autocracy, 185, 193, 212

Baal, 130, 132
Babylonia, 111
Bacon, Francis, 5
Bank of England, 137
Baxter, Richard, 102–104
Bedouins, 130
behaviourism, 277–278, 283, 285, 289, 291n4, 292
Berkeley, Bishop, 6
Berlin, 1, 206
Bernier, François, 75
Bernstein, Eduard, 210
Bible, 10, 100–101, 267
biology, 86
Blackstone, William, 11
Blanc, Louis, 206
Block, J., 60
Bonald, Louis de, 25, 27, 30, 228
Bonaparte, Louis, 88
bourgeoisie
    Durkheim on, 223
    Mannheim on, 268
    Marx on, 41, 54, 59, 61, 69, 79, 82
    Michels on, 216–217
    Mosca on, 179
    Pareto on, 162
    Weber on, 108–109, 115, 122, 124, 136, 138–139
Bousquet, G. H., 174
Brahmans, 122–125
Bramsted, Ernest K., 264
Britain, 1, 8, 20, 75, 77, 110, 245
Brody, Miriam, 14, 15n11
Brussels, 58
Buddhism, 124, 245, 254
bureaucracy
    Mannheim on, 272
    Michels on, 207–209, 215, 219
    Mosca on, 195, 197–199
    Weber on, 111–113, 115, 118–119, 139, 141–147, 149

Burke, Edmond, 8–9, 19–21, 24–25, 84
Bury, J. B., 84

Caesar, Julius, 64, 66
Calvin, John, 100, 101, 104
Calvinism, 100–102, 104
Canaan, 130
capital, 80, 144, 234
Capital (Marx), 45, 52, 62, 68, 86–87, 87, 137–138, 158
capitalism
    and Durkheim, 225, 234
    and Enlightenment, 2
    and Mannheim, 265–266, 269
    and Marx, xii, 42, 44–45, 47–48, 51, 53, 67–69, 71, 74, 79–84, 86–89
    and Mosca, 191
    and Romantic-Conservative Reaction, 25–26
    and Weber, 93, 95–96, 98–104, 108–110, 114–115, 117–118, 121–122, 126, 133–138, 143–144
Cassirer, Ernst, 4
Catholicism, 27, 30, 100, 127
charismatic leadership, 146–149
Charlemagne, 67
chemistry, 35
children, 65
China, 74–75, 78, 85, 113–121, 125, 133–134, 134, 183
Christianity, 1, 101, 104, 122, 125–127, 133, 136, 190, 225, 227, 251, 253–254, 254
class
    conflict, 35, 41–42, 82, 128, 156, 159–160, 179, 186, 202, 216, 218, 223, 234, 266
    middle, 12, 103, 125, 139, 148, 186, 198, 211
    ruling, 107, 169–172, 176, 178–187, 189, 191, 193, 196–197, 199, 200
    structure, 35, 68, 190, 192, 199, 235, 238
    working, 35, 41, 51, 135, 138–139, 148, 188, 199, 207, 211, 216–217, 219, 220
"Class Struggles in France" (Marx), 88
collectivism, 159, 176, 183, 188
communism, 48, 52–53, 158
Communist Manifesto (Marx), 69, 86, 179

Comte, Auguste, xi–xii, 19, 27, 29–39, 41–42, 83, 223, 229, 231, 235
Condillac, Étienne Bonnot de, 3, 6
Condorcet, Marquis de, 10
Confucianism, 118–120
conservatism, xi, 16, 20–27, 69, 74, 84, 87, 108, 179, 186, 204, 268. *See also* Romantic-Conservative reaction
Contribution to the Critique of Political Economy, A (Marx), 58–59, 61, 62
Corso di Sociologia Politica (Michels), 202
corvée, 71–73, 128
crime, 199, 232, 240–245
criminology, 240, 244
Croce, Benedetto, 203
Czars, 191

d'Alembert, Jean-Baptiste le Rond, 3–4
Darwin, Charles, 86, 176–177, 181
Deism, 136
democracy
    and Enlightenment, 1
    and Mannheim, 265–266, 271
    and Marx, 83
    and Michels, 204–213, 217, 219–220
    and Mosca, 176, 178–179, 181, 183, 185–188, 192–195, 197–198, 200
    and Pareto, 173–174
    and Weber, 146–149
Descartes, René, 3–5
Deuteronomy, 131
deviance, 239–241, 254
Dewey, John, 274, 285
Diagnosis of Our Time (Mannheim), 264
Disraeli, Benjamin, 202
Division of Labor in Society (Durkheim), 222, 225–226, 230, 261
Durkheim, Émile, xii, 26–27, 83
    on anomic division of labour, 234, 257
    on crime and punishment, 232, 241–245
    on deviant behaviour, 239–241, 254
    on forced division of labour, 234, 257
    on mechanical solidarity, 84, 225, 231–232, 241
    on methodological rules, 254–256
    on occupational guilds, 226, 235–236
    on order and justice, 236–239

on organic solidarity, 84, 223, 225–226,
232–234, 255, 261
on problem of order, 229–236
and Saint-Simon, 223–228
on socialism, 222
on sociology of religion, 245–247,
251–254, 261
on suicide, 257–261
on totemism, 247–251

East, the, 72, 75, 96, 99, 110, 112–114, 122.
See also Orient
Economic and Philosophic Manuscripts of 1844
(Marx), 42
economic determinism, 57, 60, 66, 88
economics, 57, 74, 89, 97, 99, 105, 137
economy, 57, 74–76, 79, 87, 95, 97, 99, 108,
110–111, 113, 115–117, 122, 124, 143–145,
150, 228–229
market, 73–74, 108, 229
political, 47–48, 58
Economy and Society (Weber), 93–94, 96, 138
Edison, Thomas, 145
egoism, 227–228, 236, 257, 261
Egypt, 74, 76, 83, 110–113, 115–116, 128–131,
247, 253
"18th Brumaire of Louis Bonaparte, The"
(Marx), 88
Elementary Forms of Religious Life (Durkheim),
245
Elite-Theorists. *See* Neo-Machiavellians
Émile (Rousseau), 8
Enclosure Acts (England), 45, 134
Encyclopedia, 5
Engels, Frederick, 55–57, 60–62, 64–78,
86–87, 95–96, 105–106, 114, 179, 194–195,
203, 210, 288
England, 6, 10–11, 17, 20, 45, 80, 86, 134–137,
189, 191, 196, 198–199, 264
"English, Dutch and American Protestants"
(Weber), 100
English Revolution, 1, 117
Enlightenment, xi, 1–10, 16–17, 19, 21–22,
25–26, 29–31, 37, 41–43, 49, 84, 122, 156,
176, 187, 292
Entäusserung, 45
epistemology, 4–5, 18, 266–267, 286–290, 292

equality, 187, 207, 208
Essay Concerning Human Understanding
(Locke), 5
Essays on the Sociology of Culture (Mannheim),
264
Essence of Christianity, The (Feuerbach), 43
Europe, 8, 16–17, 25, 27, 39, 71, 79, 83–84, 99,
127, 143, 183, 198–199, 224, 255, 257–258,
266. *See also* Western Europe
evolution, 83–87
Ezekiel, 131–132

factories, 82, 134, 146
Family, The (Durkheim), 222
farmer, 80
fascism, 148–149, 173–174
feudalism
Marx/Engels on, 66–68, 70–75, 78–80,
86–87
Saint-Simon on, 223, 224
Weber on, 95, 105–110, 117, 144
Feuerbach, Ludwig, 43–44, 55
Fourier, Joseph, 222
France, 1, 6, 8, 20, 29, 75, 88–89, 99, 171,
173–174, 206, 214, 224, 229
Frankish tribes, 105–106, 108
Franklin, Benjamin, 100, 102, 104
Freedom, Power, and Democratic Planning
(Mannheim), 264
French Revolution, xi, 1, 8, 10, 15n1, 19–21,
41–42, 73, 84, 117, 171, 225, 235
Freud, Sigmund, 283–284
Frisch, Karl von, 277

Galileo, 3, 5
Gemeinschaft, 266
General Economic History (Weber), 133
George III, 20
German Ideology (Marx and Engels), 48,
61–62, 70, 86
German Social-Democratic Party, 148
German Sociological Association, 94
Germania (Tacitus), 66
Germanic peoples, 64–66, 105
Germany, 1, 17, 21, 23–25, 29, 45, 72–73, 101,
146–148, 173, 183, 203, 209–211, 213, 219,
257, 265

Gerth, Hans, 94, 264

gestures, 275–279, 282, 289

gnosis, 125

Greece (classical), 10, 71, 84, 122, 126–127, 132, 171–172, 176, 185, 188, 247, 249

Grundrisse (Marx), 62

guilds, 69, 81, 109, 115, 117, 119, 124, 209, 226, 235, 257. *See also* unions

hedonism, 100

Hegel, Georg Wilhelm Friedrich, 19, 21, 22–25, 29, 43, 49, 56n4, 56n11, 83, 289–290 and Marx, 50–55, 58

Hinduism, 123

Hindustan, 75–76

historical materialism, 94–95, 97, 159, 203–204

History of England (Macauley), 10

Hobbes, Thomas, 155, 229–330

Holbach, Baron d', 1, 6, 10

Homer, 6

Hugo, Victor, 88–89

humanitarian sentiments (Pareto), 160–161, 169–171

Hume, David, 6, 17–19

idealism, 5, 54–55, 213, 266, 274–278, 286, 292

Ideology and Utopia (Mannheim), 264, 270

India, 8, 20, 74–75, 77–78, 110, 113–114, 133 religions of, 121–126

Industrial Revolution, xi–xii

industrialism
Durkheim on, 223, 225–227, 229–231, 234, 257, 261
and Enlightenment, 2
Mannheim on, 264, 266
Marx on, 41, 42, 44, 48, 67, 69–71, 80–82, 84
Michels on, 216
and Romantic-Conservative Reaction, 27, 30–31
Weber on, 99–100, 109, 115, 117, 124, 134–138, 144

Inquiry Concerning the Principles of Natural Theology and Morality (Kant), 4

Instinctualism, 286, 292

intelligentsia, 270–272

irrigation, 74–78, 110–114

Isaiah, 131–132

Islam, 127, 254

Israel, 114, 128–133

Italy, 117–118, 149, 174, 183–184, 210

Jainism, 124

James, William, 274, 278–279, 285

Japan, 110

Jerusalem, 131–133

Jones, Richard, 74

Judaism, 120, 123, 125, 126–134, 253

justice, 190–191, 233–239

Kaldun, Ibn, 202

Kant, Immanuel, 4, 6, 17–19, 55, 266

Keller, Helen, 282

Kepler, Johannes, 3

knowledge, 264–266, 268–270

Kshatriyas, 122

labour
Comte on, 38
division of, 38, 52, 62, 68–69, 81, 95, 103, 135, 206, 207, 223, 225–231, 233–234, 257
Durkheim on, 223, 225–231, 233–234, 257
Mannheim on, 271
Marx on, 45–47, 52, 60, 62, 66, 68–69, 71, 79–82
Mead on, 287
Michels on, 202, 206, 213–214, 217
Weber on, 93, 95, 103, 111–112, 134–138
Wollstonecraft on, 9
See also bureaucracy; guilds; unions; workers

Lafargue, Paul, 210

laissez faire, 229

language, 86, 182, 275–279, 282, 288

Laotzu, 119

Leibniz, Gottfried Wilhelm von, 3–4, 18

Letters on Education (Macauley), 10

Leviathan, 155, 229–230

Levites, 131

Liberal-Conservative party (Italy), 184

liberalism, 26, 146, 184–186, 192, 193, 196–197
Lichtheim, George, 94
literati, 118–120
Locke, John, 5–6, 18, 266, 287. *See also* empiricism
Lombroso, Cesare, 244
Luther, Martin, 100, 101

Macauley, Catherine, 10
Macedonia, 172
Machiavelli, Niccolo, 75, 121, 154–156
Maistre, Joseph de, 25, 30–31, 228
Malinowski, Bronislaw, 251–253
Man and Society in an Age of Reconstruction (Mannheim), 264
mandarins, 118–119, 125, 134
Mannheim, Karl, xii
    on ideology and utopia, 264–270
    on intelligentsia, 270–272
    on sociology of knowledge, 264–270
    on *Weltanschauung*, 266, 268
Marcuse, Herbert, 50
"Mark, the" (Engels), 64, 72
Martineau, Harriet, 39n2
Marx, Karl, xi–xii, 24–25, 39, 156, 176, 179, 187, 190, 194–195, 205, 292
    on alienation, 43–48, 51, 81, 82
    on ancient mode of production, 59, 61, 79
    on Asiatic mode of production, 59, 61, 74–79, 82–83, 87, 89, 109–114, 114, 123, 133
    on capitalist mode of production, 69, 79–83, 135
    on class, 137–142
    on division of labour, 53, 68–69
    and Durkheim, 222, 231, 233
    on economy, 59, 60, 63
    exchange-value, 74, 79, 136
    on feudal mode of production, 59, 61, 71–74, 78–79, 82
    on Hegel and Feuerbach, 51–55, 56n4, 58
    on historical sociology, xii, 89
    on history, 57, 58, 87, 89, 149–150
    and Mannheim, 265, 267
    on materialist history, 54, 60, 96, 159
    on means of production, 45, 46, 47, 52, 53, 79, 87, 139, 142, 144, 145

and Michels, 202–203, 210, 217, 219
    on modern mode of production, 59, 61, 79, 82
    on modes of production, 60, 61, 63, 69, 79, 87, 105, 108
    on natural man/human needs, 42, 43, 68
    and Pareto, 158–159
    on precapitalist modes of production, 69, 89
    on productive forces, 61–62, 67–71
    on relations of production, 51, 58–59, 61–62, 74
    on religion, 43–45
    and social evolution, 86–87
    on tribal ownership, 61–67
    use-value, 68, 74, 79
    and Weber, 93–105, 182, 192, 202–204, 264, 269
materialism, 1, 5–6, 51–52, 54–55, 60, 94–97, 99, 159, 203–204, 234, 266, 274–275
    scientific, 6
Maurer, Georg Ludwig, 72
Mauss, Marcel, 222
Mead, George Herbert, 292
    "biologic I," 283–285
    epistemology, 286–290
    gestures, 275–279, 282, 289
    meaning, 278–280
    self, the, 281–282, 282–283, 289
    and social psychology, 274
Meitzen, August, 94
Melanesia, 252–253
Memoirs of the Gallic Wars (Caesar), 66
Merovingians, 67, 108
Mesopotamia, 83, 110–111, 131
metaphysics, 2, 24, 31–33, 55, 83, 277–278, 286–287
Methodism, 102–103
Michels, Robert, xii, 148–149, 154, 156, 179, 202–220
Middle Ages, 2, 25–27, 66–67, 69, 71–72, 101, 106–107, 115, 122–123, 127, 199, 235, 266, 271
Mikhailovsky, N.K., 87
military, 64–65, 67, 70–71, 84, 105–109, 112–115, 117, 124, 142, 146, 163, 173, 178, 180–181, 192, 198–200, 208, 225
    standing armies, 198–200

Mill, James, 74
Mill, John Stuart, 39, 74
Mills, C. Wright, 94
Mind, Self and Society (Mead), 274
Mommsen, Wolfgang, 146–149
Montesquieu, Charles, 1, 74, 184–185, 187, 189, 191, 196–197
More, Thomas, 80
Morgan, Lewis Henry, 83–86
Mosca, Gaetano, xii, 154, 156, 176–200, 202, 204–205
    on Aristotle and Montesquieu, 184–189
    on "directing minority," 183–185
    on juridical defense, 185, 189, 190–193, 199, 200
    on parliamentarism, 196–198
    on "political formula," 182–183, 191
    and politics, 184–185, 186, 188, 189
    on ruling class, 176, 178–184, 187, 189, 191, 193, 197, 200
    on "social forces," 177, 180, 181, 189, 191–192, 196
    on standing armies, 198–200
    on "struggle for preeminence," 177–180, 182
    on universal suffrage, 194–196, 198
Moses, 129–130
Mussolini, Benito, 149, 173–174

Napoleon, 17, 166, 217
Napoleon, Louis, 88
nationalism, 19–22, 84, 182–183, 193, 258
naturism, 246
Near East, 110, 112
Necessary Hints to Those That Would Be Rich (Franklin), 100
negative philosophy, 29, 31, 35, 37, 41
negative-critical thinking, 3, 25, 41, 49, 53, 224
Neo-Machiavellians, xii, 154
New Christianity (Saint-Simon), 227
Newton, Isaac, 3–5, 17–18, 84
Nicias, 171–172
Nietzsche, Friedrich, 147, 267
Nile, the, 111
Nisbet, Robert A., 84–86
nomadism, 62, 64, 71, 77

North America, 194, 247
Nouveaux Principes d'Economie Politique (Sismondi), 229

Occident, 113, 115, 117, 121–122, 126. *See also* West, the
oikos, 111
oligarchy, 148, 162, 204–205, 208, 212–215, 217, 219–220
Orient, 75, 78, 83, 113, 115, 122. *See also* East, the
Oriental despotism, 75, 77–78, 112
Origin of the Family, Private Property, and the State (Engels), 86

Pareto, Vilfredo, 154–174, 176, 178–179, 184, 192, 195–196, 202–205, 214–215
Paris, 1, 58
Paris Commune, 194
parliamentarism, 196–198
Parsons, Talcott, 93, 175n3
"Part Played by Labour in the Transition from Ape to Man, The" (Engels), 288
pastoralism, 62–63
Paul, St., 102
Peirce, Charles Sanders, 274, 285–286
Persia, 75–77
Philosophes, 1–2, 3, 5, 16, 19–20, 22, 26–27, 29, 43, 224
Philosophical Enquiry into the Sublime and Beautiful, A (Burke), 9
Philosophy of History (Hegel), 23
Philosophy of the Act, The (Mead), 285
Physiologie Sociale (Saint-Simon), 224
Pietism, 102
Plato, 119, 178
plebeians, 155, 170, 183
polis, 115, 124
Political Parties (Michels), 202, 204
Politique Positive (Comte), 39
positive philosophy, xi, 29–31, 33–39, 41, 224
positivism, 29, 37, 39, 51, 56n11, 223–224, 256, 262
Poverty of Philosophy, The (Marx), 67
pragmatism, 266, 274, 286–287, 290, 292
precapitalism, 69, 82, 87, 89, 105
"Preface" (Marx), 58–62, 67, 69, 78–79, 82–83, 86

Preliminary Discourse (d'Alembert), 4
princes, 155–156
Professional Ethics and Civic Morals
   (Durkheim), 238–239, 260–261
proletariat, 41, 44, 79–81, 145, 161, 183, 192,
   202, 207, 209, 216–217, 219, 268
Prometheus, 43
property, 45, 63, 64, 69–70, 73, 75, 117,
   138–141, 195, 236–239
      private, 33, 52–53, 64–66, 75, 88, 105,
         117, 185, 188, 204
Protestant Ethic and the Spirit of Capitalism
   (Weber), 93, 97–99, 105, 133
Protestantism, 2, 25–27, 93, 96–105, 119–120,
   122, 127, 133, 135–137. *See also* Calvin,
   John; Luther, Martin
Proudhon, Pierre-Joseph, 88–89, 206
Prussia, 23, 83, 173, 210, 257
psychology, 5, 101, 164–165, 176, 178–181,
   188, 205–206, 209–210, 215–217, 240, 245,
   266–268, 276–277, 284–285
Puritanism, 102–103, 120, 136–137

race, 38, 176–177
Rationalisierungsprozess, 126
rationalism, xi, 3–4, 16–17, 20, 99–100,
   114–115, 120–122, 125–126, 129, 131, 133,
   137, 142, 146, 157, 161, 164, 166, 178, 242,
   266
Reflections on the Revolution in France (Burke),
   8, 20–21
"Reflex Arc Concept in Psychology" (Dewey),
   285
Reformation, 30, 98, 100, 122
religion, 16–17, 27, 98, 103, 105, 133, 136–137,
   165–166, 181, 190, 193, 228, 261
      in China, 114–121
      Durkheim on, 245–247, 251–254
      in India, 121–126
      Marx on, 43–45
      See also animism; Judaism; Protestantism;
         Puritanism; totemism
Religion (Durkheim), 222
Renaissance, 122
revolution. *See* French Revolution, American
   Revolution, English Revolution
Roman Agrarian History (Weber), 94

Roman Empire, 65, 70–71, 84, 105–106, 108,
   122, 127, 166, 185, 267
Romantic-Conservative reaction, xi, 16–27,
   84, 292
Rome, 174
Roth, Guenther, 94
Rousseau, Jean Jacques, 2, 8, 10–11, 13–14, 17,
   32, 42, 176, 187, 190, 206
Rules of the Sociological Method (Durkheim), 256
Ruling Class, The (Mosca), 176
Russia, 78, 86–88, 183

Saint-Simon, Henri Comte de, xi–xii, 19, 27,
   30, 34, 83, 178, 222–231, 236
Salomon, Albert, 94, 96
Sand, George, 217
Scheler, Max, 267
scientific method, 6–7, 36–37
secularism, 2, 26, 38, 102, 129, 210, 224, 226,
   236, 261
serfdom, 63, 67, 71–73, 72, 73, 80, 111, 134,
   180. *See also* slavery
Shakespeare, 277
Shudras, 122
sib, the, 115, 117–118
Sismondi, J.C.L., 229
slavery, 8, 47–48, 53, 61–64, 66, 68–69, 71–72,
   79, 132, 134–135, 138, 188, 237
Smith, Adam, 74
social
      change, 25, 30, 60, 62, 65, 78, 84, 129,
         204, 223, 238, 264–266
      democracy, 183, 193, 197
      order, 8, 20, 25, 30–32, 42, 44, 59, 169,
         190–191, 217, 219, 224–225, 228–231,
         240, 289–290
      structures, 62, 107, 110, 114, 122, 126,
         129, 141, 177–178, 180, 265, 267, 281
      systems, 32, 36–37, 41–42, 112, 124, 158,
         205, 233, 260, 266
"Social Causes of the Decline of Ancient
   Civilization, The" (Weber), 106
Social Change and History (Nisbet), 84
Social Contract (Rousseau), 187
social psychology, 139, 274, 292. *See also* Mead,
   George Herbert
social sciences, 35, 89, 93, 150, 197, 262

socialism
    Durkheim on, 222–224, 228, 230,
        231–233, 237, 239, 256
    Marx on, 52
    Michels on, 203, 204, 206–208, 210–211,
        213–217, 219
    Mosca on, 176, 192, 193, 196–197
    Pareto on, 156, 158–163
Socialism and Saint-Simon (Durkheim), 223
sociology, xi–xii, 7, 19, 27, 31, 38, 89, 93–94,
    96, 150, 158, 160, 162–163, 176, 192,
    202–203, 222–223, 254–256, 274
    of knowledge, 264–270
Socrates, 51, 241
Solomon, 128–129
Sparta, 172
Spencer, Herbert, 83, 233
Spinoza, Baruch, 3, 4
Starkenburg, H., 60
"Structural Analysis of Epistemology, The"
    (Mannheim), 264
Stuarts (England), 136–137
suffrage, 13, 163, 185, 192, 194–196, 198
suicide, 257–261
Suicide (Durkheim), 222, 260
Sumer, 111
Sun King, 148, 210
Sybil (Disraeli), 202
syndicalism, 217
Système Industriel (Saint-Simon), 226–227
Systéme Sociale (d'Holbach), 10
Systèmes Socialistes, Les (Pareto), 158, 161, 166

tabula rasa, 5, 18, 290
Tacitus, 64–66
Taoism, 116, 119–120
Tatars, 183
technological determinism, 57–58, 67, 71, 95
Teorica dei Governi e Governo Parlamentare
    (Mosca), 178
Thebes, 172
theology. *See* religion
"Theses on Feuerbach" (Marx), 55
Thirty Years' War, 73
Tims, Margaret, 10
Tocqueville, Alexis de, 83
Tönnies, Ferdinand, 207

Torah, 131, 133
totalitarianism, 38, 191, 197, 200
totemism, 247–251
Traité de Sociologie (Pareto), 158
transcendental logic, 19. *See also* Kant,
    Immanuel
Trattato di Sociologia Generale (Pareto), 203
*Travels Containing a Description of the
    Dominions of the Great Moguls* (Bernier), 75
Treatise on Metaphysics (Voltaire), 4
Treatise on Systems (Condillac), 3
tribal ownership, 61–67, 107
Turkey, 75, 183
Tylor, Edward Burnett, 83, 245, 246

unions, 123, 208–209, 211, 214. *See also* guilds
United States of America, 8, 62, 85, 93, 99,
    143, 199, 274. *See also* American Revolution
utilitarians, 102–103, 168, 229–331
utopia, 48, 130, 154, 176, 187, 203, 219, 267.
    See also Ideology and Utopia
Utopia (More), 80
utopian socialists, 158

Vaishyas, 122
Vedas, 125
Vindication of the Rights of Men
    (Wollstonecraft), 8
Vindication of the Rights of Woman
    (Wollstonecraft), 8–9, 10–14
violence, 72, 155, 168, 169, 170
Voltaire, 4

water. *See* irrigation
Watson, J.B., 277
Weber, Max, xii, 254, 292
    on ancient Judaism, 126–134
    on Asiatic mode of production, 110–114,
        133
    on bureaucracy, 111–113, 115, 118–119,
        139, 141–147, 149, 272
    on class, 137–142
    on economics and society, 97
    on feudalism, 105–110
    on historical-sociological method, 96,
        149–150
    on "ideal-type" construct, 102

on leaders, 146–149

and Mannheim, 264, 272

and Marx, 93–105, 182, 192, 202–204, 264, 269

on pariah people, 123, 127, 133

on Protestant ethic and spirit of capitalism, 96–102, 104, 122, 137

on religions of China, 114–121

on religions of India, 121–126

on Western capitalism, 134–137

Weimar Republic, 146–147

Weltanschauung, 97, 266, 268

Wesley, John, 103–104

West, the, 82, 85, 88, 96, 99, 101, 110, 113–115, 117–118, 120–123, 126, 133–134, 142, 148. *See also* Occident

Western Europe, 87–88, 110, 127. *See also* Europe

Wollstonecraft, Mary, 8–15

women, 8–15, 38, 65, 74, 188, 248

workers

Durkheim on, 226, 228, 236, 259

Mannheim on, 271–272

Marx on, 42–43, 45–48, 81–82

Michels on, 209, 210, 213–214, 216–217, 219

Mosca on, 183

Pareto on, 159

Weber on, 103, 113, 123, 134–135, 138–139, 142, 145

See also class; labour

World War I, 146, 183, 219, 258

World War II, 143, 264

Wundt, Wilhelm, 277

Yahweh, 127–132

Zasulitch, Vera, 87